WILD FOREST HOME

JJ, the first northern spotted owl I found during surveys, Mt. Hood National
Forest, 1986. USDA Forest Service by Betsy L. Howell.

WILD
FOREST
HOME

*Stories of Conservation in the
Pacific Northwest*

Betsy L. Howell

THE UNIVERSITY OF UTAH PRESS
Salt Lake City

The views expressed in this book are those of the author and do not
necessarily represent the views of the agency, department, or the United States.

 The Defiance House Man colophon is a registered trademark
of the University of Utah Press. It is based on a four-foot-tall
Ancient Puebloan pictograph (late PIII) near Glen Canyon, Utah.

LIBRARY OF CONGRESS CATALOGING-IN-PUBLICATION DATA
Names: Howell, Betsy L. (Betsy Leialoha), 1965– author.
Title: Wild forest home : stories of conservation in the Pacific Northwest / Betsy L. Howell.
Description: Salt Lake City : The University of Utah Press, [2024] | Includes bibliographical references. |
Identifiers: LCCN 2024016343 | ISBN 9781647691943 (paperback) | ISBN 9781647691950 (ebook)
Subjects: LCSH: Howell, Betsy L. (Betsy Leialoha), 1965– | United States. Forest Service—Biography.
  | Women biologists—Northwest, Pacific—Biography. | Wildlife managers—Northwest, Pacific—
  Biography. | Forest ecology—Northwest, Pacific. | Wildlife management—Northwest, Pacific. |
  LCGFT: Autobiographies.
Classification: LCC QH31.H32 H68 2024 | DDC 570.92 [B]—dc23/eng/20240509
LC record available at https://lccn.loc.gov/2024016343

Earlier versions of the following essays in this book have appeared in *American Forests*, https://www
.americanforests.org/ ("Little Critter with Big Influence," Fall 2014; "Silent Survivor," Fall 2015; "The
Fire's Edge," Fall 2016); *Earth Island Journal*, https://www.earthisland.org/journal/ ("The Whistle
Pig," June 2018); *The Wildlife Professional*, published by The Wildlife Society, https://wildlife.org/
publications/ ("Searching for Snakes," May/June 2019; "Bearing Witness," September/October 2020);
and the anthology *The Back Road to Crazy, Stories from the Field* ("The Pacific Marten," University of Utah
Press 2005).

Cover art by Larry Eifert, commissioned by Mount Rainier National Park. Used by permission.
Errata and further information on this and other titles available at UofUpress.com.

For Barbara, who believed, always.

Contents

Maps

Acknowledgments

To successfully work in wildlife conservation and land management requires a great community. I want to thank many of my colleagues who are doing this important work and who also gave generously of their time to read, review, make suggestions, correct mistakes, and clarify important scientific concepts in *Wild Forest Home*. Any lingering errors are completely my own.

Many, many thanks go to Dede Olson, John Chatel (now retired), Anne Poopatanapong, Cat Caruso, all USDA Forest Service employees, and Jerry Franklin, University of Washington, for reading the entire manuscript and providing invaluable feedback. The world of species and ecosystem conservation is a busy place, so I appreciate the time you all spent reading and supporting my efforts to document it. An additional shout-out to Dede Olson for many years of providing great enthusiasm for my work and also for being a pillar of inspiration in the amphibian and reptile world.

Similar appreciation goes to Keith Aubry, USDA Forest Service Pacific Northwest Research Station (emeritus), for reading the Pacific marten essays and also for being a wonderful, brilliant colleague during the many years we've been searching for martens in the Olympic Mountains.

Lee Webb and Dave Shea, retired Forest Service, read the essays from my early years with the agency and helped fill in pieces from long ago. Both were also very instrumental in my development as a biologist, especially Dave, who took on the unsolicited role of being my mentor.

To my current colleagues in the Olympic National Forest—Mark Senger, Cheryl Bartlett, Karen Holtrop, and Marc McHenry—who read and provided corrections to our shared histories: thank you so much. Similar thanks as well to Kristen Hauge, who provided very important guidance on describing the original people who lived, and still live, in the landscapes of the Mt. Hood, Siskiyou, and Olympic National Forests. You all inspire me with your passion and dedication to this landscape and its plant, animal, and human residents.

Many thanks go to Marty Raphael (emeritus) and Damon Lesmeister from the Forest Service Pacific Northwest Research Station, and Dave Wiens, U.S.

Geological Survey (USGS), for reviewing the essays on marbled murrelets, barred owls, and spotted owls. My appreciation and thanks also to Debaran Kelso for reviewing the owl essays, for your more than 30 years of research with the Forest Service on spotted owls, and for being so willing to share your own story as it unfolded alongside these magnificent birds.

To those I've worked with in Olympic National Park—Patti Happe (now retired), Scott Gremel, Dave Manson (now with the Lower Elwha Klallam Tribe), and Kurt Jenkins (retired USGS)—my utmost gratitude for your review of the essays on fishers, mountain goats, and spotted owls, as well as for your many years of work to restore ecosystems on the Olympic Peninsula. Many thanks as well to Jeff Lewis of the Washington Department of Fish & Wildlife (WDFW) for your impressive dedication to restoring fishers to the landscape in Washington. Being able to be a part of marten and fisher conservation and work with each of you have been highlights of my career.

Many thanks go to JD Kleopfer of the Virginia Department of Wildlife Resources for sharing your "Christmas salamander" story with me (and reviewing it), as well as so many other stories during the two days I spent tagging along on herp surveys with you and your crew in Virginia. Similar thanks to Rich Hatfield (Xerces Society for Invertebrate Conservation) for reading the piece on bumble bees, to John Rohrer (retired Forest Service) and Scott Fitkin (WDFW) for sharing your knowledge and passion for snakes with the wider world, and to Michael Best (College of the Redwoods) for sharing your fascinating research into the life of the ensatina salamander.

My appreciation also extends to old friends and colleagues William Johnson, Mary McCallum, and Carrie Phillips, all of whom generously allowed me to include them and some of their stories in these essays. I want to also thank Halle Lambeau and Dylan Hubl, who is currently completing his master's research on Pacific marten distribution in the Olympics, for bringing your immense skills to wildlife conservation and for being two of the brightest and the best of the next generation of scientists.

Paula MacKay and Robert Long of the Woodland Park Zoo have my deep gratitude for joining the Pacific marten project on the Olympic Peninsula and taking our investigations to new heights, which I was able to reflect on in the "Dodger Point" essay. Much of the work I've been involved with in Olympic National Forest has only been possible through the efforts of dozens of volunteers, too numerous to name here, but I would like to highlight Gregg Treinish of Adventure Scientists for also helping to advance understanding of martens on the peninsula, and Jack Smith (retired WDFW), Kyle Winton, and Scott

Harris (WDFW) for coordinating thousands of volunteer hours in an effort to restore habitat for Roosevelt elk. Much gratitude as well goes to Darrell Borden, now retired, for inspiring so many young people serving in the Washington Conservation Corps and for also accomplishing thousands of hours of habitat restoration work.

Many thanks also go to the people I've worked with in Partners in Amphibian and Reptile Conservation for welcoming me into the fold and for your complete devotion to these species that many people don't think twice about. Similar appreciation goes to those I've worked with in the Washington Chapter of The Wildlife Society. I've never been much of a "joiner," but it has been a rewarding experience to be part of two such fine organizations dedicated to wildlife conservation.

I also want to thank editors Zoe Loftus-Farren at *Earth Island Journal*, Keith Norris at *The Wildlife Professional*, and Ashlan Bonnell at *American Forests* for publishing some of the essays in *Wild Forest Home* and for doing so much to educate people about the environment.

This book would not exist if I'd never worked for the U.S. Forest Service in the first place. For that good fortune, I want to thank those who hired me over the years: Jeff Uebel, Rick Kneeland, Kim Mellen-McLean, Robin McAlpin, and Susan Piper. Your support and encouragement pushed me to do things I may not have done on my own.

This book also would not exist but for the hard work of several people at the University of Utah Press. Many thanks to Tom Krause, who has since moved on, for first noticing my work and being enthusiastic about its possibilities; to Glenda Cotter, who carried the manuscript through the review stage during the transition of finding a new acquisitions editor; and to Jed Rogers for seeing the book to the finish line. Thanks also to Jessica Booth, Susan Wegener, and Kristen Joseph for accomplishing all the many fine details during the production phase.

Similarly, Chelsea Feeney created the maps, did an excellent job in record time, and was a pleasure to work with. Very early feedback on the manuscript came from Liana Vasquez, for which I'm most grateful. For generously sharing their artwork and photography, much gratitude goes to Coke Smith, Alan St. John, Michael Best, and Larry Eifert.

Though they have been gone for many years, I also want to thank my parents for encouraging me to follow my own path even if they might not have always understood it.

Finally, my tremendous thanks and gratitude go to my wife, Barbara

Sjoholm. You have helped shape this book in crucial ways, held my hand during many times of self-doubt, and never stopped believing in the importance of the work. You're my inspiration and guide on this fascinating journey through the writing life.

Note to Readers

In terms of the names of different wildlife species, a few notes are important. Throughout the book, I refer to "carnivores," and in most cases, I'm referring to mammalian carnivores—for example, Pacific martens and fishers—unless otherwise noted (technically, martens and fishers are more specifically "meso-carnivores," meaning that 30–50 percent of their diet consists of other food, such as fruit, plants, and fungi). However, members of other groups of animals, such as amphibians, reptiles, and birds, can also be carnivores.

I use both "northern spotted owl" and "spotted owl," but I'm always referring to the northern subspecies, *Strix occidentalis caurina* (as opposed to the California spotted owl, *Strix occidentalis occidentalis*, or Mexican spotted owl, *Strix occidentalis lucida*).

"Invertebrates" include such animals as terrestrial mollusks, slugs and snails, and pollinators, butterflies and bumble bees.

Scientific names are included throughout the book, though not for every species, as this seemed overly detailed, particularly when I'm listing a number of species.

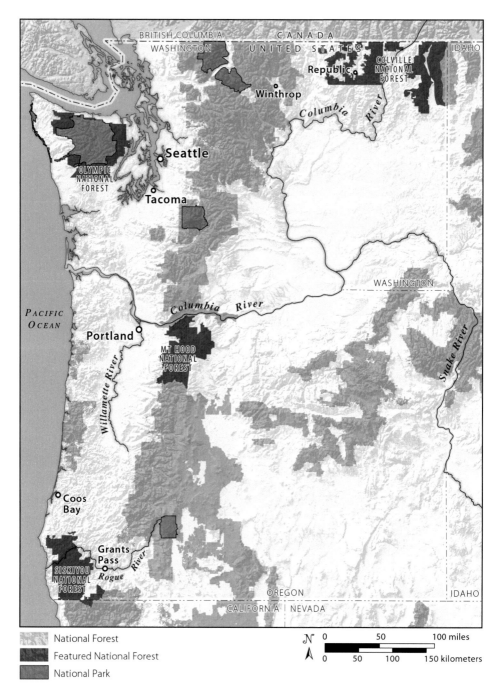

Map 1. National Forests in Oregon and Washington.

Introduction

The bed of moss and duff I'm lying on is a foot thick, the tree next to me several centuries old. Looking up, I see the intricate forest canopy, a tapestry of interlocking branches and kaleidoscopic sunlight. In this temperate old-growth stand on the Olympic Peninsula of Washington State, the past is everywhere: A log that's now melting back into the earth. Ancient trees shortened by coastal winds that snapped them like twigs. The moss bed itself a blanket of time's decomposition. Hints of the future are here too: A western hemlock seedling the size of a button growing on the log. Knee-high huckleberry bushes. The fruits of fungi no bigger than my thumb. The air and ground are verdant, filled with vibrant bigleaf maples and vine maples, sword fern, deer fern, and licorice fern.

The amount of life here is awe-inspiring. I think, as I often do when I'm in these forests, of a quote by plant ecologist Frank Egler: "Ecosystems may not only be more complex than we think, they may be more complex than we *can* think" (italics mine). Yet I have worked for many years to understand, or try to understand, the intricate ecology of these forests. As I close my eyes during my lunch break on this uncharacteristically warm, dry afternoon in the Olympic Mountains, I relax into the ringing trills of varied thrushes and the tiny squeaks of chickadees and kinglets. Suddenly, a loud chatter startles me. A Douglas's tree squirrel has noticed my arrival and determined me an intruder. Though it's true I'm only a visitor to the forest, I also know I belong here.

*

For more than 30 years, I've had the great fortune to spend many of my days in the temperate rainforests of Oregon and Washington. Since 1986, and except for a few years spent in the Peace Corps and also studying writing, I've worked as a wildlife biologist for the U.S. Department of Agriculture, Forest Service in the Pacific Northwest. I began in the Mt. Hood National Forest east of Portland, Oregon. Three years later I migrated south to the Siskiyou National Forest (now the Rogue River-Siskiyou) on the southern Oregon Coast. Most recently, since 2004, I've worked on the Olympic National Forest in western Washington State. This westside forest is similar to the other two but also unique in its "island-like" location on the Olympic Peninsula, which has saltwater on three sides and urbanization on the fourth.

I stepped into the agency during a time of great transition, just before the northern spotted owl and the marbled murrelet were federally listed under the Endangered Species Act. These two very different birds, one a raptor and one a seabird, are both dependent on the ancient coniferous forests of western North America, the very same forests that have also supported humans since time immemorial. For 10,000 years, Indigenous tribes lived with and utilized the landscape's forests sustainably. For the last century and half, after the arrival of European settlers, the use has been extractive and commodity-driven. After the owl and murrelet were designated as threatened species—in 1990 and 1992, respectively—lawsuits, uncertainty, anger, and fear consumed the region where the economy and society had depended on harvesting trees for a century.

President Bill Clinton's 1994 Northwest Forest Plan sought to provide direction for a society in turmoil. This document ushered in sweeping changes in the management of forests within the range of the northern spotted owl. Natural resource management on federal lands began moving from emphasizing products to emphasizing ecosystems. From focusing on single species to assemblages of species. From looking at animals and plants in terms of utility to humans to valuing their function in the environment apart from us. My own career as a biologist reflects this evolution. I began surveying for spotted owls, then moved into working with both owls and murrelets. Soon, I was trying to find small carnivores, including Pacific martens and fishers, as well as amphibians and reptiles. Then came songbirds and mollusks, other raptors, and invertebrates. The more species that I learned about, the more the complexity of the forest became clear. The more the connections of the forest ecosystem became illuminated, the more I wanted to learn about everything. This has necessarily meant a career as a generalist rather than a specialist, but it's a path that has suited me well.

In my early years with the Forest Service, we biologists needed to prove harm to wildlife from management actions in order to mitigate those actions, particularly for those species that were federally listed under the Endangered Species Act. After the adoption of the Northwest Forest Plan and the reduction in timber harvest levels, we, in partnership with our forester colleagues, now needed to show how our activities could benefit wildlife populations. Yet it hasn't only been changing societal values or management direction that has transformed the landscape in the last 30 years. The dynamic forces of wildfire, the arrival of invasive species, the appearance of wildlife disease, and the many-layered impacts of climate change (including drought, rising ocean temperatures, and catastrophic and sometimes unpredictable weather events) are all tremendous challenges that are happening at once. No wonder Frank Egler doubted our capacity to even be capable of understanding it all. Yet understand it we must, at least as best we can.

*

Stories are important and science is important. Making sense of the natural world requires both. *Wild Forest Home* is a blend of the two, a compilation of linked essays describing my 30 years as a wildlife biologist with the Forest Service and my experiences studying different wildlife species using evolving technology and survey techniques. It is also part memoir, as I describe my career path, how I left and returned to the agency twice, found solace working in the forest after the deaths of my parents, and decided to become a writer, in addition to being a wildlife biologist, in the late 1990s. I have my wife, Barbara, to thank for planting the seeds of the idea for this book, which she did in June 2013 as we hiked to the top of Mt. Zion in Olympic National Forest. The year before, I had met a research scientist named Michael Best and learned of his work studying ensatina salamanders. This terrestrial amphibian is common on the West Coast, and Michael had been quantifying the effects that ensatinas have on the carbon cycling of coniferous forests. The results showed that having more ensatinas on the landscape meant more carbon sequestration, an important fact in the fight against climate change that I felt should be shared with people beyond the research and land management communities.

As Barbara and I took breaks along the Mt. Zion trail, we discussed how I might write an article about Michael and his research. In the previous 10 years, I'd published essays on travel and history, but I wanted to do more science writing. I wanted to share my experiences, past and present, working with northern spotted owls, marbled murrelets, Pacific martens, and salamanders. I also wanted to write about the other people I knew, like Michael, who were doing important research. That summer, I contacted Michael and found him very keen to work with me. Our collaboration resulted in an article published in the fall 2014 issue of *American Forests*, "Little Critter with Big Influence."

I subsequently wrote more articles on other salamanders, spotted owls, and snakes. With these projects, I wanted to convey the amazing worlds of the creatures I had come to know as well as translate science into understandable concepts for the average person. From knowing more about the natural world comes a feeling of connection to it, and connection can lead to action on the Earth's behalf. With so many of my colleagues doing critical scientific research, as well as providing environmental education, there has always been much to write about. Before long, the idea for a collection of linked essays about the wildlife and ecosystems of the Pacific Northwest began to take shape.

Such a collection might begin at the forest floor and move up through the canopy. Though this final work doesn't have a straight-line trajectory, the basic structure of *Wild Forest Home* is that of describing at least a portion of the forest's complexity that I've experienced in my career. While some essays are focused on science and survey techniques, several weave in my own personal journey and the events, unexpected as well as planned, that have influenced the direction of my life in important ways. The 25 essays in this book were written beginning approximately 15 years ago. Many started as journal entries, some dating back to 1986 as I recorded my experiences and observations in the forests of the Pacific Northwest. Some essays I have kept here in the present tense, including ones that remain structured as journal entries. While the overall path of the book moves forward in time from 1986 to 2020, there's also some back and forth, as I arranged the essays somewhat thematically. To help minimize confusion, the table of contents lists, for each essay, the appropriate national forest and the year when events are taking place. Occasionally, I've inserted notations into an essay to update the reader on changes since it was written (e.g., if someone in the essay has retired or updates regarding the conservation status of different species).

*

I grew up in the forests of the Pacific Northwest. This circumstance, for which I'll always be grateful, might not have ever happened were it not for one surprising decision by my parents: to leave Honolulu, Hawaii, where I was born and where they'd lived for 10 years, and move to Tacoma, Washington. Being just a year old at the time, I had no say in the matter. If I had, I might have questioned this change. Leave the exotic island life for the fog-shrouded Pacific Northwest? Go from endless sun, warm breezes, and blue, silky ocean waters to seemingly endless (at times) rain, overcast skies, and gray, freezing rivers? Yet while my father had been stationed at nearby Fort Lewis some years before, my parents had fallen in love with the Northwest's own special beauty. This is how my mother told it: "We were deciding where to go after your father retired from the army, and one day we both got home from work and said at the same time, 'Tacoma!'"

This was an even funnier story in the late 1960s and early 1970s given the roughness of the city in those years. The Asarco copper smelter was still providing the region with the "aroma of Tacoma"; the downtown area, according to my mother, was a place respectable people didn't go; and even back then, Tacoma lived in the shadow of Seattle, its flashier neighbor to the north. However, my parents simply ignored the teasing from family and friends in Southern California and Hawaii. They found us a modest, ranch-style house in a newly built neighborhood with streets named for Pacific Northwest flora. We settled into our brightly painted yellow home on Snowberry Circle and spent weekends exploring the region's forests. We camped and fished at Spirit Lake near Mt. St. Helens and rambled around the wildflower meadows of Mt. Rainier. After my dad decided he must have a boat, we began traveling the waters of Puget Sound. Soon, my parents bought a motor home. We dispensed with the canvas, military tent, cots, and pop-up toilet for a more comfortable camping experience. Sometimes, we returned to Hawaii for vacations on the beach, but there were never any discussions about moving back. My father had grown up in Illinois and my mother in Colorado, but I think they were Pacific Northwesterners at heart.

*

In this coastal Northwest environment, I spent long hours in the forests around our home. I also dreamed of adventure in far-off lands. After reading the Born Free series by Joy Adamson, I fully expected to grow up and go to Africa and live with the lions and leopards. If not Africa, then the Yukon or Northwest Territories would work too. I was an only child, with parents who were 45 and 40 years old when I was born. Of course, I had friends in our neighborhood, but a kind of solitude also enveloped much of my early life that made me feel both lonely and exhilarated. I craved life in remote places and being close to wild animals that, though unpredictable by nature, seemed less mysterious in their intentions than people. I also felt at ease being alone in the nearby forests, a contentment that may have been innate or the result of what I was experiencing in my family life and that I wanted to distance myself from.

My father's alcoholism and buried trauma from participating in two wars were easier to see and understand. My mother's all-too-frequent cold detachment and hostility, contrasted with an often generous heart, still puzzle me. Because I spent most of my time with my parents, the withdrawal they both exhibited in different forms fostered my loneliness. Yet because they created opportunities for me to be in the natural world and taught me to love and respect our fellow species, I also found joy in my solitary journeys into the forest. This escapism as a child became a destination as an adult.

Midway through getting my degree in wildlife management from Washington State University, I took a volunteer position as a spotted owl surveyor in the Mt. Hood National Forest in Oregon. The next year, I was hired as a biological technician and then two years later as a professional wildlife biologist. I left the Forest Service twice in the 1990s: once to do a tour in the Peace Corps and once to become a writer. Otherwise, this has been my career with the agency: conducting species inventories and habitat improvement projects and working on fire crews and restoration planning teams. Throughout these many years, my appreciation for Pacific Northwest forests has only grown from the time when I saw them mostly as a refuge from my troubled childhood.

*

In 1986, when I began my career, the Forest Service was a different organization. The landscape looked different, and the conservation challenges seemed simpler compared with what we're faced with today. A computer system barely composed much of an employee's life, ditto phones. There had never been a biologist or a woman serving as chief of the Forest Service, the top position in the agency, but since 1993, there have been two of each; additionally, the current chief, Randy Moore, is the first African American to hold the position. Wildlife surveys now focus on animals many people either don't know about or rarely consider, a change I've welcomed since I, and my biologist colleagues, represent all species other than humans that also rely on these forests. Not only do spotted owls and marbled murrelets need older forests to survive, but so do some mammals and amphibians, mosses and mollusks. Wasn't this what the web of life I had studied in school was all about? In my early years with the agency, I spent most of my time in the field. From the beginning, I've had a front-row view of the forest's ecological tapestry, even as the connections between species and environmental events weren't always clear.

The technology to document the presence of certain species and record their activities has also become so advanced over the last 30+ years that many aspects of an animal's life can be learned remotely—that is, without ever observing them directly. Disease has become more prominent and is a devastating issue for snakes, salamanders, and bats. Budgets and staffing have declined while partnerships have increased. In the last three decades, a changing climate has shrunk glaciers but extended fire seasons, altered the amount of snowpack and the timing of snowmelt, and fostered range expansions for some species and contractions for others. In the early years, I worked with more men. Now I work with more women, though fire camps remain predominantly male. The need to protect the little untouched forest that remains in the Pacific Northwest has always seemed obvious to me. Yet for a society built around a timber industry and an economic structure supported by extracting natural resources, the changes in land management that altered the type and amount of that extraction have come at a price. And the corresponding transformation, to rural livelihoods and communities, hasn't been easy.

In April 1990, I attended a week-long training session for "Early Career Biologists." The two instructors for the class were Jack Ward Thomas, at that time a Forest Service research wildlife biologist who later became chief of the Forest Service, and Jim Kennedy, a professor at Utah State University who had worked for the Forest Service in the 1960s. Kennedy had been studying the social makeup of the agency since 1982. At that time, he began investigating how new employees were adapting to careers in the Forest Service culture. I remember this week as transformative, from the bonds I made with other attendees to all of us learning about the sweeping changes occurring in land management. We were living through a historic time in the agency, and I think we all knew this even then. Earlier that month, Jack Ward Thomas and the Interagency Scientific Committee he led had just delivered "A Conservation Strategy for the Northern Spotted Owl." This seminal document propelled Jack and his colleagues to national fame, and he wrote in his journals from the time, "The night we finished the report at 3 a.m., I stared at that picture for over an hour with a strange sense of foreboding. My life would never be the same" (Thomas 2004, 16). The picture he referred to was of a young girl and her dog walking down one fork in a trail. A sign above the fork read "The Rest of Your Life" while the other path's sign read "No Longer an Option." Two months later, the northern spotted owl would be listed as a threatened species by the U.S. Fish & Wildlife Service. Jack's life—as well as the lives of many others, including me—would, in fact, never be the same, as timber harvests and budgets declined on federal lands and a new era began to better understand the amazingly complex old-growth forests of the Pacific Northwest.

*

Since landscapes and the people who occupy them are constantly in flux, it's important to acknowledge the original inhabitants of the places I write about. The stories in *Wild Forest Home* occur primarily within the designated Mt. Hood, Siskiyou (since 2004, Rogue River-Siskiyou), and Olympic National Forests of Oregon and Washington. The U.S. Forest Service, the agency that manages the national forest system, came into being in 1905, barely more than a century ago. While this book chronicles my personal experiences, many of them documented in my journals from the time, during a career spent working in the national forests, I want to acknowledge that since time immemorial, these lands have been inhabited by Indigenous peoples.

Mt. Hood

Many bands of the Sahaptin, Chinook, and Molala peoples originally lived on the lands now managed by the Mt. Hood National Forest. Many of these bands today are represented by the federally recognized tribal (FRT) governments of the Confederated Tribes of Warm Springs, the Confederated Tribes of Grand Ronde, and the Confederated Tribes of Siletz Indians of Oregon, all of whom continue to have ties to the Mt. Hood National Forest.

Siskiyou

Many bands of the Takelma and Athabaskan peoples originally lived on the lands now managed by the original Siskiyou National Forest. Many of these bands today are represented by the FRT governments of the Confederated Tribes of Siletz Indians of Oregon, the Confederated Tribes of the Grand Ronde, the Coquille Indian Nation, and the Tolowa Dee-ni' Nation, all of whom continue to have ties to the Rogue River-Siskiyou National Forest.

Olympic

Many bands of the Wakashan, Quileute-Chemakum, and Central, Southern, and Southwestern Coast Salish peoples originally lived on the lands
now managed by the Olympic National Forest. Many of these bands today
are represented by the Skokomish Indian Tribe, Jamestown S'Klallam Tribe,
Port Gamble S'Klallam Tribe, Lower Elwha Tribal Community, Makah Indian Tribe of the Makah Indian Reservation, Hoh Indian Tribe, Quileute
Tribe of the Quileute Reservation, the Quinault Indian Nation, the Confederated Tribes of the Chehalis Reservation, and the Suquamish Indian Tribe
of the Port Madison Reservation, all of whom continue to have ties to the
lands of the Olympic Peninsula.

*

Additionally, the management structure of national forests can change over
time. The Mt. Hood National Forest had seven ranger districts in 1986 when I
began working for the agency, and now there are four. Parts of the Bear Springs
Ranger District were absorbed into all four of these districts, and the district
office buildings were returned to the Confederated Tribes of Warm Springs
upon whose land they sat. In 1989, when I moved to the Siskiyou National
Forest, there were seven ranger districts; now this portion of the Rogue River-
Siskiyou National Forest has three, one of which still is the Powers Ranger
District.

*

For me, there's nothing better than the moment when I seem to disappear and
the forest becomes everything. When the centuries my tree companion has
lived become less far away. When I'm no longer a biologist or an employee and
my tasks and notebooks seem less important than just being present. When
I'm simply one more living thing in a vast community of beings. Terrestrial
salamanders that may number in the thousands surrounding me in one small
acre. Millions of microscopic creatures living in a clump of moss the size of
my fist. Worms and beetles slithering and scampering all around. Nuthatches
and chickadees and other songbirds darting to and fro above. It's the moment
when I blend into the fabric of the forest, watching and being watched, and my

connection to this place grows stronger than my need to understand it. These are the blessed times. Yet they come too infrequently and leave too quickly.

For I must get out my notebook and once again turn on my biologist's eye. I must look for what's here in this stand, what I can see, and make estimates of what may be missing. I must set up a remote camera station or a survey plot or begin looking under bark and rocks for salamanders. And I must do all this without perfect understanding. Because the people of this country are paying me and my colleagues to learn about these forests. They're paying us to seek answers and solutions to complex questions of shrinking resources, declining species diversity, and increasing human needs. The work is challenging, but I know how fortunate I am. I've participated in an important era in the history of national forest management, a time that continues to evolve, influenced by our growing understanding of ecological systems and a rapidly changing environment. My career has been spent in the field, in forests that I love, close to the ground and to the wildlife species that live there as well as those high above in the canopy.

Part I

OREGON

Imagine walking through a richly inhabited world of Birch people, Bear people, Rock people, beings we think of and therefore speak of as persons worthy of our respect, of inclusion in a peopled world.

The circle of ecological compassion we feel is enlarged by direct experience of the living world, and shrunken by its lack.

—Robin Wall Kimmerer, *Braiding Sweetgrass: Indigenous Wisdom, Scientific Knowledge, and the Teachings of Plants*

I

The Spotted Owl

Mt. Hood National Forest, 1986–87

A northern spotted owl (*Strix occidentalis caurina*) sits on a branch snoozing 10 feet away from my work partner, Sharon, and me. It's a cool but sunny morning in this old-growth coniferous forest. Beams of light push down through the canopy of trees above us. Blooming rhododendron bushes, knee-high patches of salal, and delicate trillium plants grace the forest floor. Below us, down a steep, rocky slope, a stream tumbles with newfound abundance and energy from melting snow. In less than a mile, it will join another creek, then a river, then a bigger river, and finally the mighty and well-known Columbia River. The spotted owl we're now watching was known to reside in this stand, and we have merely confirmed its presence during another breeding season. Yet the experience is wholly new for both Sharon and me. Before today, we had never seen a spotted owl.

Sharon takes a mouse from a box she has carried in her backpack and sets it on a log. I'm ready with my camera. The owl, approximately 16 inches tall and weighing a bit more than a pound, opens its solid, dark eyes and looks down. It has already eaten two of our mice and stored a third in a nearby tree, yet our hope is that it will take the food to its mate in the nest tree, wherever that may be. Jeff, our supervisor, has known about this owl but hasn't been able to locate the nest. I wonder how we'll do following, on foot, an owl that is flying through the canopy of this lush, steep country. Yet this is a small worry. I am 20 years old, and Sharon is 25. Though this fieldwork is new to both of us, we're in good shape. In any case, it is a spurious concern; the owl is not interested in any more mice and continues to rest. We have likely learned all we will today, but we continue to stay with the bird. We are both in awe that a wild animal is so at ease in our presence.

*

Surveying for northern spotted owls was my first job with the Forest Service. During the spring of 1986, I saw the advertisement seeking volunteers for

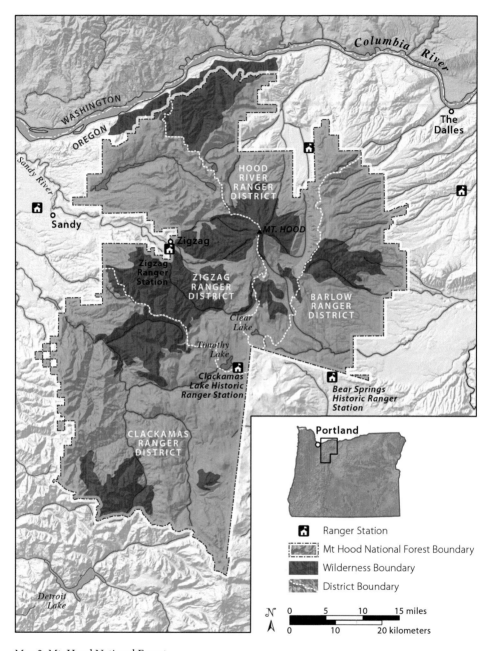

Map 2. Mt. Hood National Forest.

summer trail crews in Mt. Hood National Forest and applied. I was finishing my junior year at Washington State University, had just completed courses in wildlife management, mammalogy, fisheries management, wildlife disease, and botany and was eager to apply all this new knowledge. Though trail work wasn't exactly in my field of study, it was closer than other jobs (gardener, house painter, mailroom clerk) I'd had during college. Yet I got lucky. Noticing that I was a wildlife major, the recreation specialist at the Zigzag Ranger District passed my application onto the fisheries biologist. Jeff, who also managed the wildlife program, was looking for two volunteers to do owl surveys. Concern had been growing about northern spotted owls since the 1970s, when researchers began observing the species' presence almost exclusively in old-growth forests. These forests were also crucially important to the timber industry and a society that depended on wood and wood products.

"We have several areas with spotted owls," Jeff told me over the phone, "but we don't know where their nests are. That will be your job, to find the nests."

"How do we do that?" I asked. Jeff had already told me that I'd have a work partner, a woman named Sharon, who was moving from the Midwest to Oregon with her boyfriend, Tom.

"You'll offer some live mice to the owls," he explained, "and see if they'll take them. If the birds are nesting, then they'll carry the mice to their mate in the tree. See, it's important to know where the tree is, especially if it's in an area where we're planning a timber sale."

All this sounded extraordinary and more than a little impossible. How did one get a wild animal to come close enough to take a proffered mouse? Perhaps Jeff read my mind.

"Spotted owls are interesting animals," he continued. "They'll respond to you imitating their hoots and take a mouse right out of your hands. They're very friendly."

Before talking with Jeff, I hadn't ever heard of the northern spotted owl. After we finished talking and I'd accepted the volunteer position, I got out Roger Tory Peterson's *A Field Guide to Western Birds* to learn something about the species. A drawing of an owl with spots on its breast stared back at me from the pages. "A large, dark-brown forest owl with a puffy round head," read the description. "The large *dark* eyes and the heavily barred and spotted underparts identify this rather rare bird." The voice of the spotted owl was characterized as a "high-pitched hooting, like barking of a small dog. Usually in groups of 3 (*hoo, hoo-hoo*) or 4 (*hoo, who-who-whooo*)" (Peterson 1961, 124).

Though this was my first introduction to northern spotted owls, the species had been studied since the early 1970s, when Eric Forsman, a graduate student at Oregon State University, began investigating the owl's distribution, habitat, and basic biology. Eric, an avid birder since high school, had been interested in these owls for several years. While working during the summer for the Willamette National Forest in Oregon in 1969, Eric had his first encounter with a spotted owl. One evening at the Box Canyon Guard Station where he was assigned, he heard what sounded like barking nearby. At first, he thought it sounded like a "weird-sounding dog," but then he realized the call was similar to how spotted owl calls had been described in books. Eric found the owl that evening and began calling back to it. In a 2016 interview for Oregon State University, Eric explained that though he was an amateur at imitating the owls' calls at that time, the owls still responded. "They eventually followed me all the way back to the guard station" (Forsman 2016).

Eric would go on to complete his master's and PhD on spotted owls and become a key figure in spotted owl conservation and forest management in the Pacific Northwest. And 17 years after his first encounter with the birds, we'd be using the same simple methods of imitating the spotted owl location call to find them.

*

In late May, I arrived in Zigzag, Oregon, a small town west of Portland near the base of Mt. Hood, the highest peak in the state. Jeff, a stocky, bearded man in his mid-30s, greeted me enthusiastically and showed me around the compound of historic buildings.

"Our office is this one," said Jeff, pointing to a green and beige structure with dormers and a gabled roof. "This used to be the ranger's residence years ago, but now it's the fish, wildlife, and silviculture offices." He led me to a large back room with a stone fireplace and a disorganized collection of hip waders, boots, nets, and desks piled high with papers and folders. Jeff looked sheepish. "Sorry, it's a bit of a mess."

After clearing away a corner for me and Sharon, who would be arriving in a few days, Jeff showed me some of the field gear we'd be using: a cage to hold the mice, white cassette tapes filled with spotted owl location calls, and a megaphone for projecting the hoots (we could use our voices as well, he said). There was also the requisite Forest Service equipment: hard hats, gloves, compasses, and orange cruiser's vests.

We then visited the recreation and fire buildings, the main office, and finally the small cabin in the back where I would live. This log structure, built in the 1930s, contained one bedroom, a tiny bathroom, a living area, a kitchen, and an attic.

"Will this be OK?" Jeff asked nervously as I explored the different rooms. "I mean, it's a little dim. And rustic."

The steep roof, the decades-old smell of wood, and the dark interior made me feel like I was at last fulfilling my childhood fantasy of living in the wilderness. Though my parents and I had car camped in the Cascade Range when I was young, and we'd spent many days exploring the waterways of Puget Sound in our small boat, we never did any hiking or backpacking. Consequently, I'd never had any real backcountry experiences and had certainly never stayed even one night in a place like this.

"Are you kidding?" I asked. "It's perfect!"

That first night, I could barely sleep due to excitement. This was what I had always wanted. To be close to nature, spend time in the wilderness, and work in conservation. As I began my new job, I heard the concern in my dad's voice when I called home. He was glad I had a work partner, but on the weekends, I traveled solo. He didn't like me hiking alone, yet he didn't say too much. I'm sure he could hear the happiness and excitement in *my* voice. If I didn't say it clearly, the truth was implied: I'd found a new kind of home.

*

Can you make a living doing *that*? No one in my family had ever heard of wildlife biology as a profession and couldn't conceive of choosing to spend so much time in the forest. Blank stares met me when I returned to Tacoma that summer and explained the survey work, which included describing the long hours spent being out at night and all the equipment we carried. My cousins had no interest in spotted owls, the species' dependence on old-growth forests, or how the birds would readily come to us when we called to them. The strategy of feeding the owls mice elicited expressions of disgust. Also, didn't I care about the mice? How could I haul the rodents around for hours in my backpack; wasn't that hard on them? I explained that I did care, but this seemed to be the best way to find the owls' nests, which was also important. On it went. The hours spent thrashing through the brush sounded terrible to most of my family. What if I fell and hurt myself? What if a bear or cougar attacked me? Wasn't I afraid? Their questions were never about the work itself, only about imagined disasters.

Surprisingly, I wasn't bothered by the indifference, judgment, or teasing (one cousin took to calling me "spotted Howell"). Nothing about the new world I'd found seemed the least bit strange. The forest didn't frighten me, and the work felt meaningful. It helped immensely that my parents *were* interested and did support me. When they came to visit, they liked the cabin and other historic buildings at the ranger station. That evening, my mom and I drove out to one of our survey areas and called to the owls from the road. The stars danced above us, and the creek flowed quietly below us. As the evening progressed, my mother grew tired. She seemed a little out of place in the nighttime world of the forest, but I appreciated her willingness to give the experience a try. When they left at the end of the weekend, my father said, "We're proud of you, Bets." Even if they didn't completely understand the appeal of this job, and even if their daughter being out in the woods alone made them nervous, my parents never dissuaded me from following my dreams. For this, I've always been grateful.

*

By the time I began as a volunteer spotted owl surveyor, the Forest Service had been working since the early 1980s to develop an adequate conservation management plan for the species per legislative direction that national forests provide habitats to support viable populations of all native species. These efforts included the 1984 *Regional Guide for the Pacific Northwest Region* of the Forest Service, which documented the need for at least 1,000 acres of old-growth forest for 500 pairs of owls distributed across the national forests within the species' range (this was below the 2,200-acre home ranges for owls described in a 1984 scientific monograph published by Eric Forsman and his colleagues). After environmental groups filed appeals against the *Regional Guide*, work began in 1985 on a supplemental environmental impact statement (SEIS) on owl management. The draft SEIS came out the spring I arrived in Zigzag and proposed providing 2,200 acres of old growth for each of the 550 spotted owl habitat areas (SOHAs). The SEIS estimated these provisions had a high probability of providing a sufficient amount of habitat for a well-distributed population in the short term but a low probability in the long term. This plan also estimated a 5 percent decline in timber harvest in the national forests. Neither environmental nor timber industry groups were pleased with these numbers, and work and negotiation continued in 1986 and beyond to determine how best to provide for the needs of owls as well as people, who had come to rely on revenues and products from the forests.

I was little aware of all that was going on at upper levels in the Forest Service as Sharon and I continued surveying many SOHAs in the Zigzag and Estacada ranger districts. At Estacada, we worked for the district wildlife biologist, a woman named Karen, who was the complete opposite of Jeff with her organized and tidy office. We did a three-day trek into Bull of the Woods, a newly designated wilderness that included a dozen mountain lakes and was a relatively isolated landscape only 70 miles from Portland. We heard spotted owls during the night but couldn't find them during the day. This felt disappointing, but the breathtaking wilderness with so much to observe didn't leave any time for dwelling on what we weren't seeing. In the talus slopes, I observed my first pika, a small member of the rabbit family. These animals, with their industrious summertime gathering of food, had inspired the phrase "Make hay while the sun shines." Curious blacktail deer, enterprising chipmunks, and friendly gray jays visited our camp. "Quorking" ravens flew above us during the day; common nighthawks welcomed the twilight hour.

Sharon and I had already been introduced to nighthawks, a fabulous bird in the nightjar family that forages on insects and can make a person dizzy when trying to follow their acrobatic flying. We'd first heard them earlier in the summer. That evening as the sun set, we were listening to the rapid, high-pitched notes of a saw-whet owl when suddenly something growled very close to us.

"What was *that*?" whispered Sharon.

Though I felt comfortable being out at night, I wasn't crazy about the idea of sharing our survey site with a bear. The thing growled again, and we realized that the sound was coming from above us! The odd noises had to be from a bird, but how could that be? Later, we would learn that as the male nighthawk dives downward, the rushing of air across his primary wing feathers creates a hollow "booming" sound, an effect that's very loud and surprising when one isn't expecting it.

*

Was this really work? I had to ask myself the question because being outside every day, hiking and backpacking, learning about the natural world, and meeting the forest's animal residents seemed more like play. On the weekends, I explored different trails along the Salmon River and Hunchback Mountain and around Mirror Lake and Trillium Lake, both close to Mt. Hood. I took many rolls of photos of everything. I bought different filters for my Canon

PowerShot camera that deepened the blue of the summer sky and transformed the already-dappled forest light into starbursts. Many images of Mt. Hood's reflection in Mirror Lake accumulated in my collection. I also couldn't pass a rhododendron flower without snapping a photo. My greatest subject, however, was the first spotted owl Sharon and I found, the bird we'd named Jeff Jr., or "JJ," after our supervisor.

Below the tree canopy in the temperate rainforests of the Pacific Northwest isn't the easiest place to take photos. The uneven light casts shadows, and aiming above myself toward the sky, where the owl sat, most often resulted in a photograph that was backlit and dark and grainy. To compensate, I simply took many photos. If I'd had a digital camera back then, I would have had thousands of pictures of JJ. As it was, I was limited to 24 or 36 photos per roll of film, but I always had many rolls with me. To my satisfaction, a few came out well. They showed JJ during a typical owl day: snoozing, watching other birds, preening. I still have the best photo in a frame above my desk at home.

Though almost all my time was spent in the field, I occasionally found myself in the office. Before Sharon arrived that May, Jeff instructed me in mapping older forest stands within the known owl territories. In the 1980s, before geographic information systems and electronic imagery, this was done using overlays of plastic mylar and large poster-size aerial photographs of the landscape. I learned how different ages of forest appeared from the air. Old growth looked "fluffy" and dark green. Younger stands had a lighter green hue. Swaths of alder or maple appeared almost lime-colored. I took these overlays and transferred them to paper using a large machine called a "blue-line printer." The chemicals used in this device smelled awful, but the process worked. After feeding a large, yellow paper with the mylar atop into the machine, a blue map with the imprint of topographic lines and aerial imagery emerged. We could then carry this map during our surveys.

In 1986, the Forest Service used a computer system called the Data General, or DG for short. Chunky monitors the size of small boxes displayed glowing screens of green letters. The capabilities of the DG compared to today's systems were very simple: emailing within the agency, word processing, and a basic filing system. Being a volunteer and a field person, I didn't have a DG computer and felt glad of it. I'd had to take a computer programming class in college, an inexplicable requirement for a wildlife major, and barely scraped by with a C. Nothing about computers was intuitive to me (I shamelessly capitalized on a computer science major's crush on me that semester to get his help with every assignment). My continued lack of understanding of the world of electrons and binary systems showed itself at Zigzag that summer. One afternoon, another employee tried to tell me about sending messages to other offices.

"Each office has a different address," Gary explained, "so when you type that in, that's where the message goes."

To people like me, who didn't have much interest in technology, the mechanics of sending letters electronically were still new in 1986. "But how does that *work*?" I asked. "I mean, how does the message get there?"

Now Gary looked puzzled. Then he slowly smiled. "Oh, right. It just travels over the phone lines."

"I see," I said, nodding. Phone lines I understood. Still, I was glad I didn't need to know too much about computers.

*

We never found JJ's nest or mate that summer, though he continued to respond and fly in for mice, typically eating them on the spot. We also documented other owl species, including the (at that time) little-known barred owl. This species, similar in appearance to the spotted owl but with vertical bars on its breast rather than spots, hadn't been in the Pacific Northwest historically. That summer, we paid little attention to the barred owl. It might have looked similar to the spotted owl, but it wasn't what we were looking for.

The hard, exhausting work provided me real-life experience in learning about species and ecosystems. I began to see the challenge of trying to fully understand the complex interactions among *every*thing in the forest. In the mid-1980s, concern over the spotted owl and old-growth ecosystems, while a big focus for some environmental groups and individual researchers and research teams, was only just beginning, it seemed to me, to be understood by employees across the agency. Neither the owl nor the marbled murrelet, a small seabird that nests in older forests, had yet to be listed under the Endangered Species Act. The idea that an entire industry and way of human life could be upended by two animals that most people would never see seemed highly implausible. Yet change was coming. In January 1987, a little-known environmental organization called GreenWorld, from Cambridge, Massachusetts, petitioned the U.S. Fish & Wildlife Service to list the northern spotted owl as endangered, citing a decline in the number of owls. Though the service denied the petition the following year, the court battles had begun. In 1990, the U.S. Fish & Wildlife Service would list the northern spotted owl as a threatened species. Two years later, they'd list the marbled murrelet as well.

*

In the spring of 1987, during my senior year of college, I applied for a biological technician position in the Mt. Hood National Forest. Jeff and Karen both wrote me letters of recommendation, and a few weeks later, I got a call from the wildlife biologist in the Bear Springs Ranger District. Most of this district lay east of the Cascade Range crest and included the drier slopes and more open, warmer habitats of eastern Oregon. I accepted the job and made plans to begin work immediately after graduation. The summer seasonal position didn't come with assured funding, and there were no benefits, yet I again felt lucky; several of my fellow graduates hadn't landed jobs yet, seasonal or otherwise. I would once again be surveying for spotted owls but also doing habitat restoration work for different wildlife species.

My new supervisor at Bear Springs, Rick, said I could live in the bunkhouse on the district office compound or at a cabin at the Clackamas Lake Historic Ranger Station, approximately 15 miles away. A lugubrious look passed over Rick's round, moon face while he described the lake area as remote and the cabin as old and dusty with no electricity, but I didn't even have to think about it.

"I'll take the cabin," I said cheerily.

Rick nodded without smiling. I could see that he had none of the light-heartedness of Jeff and seemed vaguely unhappy. Rick told me he'd worked on the west side of Mt. Hood for many years and had recently been transferred to Bear Springs. This change hadn't been welcome, and though he began some good programs on the eastside, Rick's unhappiness colored much of his time at Bear Springs. By contrast, I couldn't have been more excited. Bear Springs was farther from Portland than Zigzag and had fewer visitors. For the second summer in a row, I'd be living in a log cabin, and this time, it was right in the middle of the national forest! The lack of electricity didn't bother me at all.

The ranger station, still in existence in 2023, included several buildings and sat on the edge of Clackamas Meadows and Lake, through which wended the Oak Grove Fork of the Clackamas River. The original inhabitants, the Guithla'kimas (English spelling "Clackamas") people, lived along this river, where the great salmon resources provided the foundation for their lives and culture. In 1806, Lewis and Clark estimated the Guithla'kimas population to be at 1,800. By 1851, there were fewer than 100 people. A few years later, the surviving members were relocated to the Grande Ronde Indian Reservation, 18 miles from the Pacific Ocean. A half century later, in 1905, the newly established Forest Service began using the Clackamas Lake area. A ranger cabin and barn were constructed first, and in the 1930s, the Civilian Conservation Corps built several more buildings, including two residences, a mess hall, a fire equipment warehouse, a blacksmith shop, and a horse barn. Though blacksmiths and horses were no longer needed in 1987 to manage the forests, the ranger station still housed a fire engine crew during the summer months.

As I moved my things into the cabin, I absorbed the cool, dark air and the now-familiar smell of historic buildings. This had been the "honeymoon cabin," a home built in the early 20th century for the district ranger's resource assistant and his new bride (sadly, this building I lived in burned down in 2003). A tiny bedroom separated the living area from the bathroom. The kitchen, with its small windows, faced the meadow. A fireplace and the foundation had been constructed of large, impressive stones. Without electricity, I would make good use of my newly purchased lantern, though as it was the beginning of summer, I could also remain outside reading until late. And with the fire crew living just across the road in the much larger ranger's house, I doubted I'd feel lonely.

The next morning, I woke up early to Clackamas Meadow hidden under a blanket of mist. As I stepped into the shower, I noticed a dark object on the tub floor. Sensing my presence, the quarter-sized tree frog moved. Though it had entered for the dampness, maintained by a small leak in the shower head, a full-blown spray was not desired. The frog disappeared into a crack in the wall. Over the next months, we would meet several times.

During those first spring days in the cabin before leaving for the office, I drank coffee and watched the mist rise. Blacktail deer feeding in the meadow looked up in surprise at the new resident, then returned to their activities. The dry air encouraged the yellow lupine and Ponderosa pine to release their sweet smells. Natural, forest sounds dominated. Chirps from robins and juncos. Sharp cries of ospreys flying to the nearby lakes. The haunting songs of migrant Swainson's thrushes recently returned from their tropical winter homes. The loud caws and staccato chatter of the ever-present Steller's jays, crows, and ravens reminded everyone who the bosses were here.

After almost a year away, I once again felt that I had returned home. Even now, decades later, I easily remember this feeling. A few years ago, when I read the eloquent words of Robin Wall Kimmerer describing the smells of her beloved sweetgrass in her 2013 book, *Braiding Sweetgrass: Indigenous Wisdom, Scientific Knowledge, and the Teachings of Plants*, I knew she'd captured exactly what I'd experienced so long ago as I began to live closer to the forest: "Breathe it in and you start to remember things you didn't know you'd forgotten" (2013, ix).

*

In the mid-1950s, Portland General Electric constructed a compacted earth dam along the Oak Grove Fork of the Clackamas River creating Timothy Lake, a 1,500-acre waterbody. The area immediately became a mecca for fishing, camping, and boating. Altering the ecosystem from rivers and streams to still water affected some wildlife species negatively, but it created habitat for others. Timothy Lake, as well as Clear Lake, another reservoir nearby, provided ideal foraging areas for ospreys and bald eagles, resting sites for waterfowl, and abundant populations of insects for swallows and bats. Crater Creek and Copper Creek flowed into the "North Arm" of Timothy Lake, an area narrower and shallower than the main body. It was here that I spent much of my time that first summer.

The autumn before, after the lake had been drawn down, Rick had organized the construction of several small islands in the waters of the North Arm. This human-created archipelago added habitat diversity in an area that was visited less by people. When the water came up in the spring, the islands would provide safe nesting and resting areas for waterfowl and wading birds. Rick also had other ideas for wildlife habitat improvement projects in the North Arm: planting hardwood trees on the islands and along the shoreline that would lose their leaves in the fall, contributing organic matter to the nutrient-poor reservoir; installing logs around the new islands to minimize erosion; constructing a buck-and-rail fence around recently planted aspen to protect the trees from grazing cattle; building and installing boxes for cavity-nesting wildlife; tipping over mature conifer trees into the lake to create cover for fish; and, finally, topping a nearby tree to install a platform to encourage osprey nesting. It was an ambitious plan, to say the least. Still, I felt very excited about these projects. The summer before, I had done only spotted owl surveys. Now I would begin helping to improve the landscape for wildlife species, concepts I had studied in college but had yet to put into practice.

Rick hoped to accomplish much of this work during a two-day work party with a high school group from Portland. I jumped into the planning even though I had never organized anything in my life. Unfortunately, my inexperience showed. Rick grew impatient with my many questions and lack of understanding of how to build a fence. His thinly veiled annoyance dissuaded me from further questions, but then I got in trouble for that as well.

"You need to ask questions!" he snapped one afternoon when I looked confused about the difference between a t-post and a "hard point" on the temporary fence we planned to install around the aspen until the buck and rail could be constructed.

I felt mortified at this rebuke. Fortunately, Kim, the other seasonal wildlife employee hired that summer, was easier to work with. Kim had long hair and an inquisitive stare, her eyes squinting slightly as she listened carefully to whatever was being said. She'd recently finished her master's research on pileated wood-peckers, another species dependent on older forests. Kim, very smart and very confident, didn't seem intimidated by Rick (though I knew I was a hard worker and got along well with people, I didn't consider myself particularly smart or confident). Together, Kim and I organized most of the activities for the work party. The effort was a resounding success in terms of educating young people about the natural world as well as enhancing habitat for wildlife.

That summer, I spent many days at the North Arm, monitoring the plants, watching for osprey using the platform, and looking for ducks on the islands. We installed signs explaining the project, and any time I saw campers or hikers, I discussed the work and its benefits. Given the proximity of Timothy Lake to my cabin, I sometimes visited the area in the evening. It wasn't long at all before ducks and herons had taken up residence on the islands.

*

I also spent some of that summer in another meadow complex. Salmon River Meadows is a large, open ecosystem adjacent to State Highway 26 in a valley near the base of Mt. Hood. Without natural fire, shrubs and conifers had been creeping into the meadows for decades. Small tree islands had grown up in the drier areas; dense thickets of spiraea, while good cover for some birds, had crowded out grasses and forbs nutritious for deer and elk. Indigenous people would have burned Salmon River Meadows regularly, but fire was now only a memory for the meadows. Rick hoped to change that, but it's a big operation to create a controlled burn during the right environmental conditions. The work couldn't be done during the summer, but if one waited too long into the fall, the rains might interfere.

After the big effort at the North Arm, Rick didn't seem to know what to do with me. Kim had more skills in analysis and writing. She was also working on some follow-up publications from her master's research. While Rick continued making plans and getting appropriate permissions for burning, he sent me to the meadows to "take notes on what you see." At the time, his instructions seemed vague. Though walking around in the meadows all day sounded fun and I wanted to see a new area, I wasn't sure how useful the work would really be. There wouldn't be the solid accomplishment of planting trees or building a fence. There wouldn't be the satisfaction of seeing wildlife species use something we'd created. In fact, however, the reconnaissance work helped me practice two critical skills for a biologist: making observations and taking accurate notes.

It didn't prove easy getting around the meadows. The sedges and grasses had grown waist high, hiding the bleached forms of trees long since fallen over from the forest edge. Willow towered over me near the meandering waters, and the fortresses of spiraea had to be skirted. However, a snow-capped Mt. Hood glowing brightly in the distance against the summer blue sky encouraged me onward. Throughout the meadow, the dainty pointed tracks of deer in the soft mud along braided stream channels sat next to tiny sundew plants, carnivores of the plant kingdom. Big piles of scat showed where bears had been taking advantage of the abundant summer grasses and berries. Warblers and sparrows scattered from the shrubby areas as I approached; juncos flew in protest from their ground nests if I got too close. Occasionally, I startled a deer or a grouse. The grouse especially scared me half to death with their surprise appearance and rapid wingbeats.

Mostly though, I found only evidence of wildlife. It was more exciting to see the animals themselves, but *being* seen isn't the best strategy for them. Besides, a sighting lasted at best only a few seconds. Tracks and scats, dropped feathers, or old bones, however, could be examined for many minutes. This "forest news" told a story. It was up to me to figure out what that story was.

2

Fire Call

Mt. Hood National Forest, 1986–88

The first thing that William, the fire engine foreman stationed at the Clackamas Lake Historic Ranger Station, said when I met him in the spring of 1987 was "I look forward to working with you on fires, Betsy."

I thought he must have misunderstood. "I'll be working in wildlife," I said, smiling. "Not fire."

At first, William just stared at me. It was hard to see his exact expression given his large, thick glasses; bushy beard; and the wild, curly mop of hair that covered his forehead and the sides of his face. Yet I had the distinct feeling he hadn't liked my response.

"*Everyone* goes on fires," he said at last, walking away. As I would soon learn, he was right.

*

The previous summer of 1986, I'd been excited to go on a wildfire assignment. When my supervisor, Jeff, had mentioned the possibility to me, I thought that it sounded like a great adventure. I soon met members of the Zigzag Interagency Hotshot Crew, a group of extremely fit people dedicated to fighting wildfires throughout the fire season. They told me about the excitement, the hard work, and the camaraderie of working on fires. They described riding in helicopters to remote parts of landscapes and their preparations for being able to do this work, which included doing "power hikes" up the steep trail behind the ranger station and spending much of each day engaged in physical fitness training. Hotshots, so named because they are often the first to arrive at a fire and thus work the "hottest" areas, aren't the only ones to go on wildfire assignments. For many in the Forest Service, though not everyone, this is a big part of being an employee. It wasn't officially a requirement, but there was a cultural expectation that new employees working for a national forest would be trained in wildland firefighting. I had never participated in sports in school and wasn't particularly team-oriented, but fire work appealed to me. It would be a challenge and was also a crucial part of forest management, so I felt I must know about it.

In between conducting owl surveys my first summer, I'd attended fire school. During this three-day class, I'd learned all about wildfire behavior, fire clothes, fire tools, fire weather, and how to dig a fireline, a break to stop the fire's advance. When the opportunity came later in the summer to join a 20-person hand crew for an assignment, I immediately said yes. After driving all night to eastern Oregon, we arrived at the Clear Creek fire camp. Due to our late arrival, we were assigned the night shift. My disappointment at not starting work immediately was tempered only by my tiredness.

August in the Ponderosa pine/juniper forests of eastern Oregon is hot and dry. In the camp, generators rumbled to power refrigerated semitrucks of food. Helicopters flew in and out, transporting crews to inaccessible parts of the fire and dipping water from a nearby lake to drop on the fire. All day long, hundreds of people moved around, and trucks and buses stirred up clouds of dust. At 6:00 p.m., after getting little sleep, we all staggered to the mess tent for dinner. Then we drove for two hours to where we would dig line until the next morning. As we donned our backpacks and fire shelters and grabbed lunches, I looked in awe at the scene before us.

Having now worked for so many years on fires, I don't remember what I'd expected a wildfire to look like before I actually saw one. Maybe I imagined it would be similar to seeing several campfires going at the same time: a little smoky perhaps but not that strange. Or maybe it would be like the prescribed burn I had visited on my first day at Zigzag. There would be a lot of smoke, but the fire would still be confined to a clearcut and would be burning up only slash.

This "real" fire, however, was not like in a campground, and it wasn't only happening in a timber harvest unit. Everywhere I looked, the forest burned. Tall trees, short trees, logs, and brush—they all glowed. Fire danced in the treetops, and it crawled on the ground. Sparks popped in the air like lightning bugs. Smoke wafted everywhere, cloaking the trees, as if working with the flames to hide the gobbling up of the forest. If I don't remember my impressions before that summer, I clearly remember them at our first meeting: fear.

Yet though I felt frightened, I also was determined. I felt strongly, and continued to for several years, that fire must be suppressed at all costs, a sentiment shared by many coworkers, not to mention the general public. This resolve was a good thing, as that first shift was one of the hardest I've ever worked. That night, we dug line up a steep slope with rocks rolling down around us. The smoke made seeing and breathing difficult. My bandana helped with the breathing but not much. My headlamp showed little besides all the ash in the air. The steep ground at least meant the digging went slow, and there were frequent opportunities to rest. At six o'clock the next morning, I sat exhausted with my crew where the buses would pick us up for the ride back to camp.

Much of the next 11 days was the same. Partway through the assignment, I called my parents from the one phone available in the fire camp. After waiting more than an hour in line, I finally connected with them. I survived that first assignment, but I didn't ever want to do it again.

*

Despite our inauspicious beginning, William and I became friends during the summer of 1987. He and the engine crew lived in the ranger's house across the road from me at Clackamas Lake. Though our work hours were different, with me often out at night doing owl surveys and them working weekends, we still found time to get to know each other. My opinion of working on fires also changed as I went on more assignments and grew more comfortable working on teams in challenging situations. In July, I joined William and other Bear Springs employees on a three-day excursion to a small fire in the Gifford Pinchot National Forest. With Gifford Pinchot just across the Columbia River from Mt. Hood, we didn't have a long drive. We left at four in the morning in order to get there for the day shift, which began at six. Each of those three days, we hiked down a steep slope to our work site and then back up again at the end of the day. This smaller fire seemed more manageable to me, and the fruits of our efforts could be seen. There was less smoke too.

A second assignment that summer to a fire on another part of Mt. Hood yielded less positive results. A small group of us traveled one evening to the Barlow Ranger District, east of the mountain. That night at 10:00 p.m., our sack lunches arrived. I enthusiastically spread the packet of mayonnaise on my ham sandwich. Unfortunately, after arriving back at my cabin early the next morning, I fell ill with food poisoning. William and the engine crew had left for the day, and I had no way of letting my supervisor, Rick, know I was sick. Fortunately, the forest botanist, Lois, arrived that morning to work on the district for a few days. We had planned for Lois to stay with me in the cabin, so she got word to Rick and Kim about my plight. After this experience, I understood that every wildfire would be different. It was best to be as flexible as possible and to expect the unexpected.

*

A few weeks later, I once again had the opportunity to take fire assignments. In late August, a lightning storm moved through the Pacific Northwest, setting off blazes in numerous locations. Several areas of smoke had been reported from the lookouts in the Bear Springs Ranger District. Everyone put on their fire clothes—the iconic, flame-resistant yellow shirts and green pants—and headed out. William and I were assigned to investigate smoke rising from the north shore of Timothy Lake. There wasn't good road access to this site, so we took Forest Service Boat 25, a small pleasure craft owned by the district and used for various projects on the reservoirs. As we launched from the south shore, the fire's narrow, gray-white smoke column stood out above the lake.

We easily found the blaze and began digging line around it. Measuring less than a 10th of an acre, this *was* a bit like a large campfire. After finishing the line, we regarded a large burning snag. If it fell, the snag would land outside our containment area. William used the handheld radio to request a faller. This person would take a few hours to arrive, so we continued to monitor our fireline and break apart the bigger chunks of burning fuel. When there remained little more that could be done, we took a break. I found my new friend and coworker to be a great storyteller. As we waited for the faller, he shared some of his early experiences working for the Forest Service and other organizations.

William had worked at the Mt. Hood Meadows Ski Area for a winter in the mid-1970s after getting out of the U.S. Navy and before going to work for the Coast Guard and attending school part-time to get a degree in forestry. In this short period of time, he'd become very attached to the landscape.

"I left Mt. Hood to begin my job with the Coast Guard," he remembered. "It was a beautiful, clear morning, and Mt. Hood looked stunning. I pulled over to take a last look. Then I told the mountain I would be back. I got in my car and drove away."

In the spring of 1979, William started working for the Forest Service at Bear Springs in fire. Two years later, he left again, taking a leave of absence from the agency to pursue a tour in the Peace Corps. He spent two years on the island of Montserrat in the eastern Caribbean before returning to Bear Springs. He told me about his forestry projects there, the people he worked with, and the monthly reports he submitted to the Peace Corps. He typed up these summaries on a used typewriter he had bought shortly after arriving. William laughed about how people in Montserrat didn't use turn signals when driving.

"Instead, they'd wait until the car going in the opposite direction was very close," he explained. "Then they'd point with their finger in one direction or another!"

William's stories revitalized my own desire to work in other countries, a dream I'd had since I was a child.

"It was one of the best things I've ever done," he said. "Where do you want to go?"

"Africa," I said without hesitation. "I've always wanted to work in Africa." William nodded. "Do it."

Five years later, I did join the Peace Corps. I didn't go to Africa but instead went to Argentina, where the recruiter felt my years of high school Spanish would be put to good use. Remembering William's experience, I bought a used typewriter. After selling most of my possessions, I left the rest with my mother, boyfriend, and different friends.

*

The lightning storm of August 30, 1987, hit southern Oregon and northern California particularly hard. That day, more than 1,000 strikes peppered the region, igniting numerous fires, including one along a stream called Silver Creek in the Siskiyou National Forest in southwest Oregon. Approximately 10 miles downstream of Silver Creek, where the Illinois River, an emerald-green waterway, flows into the greater Rogue River, sits the rural community of Agness. A post office, historic lodge, RV park, and the Agness Guard Station compose several parts of a community that, though small, is also host to much summer tourism. On August 31, smokejumpers from Montana and one aerial retardant plane arrived to fight the Silver Fire. However, steep, brushy terrain and a rapidly growing fire meant that more resources would be needed. In early September, the Silver Base fire camp was established in the fields around the Agness Guard Station. On September 6, the caterers arrived. On the 11th, the east winds began to blow. By September 16, Silver had grown to 30,000 acres.

Bear Springs assembled a 20-person crew, and on September 17, we began the long drive south to the Siskiyou Mountains. Back then, a typical fire assignment lasted three weeks, but most of us didn't think we'd be gone that long. When the weather shifts to cooler temperatures and higher humidities, fire activity usually begins to lessen. On the Mt. Hood, the changes had already begun. Gold and red leaves had begun falling, and a crispness permeated the early morning air. It was true that we were heading south, and it was also true that east winds could negate any fire suppression gains achieved with cooler weather. But we still thought we'd be back in a few days.

Upon our arrival in Agness, we were assigned to a spike camp, a "satellite" location away from the main base, at a private inholding in the middle of the Siskiyou National Forest. We flew by helicopter into Briggs Ranch and stayed for a week. Our work comprised improving an existing trail as a fire break between the ranch and Silver Prairie, a large, sloping meadow two miles to the south. Meals came from tins that were either flown in if the skies weren't too smoky or brought in by pack train if they were. In the evenings, we gratefully ate the tepid or cold food, then removed our boots and went to sleep. We worked, ate, slept, and did our best to avoid poison oak, which seemed to be growing everywhere. A friendly deer in camp provided some diversion. One morning, someone snapped a photo as I fed the animal grapes while holding my yellow fire shirt over her shoulders.

During our second week, we stayed in Agness and did day trips to our fireline assignments. Being able to take regular showers and eat hot meals seemed like luxury itself. One of the barns at Agness had been turned into a movie theater, with a VCR and television for those crews enjoying days off. On one such afternoon, my crew and I watched *The Fly* with Jeff Goldblum. This disturbing movie served as a welcome distraction from a fire that, despite the efforts of hundreds of people, was threatening to reach 100,000 acres. While historic fires in the Pacific Northwest and beyond had reached six-figure sizes in the past, including the Yacolt Burn of 1902 (238,000 acres), the stunning Big Burn of 1910 (3,000,000 acres), and the three fires of the Tillamook Burn (total of 350,000 acres between 1933 and 1951), it still wasn't a common occurrence. Everyone monitored the daily tally of Silver with worry and awe.

Our third and final week on Silver saw our crew flying into the Kalmiopsis Wilderness, a few miles south of Briggs Ranch. We again improved an already established recreation trail as a fire break. This was a true spike camp situation, where there was no support from the main camp, so we slept wherever we stopped digging line for the day and ate "meals ready to eat," or MREs, that we'd carried with us rather than flown-in tins of food. The MREs weren't very good, and I couldn't work up much enthusiasm for them.

By this last week, I felt bone-tired from digging line every day and breathing smoke. Poison oak rashes covered much of my body, and scratching kept me awake at night. I hadn't been eating properly or drinking enough water. Consequently, one morning, I became shaky as we dug the fireline and had to sit down.

Leonard, our crew boss, looked at me and said, "You need to get back to base camp, Betsy."

"I'll be fine," I disagreed. "I just need to take a break."

"You don't look fine. And if we need to move quickly, you might compromise the safety of the crew." This scenario seemed unlikely to me given how far the main fire was, but it was also true that Silver had been explosive on many occasions.

A helicopter soon arrived, and in seconds, I had climbed in and was flying away. Not only did I feel ill from dehydration; I also felt awful leaving the others behind. My 22nd birthday passed when I was on Silver. While I had youth to carry me through most anything, I didn't yet have the wisdom to know my limits or to stay healthy. Silver offered me a host of new experiences, including helicopter rides, working around poison oak, and many days of digging line, that tested me physically as well as mentally. I learned valuable lessons about pacing during long fire assignments and taking care of myself under less-than-ideal conditions.

After three weeks, we headed home. Silver wouldn't be declared out for another month when the fall rains arrived. This fire had broken records for its size (96,540 acres) and duration (72 days). Not until 2002 and the Biscuit Fire would another such sizable event transpire in the Siskiyou National Forest.

*

A year later, in the summer of 1988, I found myself in Yellowstone National Park on a fire crew once again. More than 100 firefighters dressed in yellow and green stood around waiting. The National Park Service ranger smiled at us. Though she'd given this presentation many times, for her, each time was new, just like an actor's role in a play.

"Contrary to popular belief," she said, "Old Faithful doesn't erupt at the

Our Mt. Hood fire crew working on the Silver Fire in 1987. USDA Forest Service by Betsy L. Howell.

same time every day. Geysers are always changing in response to water temperature, mineral content, and even earthquakes, of which there are many in the park." She looked at her watch and then at the solemn group around her. "Another eruption is due shortly."

Most of the firefighters around me didn't seem impressed with this woman's talk on Old Faithful, her smart uniform and iconic Park Service straw hat, or the impending geyser that would soon send a fountain of 200+°F water more than 100 feet above us. No one cared about the fire that lived beneath this land. We were here because of the fire above ground. We had come to stop the many blazes that now threatened the country's oldest national park, but we'd also overwhelmed the National Park Service staff. At the moment, they didn't quite know what to do with us, hence the tour.

The first wildfire in the Greater Yellowstone Ecosystem that summer was started by lightning outside of the national park on June 14, 1988. By July 20, several more fires inside the park had burned 17,000 acres. Initially, the response had been to allow the naturally caused fires to run their course. Once a prescribed amount of acres had been consumed, then attempts would be made to contain and suppress them. Conversely, all human-caused fires would immediately be suppressed. However, given the quickly evolving situation, including extremely dry conditions, the impact on America's beloved Yellowstone, and the political consequences of fires growing together into "complexes," which quickly began to threaten human communities, full-on suppression for *every* fire began on July 21. Forest Service crews, as well as those from other agencies, began arriving shortly after.

Toward the end of July, I had joined a crew from Mt. Hood headed to southern Oregon. Before our assignment, I knew only one other person on this crew. Lottie had come to the forest as a volunteer, much as I had in 1986. She worked for Jeff doing owl surveys and fish and wildlife habitat projects, and she and I had spent a day earlier in the spring canoeing around the islands in the North Arm of Timothy Lake. Everyone else came from different districts and worked in fire. I felt intimidated not knowing many people, but our squad boss, Ken, welcomed both me and Lottie into the group of far more experienced firefighters. Ken, a wiry fellow in his 40s with a thick, slightly chaotic mustache and a teasing nature, proved to be a great squad boss. He was calm and patient and unadorned by the ego that can accompany some firefighters.

We spent only a few days in southern Oregon before our crew boss, Brian, told us we were done. He said that we had the option to return home or go to Yellowstone, where fires were growing daily. As nobody wanted to go home, we began the long drive to Wyoming the next morning.

*

On our first day in Yellowstone, we picked up garbage and cleared brush around the structures at Old Faithful. During the second day, we received the tour. On the third day, we got some much-needed R and R. Needless to say, nobody was very happy about having driven all this way just to sweep around buildings and pick up garbage. The grumbling grew louder as the days passed. Finally, one morning, Brian announced that we'd be flying into the backcountry to dig fireline. He instructed us to get our gear together and have it weighed for the flight.

Three lightning-caused fires—Clover, Mist, and Lovely—in the eastern part of the park had grown together to form the Clover-Mist Complex. Started on July 9 and 11, the three fires were estimated to have grown to 68,000 acres in three weeks. The Shoshone National Forest abutted the park's eastern edge, as did the communities of Silver Gate, Cook City, and Cody, all north and east of the fire. Though Clover-Mist currently burned several miles from these towns, the fact that it had grown so quickly caused great concern. Our assignment included digging fireline to connect natural breaks, such as dry streambeds and meadows, and trying to contain the fire within the wilderness.

For the next several days, we worked in the heat under clear skies. The helicopters regularly brought meals in tins as well as sack lunches. After dropping off the supplies, they also picked up sling-loads of garbage and food rejected from the lunches. Thus, we were able to keep the moving camp relatively free of items that would attract bears and other wildlife.

Unfortunately, our efforts to hold the fire met with little success. It jumped the lines we made; it also jumped natural breaks. The fire had moved into the crowns of the trees and raced along aerially at top speed, unperturbed by any efforts to stop it on the ground. One afternoon, we escaped to our safety zone, a wide, dry riverbed where the fire couldn't come but where the smoke settled easily. We all sat or lay down as close to the earth as possible, where the freshest air remained. I didn't feel particularly frightened regarding the fire, but the smoke worried me. When I saw a deer, not far from us, turning around in circles and clearly overwhelmed by the foul air, the worry increased. This animal vanished after a few minutes, and we didn't see it again.

Soon enough, the smoke prevented further helicopter flights. The MREs appeared from the bottoms of our packs, and we began eating previously less desirable parts of our lunches: Hostess treats, packaged cheese and crackers, Capri Sun juice packs. Fruit was also retrieved from the boxes the helicopters would have picked up had they been able to come. We managed all right until about the third day of this, when even these foods had been consumed. Ken came back from one foraging trip looking serious.

"Y'all better get on over there if you hope to still find something," he said, then looked at his waist. "Dang, I hope this smoke clears soon. I had to make a new hole in my belt this morning." Ken, already a skinny guy, didn't need to lose any more weight in my opinion. He glanced over at me.

"You doing OK, Montana?" Ken had begun calling me this because I wore a ball cap with the Treasure State's name on it.

"Oh, sure," I replied. After learning my lesson on the Silver Fire, I now made sure on every assignment to drink plenty of water and eat as well as possible. "I hope they'll be able to fly soon though."

"Yeah, me too," he nodded.

"Someone saw a bear this morning in camp," said Lottie.

"Yep," Ken confirmed, apparently having already heard this. "Another good reason to get some of the food now."

I don't remember now if our crew walked out from Clover-Mist or if we left in the helicopter. I do know that after we finished this assignment, we went to Cody, Wyoming, for two days off. Shortly after, we left Yellowstone, and a month later, "Black Saturday" struck. That day, 80-mile-per-hour winds burned another 165,000 acres in just a few hours. Two weeks later, several structures at Old Faithful burned, and on September 10, the national park closed for the first time in its history. By mid-November, when the last of the many Yellowstone fires was declared out, 793,880 acres, or 36 percent, of the park had burned. Additionally, more than 400 animal deaths were documented. Collectively, Clover-Mist and the other Yellowstone fires produced the largest wildfire event ever recorded in the park.

*

The 1988 wildfires in Yellowstone stunned the country and the world. The numbers boggled the imagination back then, as did the fact that these fires had occurred in such a cherished landscape. This was only my third year working in fire and would be the only time yet that I've done so in a national park. While nothing has changed in terms of the basic ecosystemic need for fire, tremendous events like Yellowstone now occur regularly in the West and in wild, rural, and urban landscapes.

3

Backcountry Ranger

Siskiyou National Forest, 1989, 1995

The spring night air spilled into our open windows as my coworker Jerry and I drove up the winding Johnson Mountain road into the Siskiyou National Forest. It was May 1989. I had just arrived in southern Oregon after accepting a new job in the Powers Ranger District. The year before, my Mt. Hood coworker, Kim, had left Bear Springs for a district wildlife biologist position on the Siskiyou. Shortly after, Kim encouraged me to apply for a biological technician job that had recently opened in Powers. I accepted the job while traveling in Africa during the three months I'd taken off that winter. Though I'd hoped to perhaps stay in Africa and find wildlife work, I'd been unsuccessful. Instead, I'd found myself on life's often meandering path and had chosen to return home.

Not staying in Africa, where I'd always hoped to work, had been disappointing, but I also felt excited to return to the Forest Service. Having a job in my field of study was also no small thing. And I loved the Pacific Northwest landscapes. I loved the rain and the fog, the ancient trees and the high alpine country. I loved being out in the forest by myself, yet also being with coworkers who had the same love of the forests. The Siskiyou Mountains, adjacent to the Pacific Ocean, would be different from the inland Mt. Hood. Remembering my experiences on the Silver Fire with the poison oak gave me pause, though with a little alertness, I felt I could avoid this plant. Not only would I continue working with spotted owls; I would also conduct surveys for marbled murrelets, the fascinating seabird similarly dependent on older forests.

Jerry and I had come out this evening to do a spotted owl survey. Country music played softly on the radio while we chatted. He had lived in Powers a few years already and was briefing me on life in a town of just 600 people.

"Gas is more expensive in Powers, but you should fill up here every now and then," he advised. "People will appreciate it. Shop at the market too. Powers is a funny town, but there are good folks here."

As Jerry and I got closer to our destination, we met another vehicle coming down the mountain. It was after 10:00 p.m. and now dark on this June evening.

"Wonder who this is," Jerry said, slowing down.

"Let's not say we're doing owl surveys," I proposed.

"Good idea."

The other vehicle stopped as well. A man wearing a ball cap was driving while a woman I could barely see sat in the passenger seat. The man, his face in shadow, said, "Good evening."

We exchanged a few pleasantries about the warm night, then Jerry casually asked the fellow what they were up to. The man looked over at the woman and then straight ahead. "Oh, we're just out here looking at some culverts." He paused, turning back toward our vehicle. "What are you folks up to?"

I stumbled a bit, then said, "We're looking at some stands of trees."

The man nodded, pushing his ball cap back and revealing a light-colored beard and mustache. We shortly said our goodbyes and proceeded in our respective directions.

"That was weird," I said as Jerry pushed the vehicle back into drive. "Who would be out looking at culverts this time of night?"

"Who would be out looking at trees?" Jerry asked, unimpressed with my answer.

"It was all I could think of."

As we drove away, Jerry took a last look in the side mirror as the other vehicle's lights disappeared around a curve. "You know, I'm not sure," he said, "but I think that might have been Dave Shea."

*

Beginning in the 1960s, Dave Shea worked as a backcountry ranger in Glacier National Park in Montana. In 1981, he'd taken a break from the National Park Service to try a different agency in the coastal forests of southern Oregon. Dave moved to Powers and there met his soon-to-be wife, Genevieve, also known as VV. After two years, however, Dave wasn't sure if the Forest Service was right for him. He and VV returned to Glacier. They lived and worked at the seasonal ranger station in Belly River, a remote, stunning valley of lakes, meadows, and the high country of the Rocky Mountain front range. Even though Montana held Dave's heart, he loved the coast as well. In 1988, they returned to Powers, moving into a log home along the South Fork Coquille River, the waterway that bisected the Powers Ranger District. After arriving in 1989, I heard all about Dave. He was a superb naturalist, in the vein of John Muir or

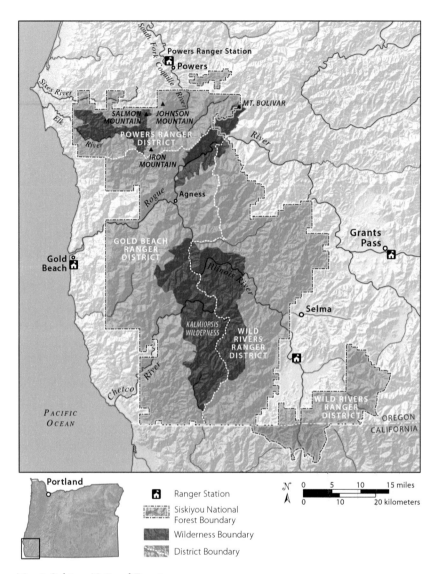

Map 3. Siskiyou National Forest.

John James Audubon. More than one person had told me, "Dave was born a century too late."

In the 1980s, it was best not to advertise one's spotted owl work. A sea change was occurring in terms of acceptable levels of timber harvest and viewing forests as more than just commodities, and people's lives and the expectations they'd always carried for their futures were also being transformed. I never felt personally threatened as a surveyor of the species most people now blamed for these shifts. Similarly, during my years in the Mt. Hood National Forest, I hadn't directly observed spotted owl antagonism, though it had surely existed. On my first trip to southwest Oregon, however, I immediately saw many bumper stickers and signs with messages such as "I like Spotted Owls . . . Fried" and "Save a Logger, Eat an Owl." Not being certain of people's reactions to my new job, I at first explained my wildlife work in general terms, emphasizing habitat improvement projects for species everyone loved, such as deer and elk or waterfowl. Later, though, as I got to know the community, I became bolder, once even wearing my "Spotted Owl Monitoring Team" T-shirt to the Timberline Tavern in Powers. Others were also circumspect about this work. Dave and VV had been surveying for owls that night on Johnson Mountain, as Jerry and I had been. We didn't realize until later that we'd first met on the mountain in the dark, but when we did, we laughed at how we'd tried to throw the other off the scent of the owl surveyor.

Dave was a wildlife biologist, but his interests encompassed everything in the natural world. In Powers, he started a plant collection for the district. He also relocated several muskrats from a city wetland that had once been an old mill pond to another wetland in the district called Cedar Swamp. There weren't any muskrats in Cedar Swamp, though they'd clearly been there at one time.

"That's just what you do," Dave told me when I asked why he'd moved the muskrats. As biologists, we needed to restore ecosystems. To Dave, who had spent almost three decades in Glacier getting to know grizzlies, wolves, eagles, and other wildlife species, this made sense. To the Forest Service, with a mission that focused on habitat rather than individual animals, such activities were not a priority. After returning to Powers a second time, Dave taught wildlife classes at the local community college in Coos Bay. He also returned to Montana in the summer to teach field courses at the Glacier Institute, a nonprofit, educational organization associated with the national park. Dave didn't need or desire more work. Fortunately for me, he changed his mind a few years later.

*

In August 1992, Dave returned to the Forest Service full time, taking my place as I left for an assignment in the Peace Corps. I hadn't forgotten my dreams of international work, and after my first year in Powers, I applied to the Peace

Dave Shea and me during a field day, Siskiyou National Forest, 1995. USDA Forest Service by Betsy L. Howell.

Corps. However, a few months later, I pulled my application. My father had been diagnosed with colon cancer, the rapid progression of which took his life a short two and a half months later. After another year of helping my mother settle into her new life, I applied again. This time I was accepted into a new program starting in Argentina. Even though I wasn't going to Africa, I would be working on a wildlife project, though I didn't know exactly what that would be.

"Out with the young and in with the old, eh?" Dave asked the afternoon he came to the office for a briefing on our different projects. He was just 52 years old then, a quiet man from Minnesota, of Irish heritage with red hair and a beard. Dave spoke softly and chose his words carefully, and people listened to him. He knew more about wildlife than anyone around Powers, living the life of someone with most of his soul in the natural world and only a reluctant toe or two in the world of humans.

Since our first meeting on Johnson Mountain three years before, I hadn't interacted much with Dave. Though I was off to my overseas adventure, I also felt envious of my supervisor Sue getting to work with and learn from him. But in January 1995, upon my return from the Peace Corps, the situation would be reversed. While I was in South America, Sue had left Powers for another job. I'd applied, and been selected, as the district wildlife biologist, while Dave was now the district botanist. I felt glad to have both the job and Dave's presence, but it seemed a little absurd too. He knew much more about wildlife than I ever would. Fortunately, Dave's knowledge, coupled with modesty and a dry wit, didn't encourage my insecurity. After my return to Powers, he began his winter wildlife class at the community college. Though I had a degree in wildlife management, I also knew there was much I could learn from him and immediately signed up. I also enjoyed many dinners at the Shea log home along the South Fork Coquille River. There, as we sat surrounded by their natural history library and Dave's collections of skulls, tracks, and antlers, the conversations centered on stories of wild animals and adventures in the woods.

*

"I spent a lot of years packing a mule," Dave said one afternoon as we returned to Powers from a day-long meeting on the Oregon Coast, "and I'm not sure what we just sat through has anything to do with the real world."

I couldn't disagree. Meetings to talk about managing the forest didn't always seem like the best way to actually manage the forest. As a Forest Service biologist, I was a generalist and was required to know something about every species on the lands we managed. The positive aspect of this included encountering the diverse tapestry of life that makes ecosystems function. The downside was that I never felt like an expert on anything. Still, part of being a biologist is knowing where to look for answers. Many answers come from spending time in the field. Out in the woods, I could be observing and learning and forming a better understanding; in meetings, I only felt trapped, uncomfortable, and generally inadequate.

"I guess it's just part of the job," I said glumly.

Dave shook his head. His suspicion of the present-day duties of a biologist extended to the Forest Service computer system as well, the DG that I'd first encountered almost 10 years earlier. Dave's return to the agency meant he needed to use the computer, but he wasn't one bit impressed. Under great duress, he agreed to look at email, or what one of our coworkers called "a way to get your bullshit message out to the world." While I typed up my wildlife reports on the DG, Dave wrote his in pencil and then asked the administration department to type them up. As the '90s unfolded and personal electronics became more integrated into human daily life, Dave refused to buy in.

"While I breathe, a computer will never enter my home," he vowed.

*

One summer evening in Belly River in Glacier National Park, Dave had been returning late to the ranger station. The job of a National Park Service back-country ranger includes spending long days patrolling, assessing resource impacts from people, assisting visitors with emergencies, conducting searches and rescues, and knowing the landscape and its residents intimately. A person must be in top physical shape. He or she needs to be comfortable in a variety of situations, many of which will be completely unpredictable. On this particular day, as golden light filled the eastern side of the valley and shadows grew long, Dave met a cougar sitting in the path. The animal immediately jumped off into the bushes. Yet it didn't go far. As Dave stood still, the cat returned. It was a big tom, with greater curiosity than fear, perhaps from an understanding that living in a national park meant people weren't as big of a threat. The human and cougar regarded each other.

"What happened?" I asked.

Dave nodded. "I lay down on the trail."

"What? Why?"

"I was curious to see what it would do."

The cougar, it seemed, was also curious. It lay down as well, and the two of them continued to share the moment and space on the trail for some minutes. Soon, the animal decided to continue with its travels. It vanished into the bushes, for good this time.

Another time, Dave was out with a younger ranger in Glacier when they came upon a grizzly bear. The animal charged them. The other man immediately ran, an understandable, though potentially fatal, response. Even worse, he hid behind Dave! Again, I asked what happened.

Dave thought a moment. "I started talking to it. The bear then stopped. It was bluff charging, see? When we didn't move, it started eating grass. Classic displacement activity."

Chief Mountain sits on the eastern edge of Glacier National Park. During one hike there, Dave had several interesting wildlife encounters. The first involved a pair of evening grosbeaks. The male bird flew very close to Dave and landed on his boot. This was surprising enough, but then the bird flew up and perched on his ball cap! All Dave could see were the black tail feathers as the grosbeak chirped excitedly. After it flew away, Dave continued hiking. He next found wolf tracks, which he subsequently followed. These led to a depression in the ground where a perfect basalt point lay. As he was looking at this ancient tool, a golden eagle flew overhead. The raptor began to call and then dropped a feather on the trail near where Dave stood. The finale for the day included finding a buffalo pelvic bone, evidence of an animal that had long since vanished from the lands in the eastern part of the park. Dave wrote about these events in his 2007 book *Chief Mountain, Home of the Thunderbird*. A "good medicine day," he called it, using a term from the Blackfeet people (Shea 2007, v). The very best kind of day for a wildlife biologist.

I have concluded over the years that there are some biologists who live completely different lives from the rest of us in the profession. They spend a huge amount of time in the natural world and have unique experiences to match. Though I've met a few people like this, I've never known anyone so aligned with the natural world as Dave. This doesn't mean, however, that he had a sentimental view of wildlife. Dave trapped for many years. When I met him, however, he no longer did. "I've killed a lot of animals in my time," he told me once. "I don't want to do that anymore."

*

Dave had several scientific collections that he'd started decades before. Scats and skulls of different animals, feathers from birds, and casts of tracks were all impeccably organized and labeled, as if they resided in a museum or laboratory. I knew from my college mammalogy course how important such collections were for research and education, but I'd also been disturbed by an assignment where we'd had to trap a small mammal, euthanize it, and then make a study skin that would become part of the department's library (I did all this, but I remember a fellow student who absolutely refused). Yet Dave's collections mostly consisted of items that he'd found; some skulls came from animals he'd hunted or trapped, but many were from natural deaths.

As a child, I'd always been a collector. From funny things like pennants and ceramic statues of cats to natural history objects like seashells and rocks. Dave's skull collection in particular impressed me. Those of the black bear, coyote, deer, and elk, among others, were all very white and clean and arranged by taxonomic group on shelves he'd built. The most unique pairing included a cougar skull that sat next to a saber-toothed tiger. The latter had been constructed by a company that made replica skulls, which Dave had purchased for educational purposes. The prehistoric feline was mounted on a stand with its jaws open to display the massive canines. As Dave showed me these one evening, he held the cougar skull in the same position. Apart from the canines and general size, there was little difference between the two.

"Cats have had no need to evolve," Dave said, respect in his voice. "They were made perfect to begin with."

Seeing Dave's years of work in 1989 inspired me to start a skull collection in Argentina, but I became more devoted to the effort after returning from the Peace Corps. As I began remote camera surveys for forest carnivores in the fall of 1995, I obtained different skulls from local trappers, who had agreed to help supply me with bait for the stations. I also opportunistically found different skulls in the woods. Both of these methods, by gift and happenstance, were the easiest ways to build up my collection. The hardest was if I had to prepare the skull myself after finding a dead animal in the woods or along a road. Animals hit by cars didn't usually yield undamaged specimens, but sometimes I got lucky. I bought an old pot at Goodwill and set up my single-burner, propane camp stove in the driveway. I'd cut off the head and as much meat as possible, then put the skull in the boiling water. A wire brush and tweezers helped remove the flesh that didn't fall off easily; teeth that loosened were glued back in later. Obviously, I tried to boil skulls only when my neighbors weren't around.

One evening, while returning from a day in the field, I saw a house cat on the forest road adjacent to the South Fork Coquille River. This spot was more than four miles from Powers. The cat had either been dropped off in the woods or been feral for some time. I stopped, but it instantly vanished into the understory. A few days later, I found the cat dead, hit by a vehicle and partially scavenged, yet the head seemed intact. I'm a cat lover, but somewhere along the line, I'd also grown less sentimental. Dave had given me an extra cougar skull he'd had, and my trapper friend had given me one of a bobcat. A house cat skull would round out my feline collection well. More than 20 years later, the cougar, bobcat, and *Felis domesticus* remain together in my home on a shelf with a glass door for easy viewing.

I still need the saber-toothed tiger, however.

*

Apart from my growing skull assemblage, I also began gathering feathers and scats and making plaster casts of tracks. The feathers and scats were simple. I just collected whatever I found and noted the stories that could be learned, or inferred, from the animal that was no more. Feathers from a cedar waxwing on a trail in Powers taken by either a house cat or a coyote. The black-legged kittiwake, a pelagic bird, dead at the old Powers mill pond that must have gotten blown inland during a storm. Feathers I found had most often simply been dropped in the normal course of shedding. Songbirds especially, due to moving through the tight world of bushes and other undergrowth and wearing their feathers out frequently, are always dropping them. Because the Migratory Bird Treaty Act of 1918 prohibits possessing any part of most bird species, I applied for a permit from the U.S. Fish & Wildlife Service to have the feathers for educational purposes. Riker mount boxes, commonly used to display butterflies and other insects, also worked well for feathers. Into one large Riker box went the kittiwake feather and two tail feathers from other species. One came from a red-tailed hawk and one from a bald eagle, this last another present from Dave.

For scats, I bought a clear fishing tackle box with compartments I could make smaller or larger depending on the size of the scat. Very fresh or very wet scats needed to be dried before storing. Using the oven for such a use proved unpopular with my housemate, so I simply wrapped them in newspaper. They still dried, but the process took longer.

In Argentina, my project had been to study mountain lions. During many field days, I'd made molds of tracks of *el puma*. Now I hoped to get a bobcat and a North American cougar to add to the collection. I bought plaster of paris at the drugstore and several sizes of hose clamps at the hardware store. When I found a good, clear track in the mud or sand, I placed the clamp around it, then mixed up some plaster to pour in. Getting the right consistency was a challenge. There couldn't be too much water or it wouldn't set up. There also couldn't be too little or the plaster wouldn't settle into the small spaces of toe or claw marks. I made many impressions of cougars and bobcats, coyotes, raccoons, great blue herons, squirrels, and black bears. I also got a mold from our compound cat, Gus. It had taken some encouragement, but Gus finally walked through a bit of mud for me. My collection of wildlife objects grew, filling up the space around my desk at work and my bedroom at home. I had plans to use all these materials for education, to display in our front office or at county fairs and other events.

Of course, there were many species whose scats, tracks, or skulls I wouldn't be collecting, including those of grizzly bears, a creature with the unfortunate, in my opinion, scientific name of *Ursus arctos horribilis*. These animals hadn't been in Oregon since the 1930s, but because of Dave's many stories about them from Glacier, they were on my mind. When I learned that my friend sometimes "made" tracks for his classes to find, I decided I could do the same. Dave's 1986 book *Animal Tracks of Glacier National Park* had illustrations of life-sized prints that I could use as a guide. With the book in hand, a measuring tape, and a set of grizzly claws Dave loaned me, I set about my task. A patch of soft, bare earth in the backyard provided the perfect place to install the track. With a spoon, I scooped out the five toes and massive palm of a left-front grizzly track. After the proportions all looked correct, I carefully pressed the claws into the earth above the toes. Connecting two large hose clamps together was necessary to encircle such a big track, as was making a large amount of plaster. As it set up, I waited, hopeful.

Dave often said that a landscape is a completely different place with grizzly bears in it. "They're just really fine animals," he told me many times. During his years working in Glacier, he'd seen them up close and from afar. He'd found their great piles of scat many times, filled with berries, hair, grass, or bones. Once a mountain lion had stepped in a pile of grizzly poop. Dave never felt afraid of the bears, but their presence heightened his awareness of his surroundings, of the possibilities for encounters, and of a world that once was, where animals and humans lived with greater connection and acceptance of each other.

Dave's admiration for grizzlies ran so deep, he'd once told VV that after he died, he wanted to be left on the side of a mountain in Glacier for the bears to scavenge.

"What did she say?" I asked.

"'You're not doing that!'" he said, adopting a firm tone. We both laughed. Then Dave became serious. "Why should I be different from any other animal?" he asked. "I'm no different from an old coyote that dies in the woods. I should be recycled just like the old coyote."

I thought about this. "I'd like to be recycled through a mountain lion."

Dave nodded. "I'd like to be recycled through a grizzly."

*

My grizzly bear track turned out very well. Of all my collecting efforts, the tracks group was now the most complete. I had enough predators, ungulates, birds, and squirrels to do an educational display in our front office. A triangular glass case sat in one corner of the reception area and was most often filled with items of Forest Service history: old compasses and binoculars, black-and-white photographs of fire lookouts and other historic buildings, stereoscopes, and early aerial photographs. These were all fine, but I thought something on wildlife would be of interest. The administration officer, Tina, agreed. I began making labels for all the tracks.

*

Dave and I worked together on several projects, and we also had our own endeavors. He did all the plant surveys for our timber sales and other projects, as well as transect surveys for neotropical migrant birds and pellet counts for deer and elk. He also organized contracts to grow native seed. With different partners, Dave completed surveys and habitat enhancement projects for amphibians and reptiles. I focused on forest carnivores, including martens and fishers, and coordinated surveys for spotted owls and marbled murrelets.

In May 1995, just after I'd returned from the Peace Corps, Dave organized a western pond turtle habitat improvement project at the old mill pond in Powers. The pond that had been used for decades to store old-growth trees from the surrounding mountains before processing them into lumber was now an open, shallow-water habitat for wildlife. In the winter, scores of American coots and American wigeons arrived and covered the lake. In the summer, osprey and swallows took advantage of the stocked fish and insect life, respectively. Mallards and great blue herons lived at the pond year-round. Canada geese and various gulls passed through during migration. It was also the home of several western pond turtles (*Actinemys marmorata*) a state-listed sensitive species. That spring, Dave and a biologist with the Oregon Department of Fish & Wildlife installed three log rafts in the pond as basking structures for the turtles. These rafts immediately became very popular with the reptiles. Dave regularly received reports from park visitors on when and how many animals were using the rafts. In this way, we also learned of the presence of a western painted turtle (*Chrysemys picta bellii*), a species not historically found in this part of Oregon.

Dave also organized surveys for salamanders and pond turtles in the forest. At that time, I knew little of this group of animals, known collectively as herptiles—that is, amphibians and reptiles. We inventoried small natural ponds as well as human-made ones that had been constructed for fire suppression. The most common resident at both types of water bodies was the northwestern salamander (*Ambystoma gracile*), a species of "mole" salamander, terrestrial amphibians that spend most of their lives underground. We commonly found northwestern egg masses—firm, softball-sized balls of gel attached to grass stems or sticks with anywhere from 30 to 270 individual eggs inside. The adults come to the breeding ponds in late winter. They lay their eggs and then return to their underground burrows. Consequently, we never saw them, though occasionally we'd observe a "neotenic" animal in the water. These individuals are adults but also retain their juvenile characteristics, such as the long gills needed to capture oxygen in water (terrestrial adults lose these gills when they move onto land).

One day, Dave and I met Lee Webb, the forest wildlife biologist for the Siskiyou, and did a reptile survey on Mt. Bolivar on the east end of the Powers Ranger District. An early land surveyor had named the mountain after the Venezuelan-born leader who liberated Peru and Columbia from Spanish rule. Mt. Bolivar is drier and rockier than many parts of the district. There are great wildflower shows here in the spring, and the trail, at only 1.4 miles in length, isn't too hard or long a climb. I especially liked Mt. Bolivar because Howell's manzanita, a shrub native to the coastal mountains of southern Oregon and northern California, also grew here.

On this day, we found a young western skink (*Plestiodon skiltonianus*), a lizard that is very fast and not easy to catch. Peterson's *A Field Guide to Western Reptiles and Amphibians* warns not to "grab the tail; it is easily shed" (Stebbins 2003, 310). The breaking off of the skink's bright blue tail is a predator defense mechanism. As the predator is being distracted by the tail in its paw, the skink escapes. Since the tail grows back, the damage is minimal, particularly relative to being eaten. As we turned over rocks and pieces of bark, Lee spotted the skink. Then Dave quickly grabbed for it.

"Don't get the tail!" warned Lee, too late, as a piece of tail broke off. Dave reached for the escaping animal again and broke off more of the tail. Finally, he got the skink. I have a photo of Dave's hands, palms up, with the skink and its tail in two blue pieces, both of which were flopping around. None of us were happy about this. Even though the tail regenerates, it's still hard on the animal. Also, until it does regrow, the skink wouldn't have this ability to evade predators.

*

The morning I set up my track collection in the display case, I cleaned the glass doors and dusted the shelves. I felt as excited as I had in the third grade when I brought my new microscope to class for show and tell. On the middle two shelves, I set the wild cats and hooved animals. The bottom and top shelves included a mélange of species, including river otter, raccoon, and muskrat, as well as a domestic dog track, useful for comparing the differences between canine and feline prints. I didn't include the homemade grizzly bear track only due to its size. This track would have taken up one shelf on its own.

Later in the day, Dave came to the front office to see my creation. He looked it over carefully.

"You're making good use of your time, Bets," he said, nodding in approval.

I beamed. From a man who had made very good use of his time during a life and career spent in the natural world, this was high praise indeed.

4

A Bobtailed Horse

Siskiyou National Forest, 1989–91

I had done a very foolish thing. I had gone walking in the hills around Powers, Oregon, even though Guy, my boyfriend at the time, had said gravely, "There's poison oak everywhere up there, Betsy."

"I'll be careful," I'd assured him, feeling his concern to be excessive. At this time of year, in the fall, the bushes with their "leaves of three" were changing colors, making them much more obvious. Also, the plant *wasn't* everywhere. I'd just walk between the vibrant clumps and keep my hands in my pockets.

By that evening, the rash had begun. The backs of my hands, my face, and neck had all turned red and started to swell. The next morning, I sat in the town's clinic waiting to see the nurse practitioner.

"Looks like you got into some oak there," he said, trying unsuccessfully to hide his amusement.

"Yeah," I mumbled. The rash had covered my lips and mouth to the extent that speaking was difficult.

"Well, don't worry," he continued in a jovial tone. "We'll get you fixed up shortly."

"Getting fixed up" involved receiving a cortisone shot and being sent on my way. I think the shot probably did help but not before the plants' oils worked their way across more of my body. My left forearm swelled so much that it resembled the limb of a certain cartoon sailor. Rashes, small and large, appeared in the most inconvenient places. One eye grew puffy and red. The next two weeks unfolded in misery.

"Don't scratch!" people said, and I wanted to hit them with my Popeye arm.

"Interesting," others mused before adding, "I can trim back poison oak all day in my yard and never get it." Of course, I hated them.

Fortunately, there were those who had as much susceptibility as I did. They looked at me with great expressions of sympathy. We didn't speak much about it, however, since they didn't want to get too close.

*

In 1905, President Theodore Roosevelt created the Siskiyou Forest Reserve, a steep, rugged landscape of temperate rainforest, exceptional botanical diversity, and maritime influences. Two years later, the reserve was renamed the Siskiyou National Forest. The word *Siskiyou* means "a bob-tailed horse" in Cree, the language of Indigenous people who lived primarily in Canada (Gibbs 2005). The story went that these coastal mountains were named when a bobtailed racehorse of a fur trapping party, which had French Canadian members, was lost during a snowstorm. By the 1950s, a few land exchanges had settled the forest's final acreage at just over a million acres.

In 2004, the administration of the forest was combined with its nearest neighbor, and together they became the Rogue River-Siskiyou National Forest, a now larger area of 1.8 million acres encompassing lands in both the Siskiyou Mountains and the Cascade Range. I worked in this part of southern Oregon from 1989 to 1998, in a landscape of old-growth forest, spotted owls and marbled murrelets, forest carnivores, wilderness and wild and scenic rivers, and yes, hillsides of copious poison oak.

My work on the Powers Ranger District, the farthest north of the five districts comprising the Siskiyou National Forest, was similar to what I'd done on Mt. Hood. I conducted species surveys, planned habitat enhancement projects, and worked on environmental assessment teams. That first spring, however, one focus took precedence over all others. Lawsuits against federal agencies, including the first from GreenWorld in January 1987 to federally list the spotted owl as endangered, culminated in a crisis in early 1989.

Environmental groups had successfully obtained a court injunction against the sale of old-growth timber on federal lands managed by the Bureau of Land Management and the Forest Service within the range of the northern spotted owl. This happened in spring 1989 and followed a court decision the previous fall determining that the U.S. Fish & Wildlife Service's decision to not list the owl in 1987 had been arbitrary and capricious and went against all expert opinion regarding the species' population viability in the face of continuing timber harvest. With listing now inevitable, timber sales halted, and pressure from the timber industry, then senators Mark Hatfield of Oregon and Brock Adams of Washington attached a special rider to that year's congressional appropriations bill. This rider, known variously as "Section 318," "Northwest Compromise," the "Hatfield-Adams Amendment of 1989," and the "Rider from Hell," directed the federal agencies to sidestep the ongoing litigation. The reason: to avoid fostering a crisis in the timber industry and communities dependent on timber extraction. This rider suspended nearly all environmental review for 7.7 billion board feet of timber for fiscal year 1990, but it also directed the Forest Service and Bureau of Land Management to delineate "ecologically significant" old-growth stands for interim protection while these timber sales moved forward. Several provisions in the rider addressed how to determine such stands, one of which included considering any new information gathered on the presence of spotted owls in these areas. Consequently, we needed to do a lot of surveys very quickly. If we found spotted owls, then those stands would be protected. If we didn't, the stands would be sold and harvested.

As a result, many in our office who had never done wildlife surveys before were recruited. These people included foresters, engineers, office administrators, and recreation specialists. All began working at night and learned how to imitate the owl's four-note location call. Kim developed a schedule of teams of two that would tackle the many timber sales planned across the district. I found myself paired with different people, including Jerry, whom I'd been with on Johnson Mountain the night we met Dave Shea, and Dixie, a woman who worked in our front office and whose husband and sons were all loggers. Given Dixie's background, I wondered how our work together would go, but I needn't have worried. We had interesting, honest conversations about the big changes coming to the management of Pacific Northwest forests as we drove between calling stations during those long nights. Dixie was also delighted when we heard the animal that had become more a symbol of struggle than what it simply was: a species native to these forests trying to survive.

It was a busy few months, with excitement and energy suffusing the office as well as anger, frustration, and worry. Depending on people's professions and biases, the owl survey work was either viewed as supporting a hijacking of the environmental review process and a blatant push to simply harvest timber, or it was a constricting, unnecessary effort to save old-growth stands that weren't needed by the species because, really, the owls could live anywhere. One morning, two of our seasonal biologists returned to the office after finding an owl the previous night, and they shared the news triumphantly. Later that day, I got a talking to from the logging engineer who had been in Powers since the late 1960s.

"They shouldn't come in here bragging like that, Betsy," Pete said in a quiet voice that belied his irritation. "And you shouldn't either. People have worked extremely hard on these sales. It isn't right."

"Maybe it isn't right to cut down all the trees," I responded, more peevishly than I'd intended. Pete was a nice man who had been very welcoming to me. He'd also helped me find housing in Powers.

His irritation grew. "That's not quite how it is. I don't think you understand. Please talk to them."

This wouldn't be the last time I'd speak quickly in defense of spotted owls or old growth, but in 1989, everything was new for all of us. Tempers could be short, and the uncertainty weighed on everyone. Biologists weren't always welcome in meetings or the workplace in general, and we certainly weren't often appreciated. Yet I had stepped into a very good situation in Powers. Kim had been here less than a year, but she'd already done a tremendous amount to foster good relations with other departments. She was smart and also reasonable, personable but also professional. She knew wildlife science as well as the constraints that managers worked under. Kim got things done, for wildlife and in support of the agency's mission.

By that spring in 1989, Kim had hired a large team of specialists, including me, a fisheries biologist, a geologist, a hydrologist, and the summer technicians. We walked into a pleasant atmosphere of positive relationships only occasionally colored by disagreements and misunderstandings. Many in the wildlife profession remember these days as the time of "combat biology." This phrase is too strong for what I experienced. I know screaming matches at environmental planning meetings in the early to mid-1980s were common in Powers, but thankfully I never witnessed them. Still, change is difficult. Many employees had been in Powers a long time. They remembered the "good old days" of the one-page environmental assessment and the great harvest that employed people and kept mills operating. They were now in their 40s and 50s and felt that my peers and I, in our early 20s, didn't understand what was really important. Of course, we felt the same about them. Most of the Pacific Northwest's older forests were already gone, and what remained should be saved. *That* was important and, for me, had always been important, long before I understood much of the science behind keeping ecosystems intact and functioning.

Three decades later, much has changed. Our knowledge of these forests, ecologically, economically, and socially, is light-years from where it was. Still, time and experiences often seem to circle back on themselves. I have found myself in the late 2010s having conversations about owls and old growth eerily similar to the ones I had in 1989.

*

On the eastern end of the Powers Ranger District is an area called Eden Valley. This landscape is the least steep part of the district, which isn't to say it's all flat. Eden Ridge rises above the valley to the north whereas the rocky formations of Mt. Bolivar, Saddle Peaks, and Hanging Rock stand guard to the southeast. The South Fork Coquille River moves through Eden Valley, fed by streams named Foggy, Wooden Rock, Panther, and Buck Creeks. Wooden Rock is a particularly lovely waterway. It travels softly during much of the year over petrified wood and blue, red, and brown stones.

Similar to my experiences on Mt. Hood, I found the spotted owls in Powers readily responded to tape-recorded or human-created hoots. At one site adjacent to a road, just the slamming of the vehicle door brought the birds in. They had obviously learned that the appearance of people also meant the opportunity for an easy meal. Yet some genetic or evolutionary aspect was no doubt in play also. The species, tucked away deep within the dark, protected world of the old-growth forest for thousands of years, had not needed to fear humans. This circumstance, while helpful for surveying, could also be fatal. Those people who wished the owls dead could call them in just as easily.

One summer day, the district geologist, Linda, and I accompanied our forester colleague, Joe, out to a timber sale called Buck Country. These units lay in a patchwork across the hillsides above Buck Creek, and Joe wanted us to see one in particular. He oversaw the presale department and the laying out of timber sale units once they had cleared the environmental review process. Joe and his crew marked the boundaries and stream buffers of the units. They also "cruised" the trees to determine the amount of timber volume available to sell.

Joe was the quintessential forester of the time. Each day he came to work dressed in red suspenders, a hickory shirt, well-worn jeans that stopped several inches above his ankles (to prevent tripping on uneven ground filled with woody debris), and a similarly well-used wool hat. Joe wasn't shy with his opinions or his allegiance to the Forest Service's mandate to supply timber to society. Consequently, he regarded us youngsters, or "ologists," with a certain level of suspicion. Yet he was also easy to like, with a good sense of humor he wasn't afraid to turn on himself and a booming laugh.

We left the road that afternoon and began hiking through the stand.

Sunlight pushed down through the canopy, falling around us in square and rectangular shapes, ovals, and stars. The temperature was pleasantly warm, and there was no wind. Because the stand was fairly flat and because we hadn't found any owls during our night surveys here, I wasn't sure what Joe needed from us. There were some large snags that would be important to save as wildlife habitat if the fallers could work around them safely. Linda offered her thoughts on how best to remove the trees while minimizing damage to the soil. Close to noon, we stopped for lunch. Joe and I got into an argument after he drank a V8 and then stuffed the empty can under a log.

"Joe!" I said. "That's littering!"

"It's not littering!" he shot back. "It's just metal. It'll rust and break down. Besides, I'm hiding it."

"That's ridiculous! It'll be years before it breaks down. If you don't take it out, I will."

He shrugged. "Suit yourself."

On the way out of the stand, we stopped to discuss something. Joe talked as Linda and I looked around at the extraordinary sweep of forest. Douglas fir, western hemlock, and western red cedar trees six feet in diameter had been growing here for hundreds of years. Logs of similar diameters that now lay quiet on the forest floor had been transformed into "nurse" structures where tiny seedlings, mushroom colonies, and yellow and orange molds grew. Young trees, midsized trees, shrubs, and snags provided structure for nests and dens and resting places for wildlife.

As my gaze took all this in, I suddenly felt another's presence. I looked back at Joe. Then my eyes focused beyond him. Not 10 feet away and just above our heads on a branch sat a spotted owl! With its ability to fly silently, it might have just arrived, or it might have been there all along.

Unlike the quiet bird, I yelped, "There's an owl!"

In contrast to us, the bird didn't seem surprised at all. Paying little attention to Pete's earlier advice, I couldn't help making my pleasure known. Joe looked at the owl for a long while. Then he threw back his head and laughed.

"There you are, ladies!" he said. "Welcome to Joe's Spotted Owl Service!"

*

I'd been in Powers about a year when the district decided to do more public outreach. Much of the Forest Service's work is focused on understanding and managing ecosystems, vegetation, and wildlife species. The agency hires people with the skills necessary to spend long days and weeks in the backcountry, but those same people aren't always excited about communicating their work to others. Still, many realized the importance of such efforts. Joann, our computer specialist, organized with the *Myrtle Point Herald*, the local newspaper, for a column on news and events from our corner of the national forest. She then sent a message to all employees over the DG explaining the new column. It would be called "Fir, Fur, Fish and People." Anyone who wished could submit articles about their areas of expertise as well as any general experiences of being a Forest Service employee.

Apart from my earliest desires to live in the wilderness and be a biologist, I also wanted to be a writer. In school, I always did best in English and history (interesting for someone who ended up going into a science field). I loved researching different topics and then writing term papers about them. Spending time in the library, looking through all the encyclopedias, making note cards filled with bits of information, and then organizing these into chapters was all work I loved. Now my opportunity had arrived to write and publish an article!

The first piece I planned to submit would be an overarching summary of my work with the Forest Service. I'd always gotten a lot of questions about what I *did* all day as a wildlife biologist. Some of the queries from coworkers could be snarky. There was the engineer who asked if I spent most of my time out in the woods petting bunnies. There was the timber sale administrator who asked me every time I saw him how the "dickey birds" were doing. Members of my family continued to be amazed that I could support myself in this line of work. Conversely, there were also those who felt I'd landed a dream job, believing I spent all my time in the forest communing with nature. It seemed worthwhile to set the record straight.

I diligently set to work on my article. I outlined the basic scope of my work: species surveys, habitat improvement projects, planning teams. Yes, I did have a great job and spent a lot of time in the woods, but this also only amounted to about 50 percent of my time while, as I explained it, "the other half is spent being what we affectionately term an 'office maggot.'" Rereading this article today, I don't believe there was much editing supplied by the *Herald* staff. It's very folksy and a bit disorganized. The title they supplied, "Wildlife Biologist's Life Seldom like That of Grizzly Adams," seemed appropriate enough given that I'd mentioned Grizzly Adams and Daniel Boone in the article. A photograph taken of me on an evening cruise on Lake Tahoe accompanied the piece.

I concluded with a friendly "If you have any questions about what wildlife biologists do, please feel free to call me at the Powers Ranger District."

The next few articles were less personal and addressed such topics as the importance of meadows to wildlife, reporting wildlife sightings, and leaving young animals alone during the spring. One piece also explained great places to go in the district for mountain biking and all the health benefits to be obtained by getting out in the fresh air. Though writing for the paper was not one of my official duties, I found it to be some of my most interesting and rewarding work. Coworkers told me I wrote well. Tina, from the administration department, said, "You're a good writer, Betsy. I love your emails! They sound just like how you talk."

At the time, I basked in this praise. It wasn't until many years later, as I tried getting published in competitive places like environmental magazines and larger newspapers, that I realized something important: writing that sounded like how I talked was not the best thing.

*

Lee Webb had been the forest wildlife biologist on the Siskiyou since 1975 and had extensive knowledge of the wildlife, botany, and history of our forest. His office was at the then forest headquarters in Grants Pass, Oregon, a three-and-a-half-hour drive from Powers, so I didn't see him much. However, after I returned from the Peace Corps in 1995 and became the district biologist, I called Lee often for direction and advice.

"Lee," he'd answer, in a quiet, vaguely bored-sounding voice upon picking up the phone. Initially, I always worried I was bothering him with my questions and frequent confusion about everything. But his patience and unhurried explanations indicated my worries were unfounded. I also found his mellowness and imperturbability reassuring. Later, his support would prove invaluable when I left the agency and then also when I wanted to return to it.

Lee didn't get out to the forest as much as he would have liked, so I took every opportunity to invite him to Powers for different field projects. One such invitation involved an overnight trip to do an early morning marbled murrelet survey in the Sixes River watershed, a part of the forest where I hadn't spent much time. I had two friends visiting from South Africa, Lyndy and Chris, and they were also keen to come along. Additionally, my new supervisor, Sue, wanted to join us. Lee arrived later than expected from Grants Pass, so we didn't get to the spot where we'd park and start walking into the site until near dark.

The survey stand was along Big Creek, a tributary to the Sixes River, an important waterway that drains into the Pacific Ocean. Big Creek flows within a funny block of national forest land that resembles a periscope on the map, rising north above the bigger, main part of the Powers Ranger District. On three sides of the block were parcels of private land, long since harvested. This made the remnant older forest along Big Creek, just 15 miles from the Pacific Ocean, even more important for marbled murrelets.

With a murrelet survey, there was no "calling" to the birds as we did with spotted owls. It was solely a listening and looking exercise. During the breeding season, the adult birds travel back and forth between ocean and forest generally at dawn and dusk. The pair is exchanging incubation duties (studies have observed this exchange every 24 hours and only at dawn, often before sunrise) and, after their one egg hatches, bringing fish to their young (which can happen throughout daylight hours, but most visits are in the morning). Our early surveys at sunrise found us listening for the adults' distinctive "keer-keer" cries and watching for their speeding movements in the treetops.

"There's no trail," I said cheerily, pointing into the shrubs and young growth down the slope from the road. "But I looked at the aerial photo and we can just go through this old, harvested unit to get to our site."

Lyndy and Chris looked a little uncertain, but they were also trekkers and up for an adventure. As the light grew dusky and we donned our packs, Lyndy said, "We'll be needing the torch soon." Sue chuckled at her calling our flashlight a "torch." Lee, happy to be out and seeing some new country, brought up the rear, and we were on our way.

Old clearcut units are not fun to walk through. In a harvested area, the new shrubs and trees have grown rapidly due to the sudden influx of sunlight. Additionally, the remains of the logging operation, the pieces of trees not removed, the branches cut off before the tree is dragged to the landing, the punk snags too rotten to haul out, are all left, making getting around a true challenge. All this is even worse to navigate in the dark. I did my best to choose a good path, but it was getting harder to see as it got later. Soon, several torches and headlamps were out and turned on. We continued down the slope among vegetation that pawed at us and shadows that made the ground seem as if it was moving.

Fortunately, it wasn't long before we arrived at the edge of the old growth and our survey stand. A few more obstacles presented themselves with trees from this now exposed edge having fallen during different storms. When at last we got into the stand, all were tired but grateful. We ate dinner and immediately crawled into our sleeping bags.

Sometime in the night, I felt my lower back itching. I didn't think too much about it, figuring this was the result of mosquito bites. The next morning, however, after our survey and with increasing daylight and more visibility, Lyndy said, "Your face looks a little red, Betsy."

Sue looked over at me. "Uh-oh."

I carefully felt my chin and cheeks, then my lower back. Sure enough, familiar warm, rough bumps met my fingertips. Poison oak does very well in new openings such as clearcuts, but I hadn't seen it. Then again, for most of the hike in, I hadn't been able to see much of anything.

Our survey being a success since we heard murrelets, we began hiking out. I tiptoed around the now obvious poison oak, but the damage had been done. By that afternoon, the rash was prominent across my hands, arms, face, and back. By that evening, one eye was swollen shut. The next morning, the other had partially closed. I returned to the Powers clinic for another cortisone shot. As I waited in the lobby, Cindy, our district receptionist, entered the clinic. She glanced at me, then looked away quickly.

"Hey, Cindy," I said glumly. "It's Betsy."

She looked my way again. Then her eyes grew big. "Oh, you poor thing. I didn't even recognize you!"

5

The Pacific Marten

Siskiyou National Forest, 1991, 1995–96

One fact about Pacific martens (*Martes caurina*) that always surprises people is the animals' relatively small size. At just 1–2 pounds and 18–28 inches long (one-third of which is its fluffy tail!), a marten is about the size of a house cat and one of the smaller carnivores in the mustelid, or weasel, family. What they lack in body size, however, they make up for with fierceness. In the 1949 manuscript *Mammals of the Olympic National Park and Vicinity*, Dr. Victor Scheffer, a U.S. Fish & Wildlife Service biologist, describes the following under "food habits" of the marten: "On one occasion, when a marten and a spotted skunk were held in captivity in adjoining pens, the marten forced its way through the partition and 'in spite of a gas attack' killed the skunk and ate one of its legs!" (1995, 89).

Similar to wolverines, their larger cousins, martens brook no argument on any topic. The sounds of a snarling one in a box trap will make a person believe that a much larger animal has been caught. As illustrated by the skunk story, they will kill and eat animals larger than themselves. And though their legs are short, they are able to traverse great distances. While other species hibernate or move to lower elevations in the winter, martens are very well adapted to living in snow, able to hunt both above and below the snow layer. This adaptation to a subnivean life is unique to martens; neither wolverines nor fishers, another member of the mustelid family, are so capable.

Martens must be bold because their smallness can make them vulnerable. They must be fast and must be able to hide. Habitats with what is often referred to as "complex structure" provide ideal cover. Old-growth coniferous forests are rich in such elements: different kinds of trees, living and dead, of many sizes; logs of all shapes piled in messy conglomerations; a density of growth that not only provides a diverse and abundant prey base for martens but also makes it challenging for predators to find *them*. Martens, similar to fishers, need hollow trees and logs to raise their kits. Pacific Northwest forests, with their centuries of forest stand life and death, provide this unique environment, but as this world has diminished with past harvest practices, the status of martens, like spotted owls and marbled murrelets, has become uncertain. Questions abound. Can marten populations survive in the older forest that remains? If not, can they survive in younger stands, and can such stands be managed to improve conditions for martens? Are populations of martens connected by high-quality habitat that allow animals to find each other without being predated by larger carnivores?

In many individual national forest management plans, martens are listed as a "management indicator species" for old-growth forests. With this concept, they serve as an umbrella species: if martens are present on the landscape, then there should also be sufficient habitat for other species dependent on older forests. Consequently, knowing where martens are found is crucial. Yet this isn't an easy thing to know. Notwithstanding the occasional snarling when trapped, martens generally don't vocalize. Their tracks and scats are rarely visible in the needle- and leaf-strewn ground of the Northwest. Martens are also largely nocturnal, and even if out during the day, their mostly brown-and-tan coloration blends in well with the color palette of the forest. On top of all these challenges, they live at naturally low densities.

We needed to find the martens, but how?

*

In 1991, I was four years out of college and had been working in the Powers Ranger District, Siskiyou National Forest, for two years. Powers is the last town on State Highway 242 in southwest Oregon, just four miles north of the national forest and adjacent to the emerald-hued South Fork Coquille River. It was a small place people-wise, with just 500 or so residents at that time, but a big place personality-wise. The town had been built around the logging industry, and people were tough and independent. They were also kind and welcoming. Though I had come to Powers to work as a biologist, no one seemed to hold that overmuch against me.

Powers was also a great place for me at 26 years old. I wasn't married, didn't have children, and had no great financial responsibilities. Those first two summers in southwest Oregon felt like being at camp. My coworkers and I spent many evenings and weekends swimming in the South Fork. We hiked and rode our mountain bikes to places called Iron Mountain, Hanging Rock, and Big Tree. The Siskiyou Mountains are rich in biodiversity with many endemic species and impressive landscapes. Serpentine, an uncommon soil type vulnerable to erosion and high in concentrations of heavy metals, gives rise to unique ecosystems. Wetlands in serpentine areas are full of the carnivorous California pitcher plant, also called the cobra lily, and California lady's slipper. Rainfall of approximately 60 inches per year sustains the ancient Douglas fir, western hemlock, and Port-Orford-cedar trees. The forests and streams became playgrounds for us young biologists and botanists.

Despite the many good things in my life during those years, one event in early spring 1991 changed my life forever. In March, my father died of colon cancer. On New Year's Eve, my family had learned of his terminal diagnosis; two and a half months later he was gone. It all happened so quickly that a sense of unreality lingered. After helping my mother reorganize her new life, I returned to Powers. I had applied to the Peace Corps the previous year, but after my father's diagnosis, I'd pulled the application. My plan for international work would have to wait.

As March became April and April turned into May, the gray, painful winter faded. The spring season of life began again with wonderful enthusiasm. Blooming rhododendrons and azaleas, returning songbirds and ospreys, and rivers and streams bursting with snowmelt filled the Siskiyou landscape. For our owl work, we stayed out all night. For the murrelet surveys, we arose early in the morning and were done by early afternoon. In short, life went on.

One summer afternoon, information came across my desk about how to set up "remote" cameras to survey for rare and elusive wildlife species, including forest carnivores such as martens and fishers. The camera design was so simple, I felt sure even I could build and install the setups. It was also cheap, which, given government budgets, helped in garnering approval for the work. The most expensive items would be the 110 Instamatic cameras, the flash tower, and the film, and none of these were very expensive. The rest, a three-foot-tall post to set the camera on, some flexible wire and fishing line, a washer, an eye screw, and a coat hanger, could mostly be found in our district warehouse (the coat hanger I would donate from my closet). Chicken wings from the grocery store would provide the bait. I purchased enough of everything to install four cameras around the South Fork Coquille River.

As I write this in 2023, more than 30 years after my first endeavors with remote cameras, the technology for documenting the presence of wildlife species has advanced light-years. These first "line-trigger" systems, as they were known, captured the target animals for which they were designed, including rare forest carnivores such as the marten, yet they were also incredibly labor

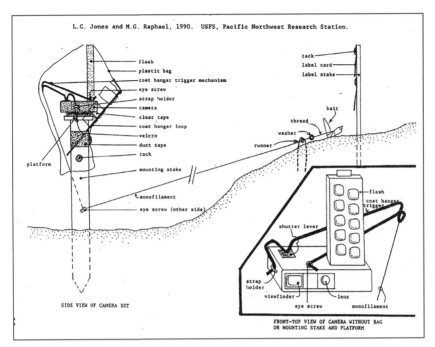

Diagram of a line-trigger remote camera system, 1990. USDA Forest Service, Pacific Northwest Research Station.

intensive. The 110 Instamatic camera could only take one photo at a time before someone (me, in this case) had to return to the site and manually advance the camera. Additionally, we had to wait several days or weeks for the film to be developed. Still, at the time, this method was revolutionary. It provided us a window into the forest world that had been previously closed.

I installed the "camera trap" stations in areas of proposed timber sales, as well as stands of older forest habitat that had been designated "pine marten habitat areas" in the 1989 Siskiyou National Forest Land and Resource Management Plan. My coworkers expressed great interest in this new and unusual work. One day, Cindy, the district receptionist, accompanied me to check the stations. At the first site, I explained how the setup worked, how an animal, interested in the piece of chicken, which was attached by the fishing line to the coat hanger set above the camera, would pull on the bait. This tugging caused the hanger to press down on the shutter button. I felt very pleased as everything had worked: at this station, a photo had been taken!

Cindy nodded, not quite as impressed as I'd hoped she'd be. "What do we do with that?" she asked, pointing to the fly-ridden meat. "It stinks pretty bad!"

"Yes," I agreed, "but it's good for getting the animals to come in."

We replaced the dried, smelly wing with a fresh one, but Cindy didn't help me again with the camera stations.

That year, the cameras along the South Fork documented little beyond small rodents and one long-tailed weasel. The following summer, I again installed the cameras in timber sale units and marten areas. This time, several black bears came calling and destroyed the flimsy setups. My next effort, I realized, would need to be done during the winter, when the bears were less active. This would have to wait, however. I had resurrected my Peace Corps application and was heading to Argentina at the end of August. Though I was sorry to leave the Pacific Northwest and knew I would miss my mother, friends, coworkers, and boyfriend, working in wildlife conservation in another country had been a dream of mine for as long as I could remember. Besides, I would be back. The Forest Service had granted me a two-and-a-half-year leave of absence. I could return to my job in Powers after the Peace Corps.

*

In Argentina, I had the good fortune to work on a research project assessing mountain lion–livestock interactions and developing recommendations for coexistence. I learned much about predators and people living together, as well as tracking and other survey methods. There was also an opportunity in South America to apply my camera experiences from Oregon. At a market in Bolivia, I purchased more Instamatic cameras and set them up around the research station where I worked. We hoped to photograph *el puma* or any of the several small wildcats in the area, including Geoffroy's cat, jaguarundi, and pampas cat.

Unfortunately, all I ever photographed were the legs of cattle, also numerous in the area and not put off by the smell of rotten chicken. Overall, my Peace Corps experience was rewarding and frustrating and placed me far outside my comfort zone. Part of me wanted to stay and continue the work, but a bigger part desired to return home. My mother was not in good health, and it seemed prudent to spend time with her while I could. Additionally, two very smart and capable Argentine biologists had taken over for me on the mountain lion project. I had no qualms about leaving.

In January 1995, I returned to Powers and my job in the Siskiyou National Forest. Since I hadn't enjoyed much success with the line-trigger systems in either North or South America, I was most pleased to learn the next advancement in camera technology had arrived. TrailMaster 35-mm cameras captured an animal on film by detecting body heat and motion and didn't require the creature to tug on a piece of bait. The new cameras advanced the film to the next frame automatically and used larger rolls of film than the Instamatics. Now either 24 or 36 photos could be taken before the station would need to be checked and the film replaced. True, one might end up with 36 photos of a raccoon, but one might also find several species of wildlife on any one roll. With permission from my supervisor, I purchased six TrailMaster cameras that spring.

In August, the publication *American Marten, Fisher, Lynx, and Wolverine: Survey Methods for Their Detection*, edited by William Zielinski and Thomas Kucera, was published. This book, easy to follow and well organized, outlined the conservation concerns for these four species: low natural densities for all, dependence on old-growth habitat that had been overharvested (fishers and martens), trapping pressure that had reduced populations (fishers, martens, and lynx), and the need for large swaths of undisturbed landscapes (wolverine). It also described a protocol for doing the surveys and provided step-by-step instructions for installing the cameras, bait, and, something new, a scent lure strong enough to draw the animals in. Detailed lists of supplies and setup tips ensured success. I ordered chicken wire and a 1/8-inch cable for securing the bait. I bought the lure, skunk scent, from the M & M Fur Company in South Dakota. For better bait than a small chicken wing, I applied to the Oregon Department of Fish & Wildlife for permission to collect roadkill. The local fish hatcheries donated salmon carcasses they didn't need. Finding a local trapper, I asked if he would let me know when he had trapped any beaver, the prime rib of the carnivore world due to the oils in their bodies and fatty tails.

Though a few years had passed, my coworkers remembered my earlier attempts with cameras and smelly bait. Still, the scent lure arriving via UPS caused a new type of anguish. Though the package had been wrapped tightly and taped, the unmistakable odor of skunk had permeated the front office by the time I came to collect it.

"Should I open the box to confirm its contents?" I asked Nancy, our purchasing person. This was standard procedure with packages, but she looked frightened at the thought.

"I don't think that will be necessary," she said, holding her nose. "But if you want to, please go outside."

Roadkill and salmon carcasses began to accumulate. My now ex-boyfriend, Guy, who still remained a friend, cut up a deer that I had found on the highway. My personal freezer filled, as did the one in the bunkhouse. This might have gone unnoticed if not for the guest employees from other districts staying there who alerted our administrative officer to the unusual bags taking up space. When I began sneaking chunks of bait into the freezer of the lunchroom fridge, Tina called me into her office.

"At least it's not skunk scent," I defended myself.

She nodded. "Maybe you should get your own freezer."

*

The infrared, 35-mm cameras worked substantially better than the line-trigger systems. Yet I still wasn't getting any martens or fishers. Part of the problem had to do with the location of the stations. Owing to my other job responsibilities, I had limited time for camera surveys that winter. Consequently, I installed them close to our office in more lower-elevation, managed habitats than those typically occupied by these species. Still, I did get very nice photos of raccoons, skunks, and bobcats. I also learned a few valuable lessons.

For example, carrying a whole beaver carcass through the forest to a station proved difficult, impractical, and unnecessary. Even though I was young and in good shape and *could* get a 50-pound beaver to a site, I still couldn't lift it above the ground. This had resulted in tying the bait to the base of a tree, not ideal given that I didn't want it stolen by some enterprising bear. My trapper friend suggested cutting the carcasses up while they were partially frozen. He claimed that it wasn't hard or messy. Though I found the process to be a little of both, it did yield manageable pieces of bait. This work, unfortunately, put me in the doghouse with our groundskeeper, Dorothy. Dedicated to maintaining a tidy landscape, she largely kept her own counsel when observing me swinging an axe behind the warehouse. One morning, however, my efforts proved too much for her to maintain her silence.

"Looks like you're killing the grass," she said before walking away.

I also confirmed the utility of Zielinski and Kucera's recommendation to have two people for setup: one to handle the smelly items and one to manage the cameras and infrared devices. Because I was doing both tasks, I invariably ended up transferring smells to the equipment. This resulted in bear damage in the early spring as the animals grew more active. Again, I tried to enlist help from my coworkers. Unfortunately, now that skunk lure was involved, there were no takers. I could hardly blame them. The process of using an eyedropper to extract a few drops of liquid that had been obtained straight from the anal glands of a skunk was simply not pleasant. I wore a bandana and held my breath, but I gagged every time.

The manual recommended checking the stations every week. I changed the film and the batteries in the cameras and infrared units, feeling triumphant if most of the roll of film had been used. No matter the condition of the meat, I put out fresh bait. I also dribbled new scent lure onto cotton balls that were housed under the top half of a milk jug I'd cut (to prevent the rain from saturating them). I took notes at each site on signs of wildlife, vegetation present, the approximate elevation, and the aspect, as well as photos with my other camera. Despite getting much rain that winter, my government vehicle maintained a redolence of sour meat and eau-de-skunk. My rain gear also became saturated with the smells of dead salmon, beaver, and deer. Other employees soon requested that I park on the other side of the compound and toss the rain gear in the dumpster. The latter was impractical, but I did move the truck.

Spending a winter outside in the Pacific Northwest isn't for everyone. It's wet and gray, the days are short, and the damp seeps into one's bones through many layers of clothing. Some wildlife species have left for warmer climes; others are hibernating. Those that remain are quieter and less visible. Everything about this time of year encourages staying inside by a warm fire with a good book and a large cup of hot chocolate.

But I grew up in the Northwest. Even if the thought hadn't been fully articulated in my childhood mind, I always knew that rain was crucial. The big trees, the many shades of green, the lush and dark world of the coniferous forests, essentially everything I loved about the outside, would not be possible without copious amounts of rainfall. Sometimes the plain, gray skies weren't so interesting. At other times, the clouds would descend for a visit. They'd hang up in the tall trees, turning the forest community into another world of ghostly shadows and secrets. Intertwining with the land, the clouds appeared as dragons, seals, or galloping horses. For my younger self, the darker and wetter the day, the better. The more abandoned the world felt, the better. Many afternoons in the woods behind our house in Tacoma, I played alone, reveling in the solitude and my own imaginary world of wilderness survival, storms, and wild animals. My work with the Forest Service had turned the imaginary into the real.

We didn't have a drugstore in Powers, so I traveled to the nearest, larger town, Myrtle Point, to get the film developed. They, in turn, sent the rolls out for processing. A week or more might pass before I got to see the photos, a moment that felt like Christmas morning. Spotted skunks and bobcats were frequent visitors to the camera stations, followed by blacktail deer, Steller's jays, and raccoons. As I pulled the last stations down in March, I knew the following winter I had to get into the high country if I wanted to find the elusive martens and fishers.

*

The months of spring 1996 passed. In July, I traveled with my mother to Hawaii, where we spent two weeks together on the Big Island. She looked thin, and her red-rimmed eyes stood out above drawn cheeks. A smoker most of her adult life, she could now walk only short distances without needing the assistance of an inhaler. She'd also started using a portable oxygen tank at home but still downplayed the true state of her health. Consequently, I chose to see only what I wanted to see, that she was doing okay. She still worked at my old elementary school, where she had been since the early 1970s. She could still travel; she could drive. She continued going out with friends and being engaged in the world.

Still, life ultimately moves only toward death. One will eventually replace the other, sooner or later, surprisingly or predictably. I grew up in a family that maintained the "if I don't think about it, maybe it won't happen" attitude around this truth. Consequently, few of us were ever prepared for its arrival. Though death *had* come for my father, my coping mechanism was to not think about it even after the fact. His leaving hurt me deeply. Despite his alcoholism, he and I shared a loving, easy connection, something I had never had with my mother.

In 1974, when I was eight years old, my mother suffered serious head injuries after being struck by a pickup truck while walking in our neighborhood. She survived, but in the weeks that followed, she experienced blinding headaches and couldn't turn over in bed without great waves of dizziness engulfing her. Mom also lost her senses of taste and smell, permanently it would turn out. Whether from the emotional trauma of these changes, or other physiological effects, my mother's personality changed dramatically after the accident. She became cold and angry. She withdrew from both my father and me, sometimes ignoring us for several days. Because my father worked the swing shift, I often suffered her silence alone during many long evenings. After some unpredictable amount of time, the mother from before would pop back into our family as if she'd just been away on a short trip.

This transformation was hard and confusing for me as a child. I needed my mother for many reasons, not the least of which being that I had my own pain to process because I'd witnessed the accident. I'd watched the truck slam into her body, carry her forward on the grill, then stop abruptly and drop her to the ground unconscious. That she lived was an enormous relief. That both the mother I'd known and the childhood illusion I'd carried of a "safe" world had vanished forever have affected my life ever since.

My parents and I sought our own sources of comfort through this tragedy. My father had alcohol, and my mother also drank too much, relying on anger and punishing others as coping mechanisms. I escaped to the forests in our neighborhood. Any uncomfortableness I felt outside, from the cold or the wet, paled in comparison to the shifting emotions and uncertainty I felt at home. And unlike at home, I never felt afraid in the woods; I liked being alone there. The world of trees and plants and animals seemed at once welcoming as well as indifferent to my presence. This seemed right. At home, the disregard from both my parents cut deeply.

As my mother grew older and I left for college, our relationship improved. To my surprise, it continued to do so after my father died. I think we both knew we had to rely on each other. We didn't talk much about him, a circumstance I insisted on and one that she wished were different. For me, discussing my father was too painful; he'd been such a big presence in our family, the parent who, despite his faults, was easygoing, funny, and generous. I also couldn't select one strand of the past to investigate. If we spoke of him, we needed to speak of it all, including her neglect and emotional abuse of me, and I felt sure she didn't want that. Occasionally over the years, I considered asking about the accident and why she had treated me the way she had, but I never did. I simply felt grateful that by October 1996, when she died of congestive heart failure, we had largely mended fences.

*

Back in Powers that November, after my mother's funeral, the snow began to fall. Over the summer, I'd purchased four more cameras, so now a total of 10 stations could be set up. This time, they all went to the highest places I could access: Hanging Rock, Mt. Bolivar, and Salmon Mountain. Right-sizing the bait helped immensely. So did my new strategy of placing the already scent lure–soaked cotton inside film canisters before leaving the ranger station. In this way, I didn't need to take the whole bottle of lure to the woods.

The white, winter world of the forest comforted me in my loss. It was cold and quiet. Golden-crowned kinglets still called gently from the midcanopy. An occasional Douglas's squirrel scampered across the path in front of me. After getting the stations installed, I checked them twice before the end of the year. The usual suspects had come to investigate (though no bears, fortunately) but not the martens and fishers I hoped for. Nonetheless, I remained confident that this would be the winter for finding them. I had worked hard to select locations in the best habitat, and I had dragged a lot of equipment through deep snow and below-freezing temperatures. Something good had to come of it all!

Though the work helped distract me from the pain of my mother's death, it couldn't mend my own drinking problem (though I'd hated my parents' drinking, I'd followed easily in their footsteps) or the insomnia I now suffered. Consequently, a deep depression engulfed me. In January 1997, I took a month off to recover. I stayed in Portland with a friend, began seeing a counselor, and stopped drinking. After many days, I began sleeping again. When I returned to Powers, there was much work to catch up on. More snow had fallen, and some camera sites were now inaccessible. It was the end of March before I was able to return to the last two stations on Salmon Mountain. The other rolls of film had all been developed. Nobody unusual had visited the sites, just my usual raccoon, skunk, and bobcat friends. I waited with little hope for the last two rolls to be developed and wasn't surprised when photo after photo revealed more of the same. As unlikely as it seems, however, the very last picture on the last roll yielded my reward. At last, there on the tree just below the bait, a Pacific marten, with its head turned back toward the camera, stared at me!

6

The Marbled Murrelet

Siskiyou National Forest, 1992

One month before I left for the Peace Corps in August 1992, an unexpected visitor arrived at the Powers Ranger District office. A man visiting the national forest had found a bird unable to fly along the paved road adjacent to the South Fork Coquille River.

"It's very unusual looking," he said before opening the box in which he'd transported it to our office. "Got funny feet, all black and white, and I don't know, it's just a bit *strange.*"

As I listened to his story, I felt a familiar sinking feeling. People regularly brought in birds they'd found in the forest. Maybe they were owls or songbirds, frequently hit by cars or, like this one, just "sitting there" along the road. Maybe a young robin, or a young wren, or one of the many summertime sparrows had left the nest too soon with shaky flying abilities. Perhaps a spotted towhee, a species that is often in low shrubs, had made an ill-timed dash from one side of the road to the other. No matter the circumstances, the rescuers always expected us to save the bird.

Much to my surprise, the bird on this day was not a robin or a sparrow. It also wasn't a wren or a Steller's jay or a towhee. In fact, it wasn't any kind of a songbird. The black-and-white youngster offering high-pitched chirps from the bottom of the box was a marbled murrelet (*Brachyramphus marmoratus*). For the past three years, since moving to southern Oregon, I had done many inventories for these birds. The dawn surveys involved listening for the murrelets' calls and watching the adults flying rapidly into and out of the tree canopy as they exchanged incubating duties or, later in the season, brought fish from the ocean to feed their young. On many occasions, I'd heard the parents' *keer-keer* calls. Sometimes I saw them as well: small, black bullets of movement.

Until this very moment in our office, however, I'd never been closer to a murrelet than about 200 to 300 feet, or the height of an old-growth tree, with the birds at the top and me at the bottom. Of course, I'd seen photographs of adults sitting on the few mossy nests that had been found high in the canopy and juveniles and adults floating atop the Pacific Ocean or other salty, inland waters of the West Coast. One of the most difficult species to study due in part to its double life at sea and on land, the murrelet is not often observed up close.

This man looked at me hopefully. Like all animal rescuers, he had the best of intentions. His concern that this bird would be hit by a passing car was valid. Forest Service Road 33 is located south of Powers, Oregon, along the South Fork Coquille River. This section of road up to Agness Pass is paved, and though narrow and winding, a vehicle in a hurry can pick up great speed. The stunning Douglas fir trees growing in a ribbon along the river will make any tourist turn her gaze away from the roadway. Looking at the little chick, I wondered *why* a murrelet would be on the side of the road. A study published the previous year had concluded that murrelet young appeared to fly directly to the ocean upon leaving the nest rather than exploring the surrounding forest first. Apart from shuffling along a tree branch, murrelet feet never touch anything solid; they are either in the air or on the water. This youngster would not have been planning to end up on the road. It also would have had great difficulty getting airborne again if it had stayed there. Fortunately, it didn't appear injured.

I told the man what he had found and described the bird's rarity and the fact that it lived in both the forest and at sea. "Its survival is threatened," I added, "by loss of forest habitat, as well as events in the ocean, like oil spills and gill netting. Currently, it's proposed to be listed under the federal Endangered Species Act."

He nodded. "Kinda like another spotted owl, huh?"

I acknowledged this vaguely, not wanting to get into a big conversation about spotted owls. Looking more closely at the murrelet, I admired the legs that sat very far back on its body, an adaptation that, along with the short, pointed wings, makes the murrelet a tremendous diver. The thick, short bill would eventually serve it well in the grabbing of small fish. The black-and-white coloration would provide a disruptive pattern to help the young bird blend into shimmering water surfaces.

"Can I leave it with you, then?" he asked. "Be a shame for it to die."

"Of course," I said with more optimism than I felt. Caring for a seabird was even less a part of my ad hoc rehabilitation experience than helping common birds such as robins and jays. Yet I knew enough to seek immediate help in this effort. Free Flight Wildlife Rehabilitation Center was only an hour's drive away in the coastal town of Bandon. I knew the director, a passionate advocate for injured wildlife, and was sure it would be a simple matter for me to take the murrelet to Free Flight. I carried the box back to my desk and called them.

"We don't have any room right now," the woman who answered the phone told me. "In the next week, we're planning to release some of our animals, and then space may open up. But right now, we can't take any more."

She suggested calling the Oregon Institute for Marine Biology, also nearby on the coast in Charleston, Oregon. However, the institute, although a research station for investigations into anything connected with the marine environment, was not set up to house injured or orphaned animals. For now, I would have to care for the murrelet myself.

I closed my eyes. In two weeks, I was leaving for Santiago, Chile, to begin Peace Corps training. I had to wrap up several projects at work; prepare for a garage sale to get rid of many of my possessions; transfer whatever didn't sell, along with my two cats, to my mother's house in Tacoma, Washington; and say goodbye to my friends and family. There simply wasn't any time to care for a baby murrelet. A hint of desperation entered my voice as I pleaded with the woman to make room for the bird.

"No, I'm really sorry." Then she added cheerfully, "But we could give you some herring to feed the little guy."

*

Descriptions of marbled murrelets aren't flattering. Words like *chunky*, *cigar-shaped*, and *neckless-looking* fill field guides, newspaper articles, and magazine essays. Various descriptions also include "a flying baked potato" or "a baked potato with wings." The murrelet is given high marks for its diving prowess but mildly ridiculed for its less-than-skillful landing on tree branches. The earliest observers of the species from the 18th and 19th centuries initially believed that marbled murrelets nested with other members of the alcid (diving seabirds) family on offshore islands. If you're good at swimming and diving and you eat food from the ocean, it stands to reason you'd want to stay near these resources. Yet nearly two centuries passed between the first description of the marbled murrelet in 1789 and when the first nest was confirmed in the redwoods of northern California in 1974. Of course, there were suspicions during that long stretch of time that the birds were in the forest. Several woodland observers noted the "gull-like" cries in the treetops. At the same time, sightings of the bird could not be confirmed during the breeding season where its brethren, the murres, auklets, and puffins, were nesting. Little did anyone fully realize that this bird led a life like no other: a dual existence between the Pacific coast's ancient forests and the saltwater seas.

*

As the murrelet chick peeped on my desk, I considered the problem of where to house it. My two cats were not going to tolerate a newcomer in our midst. Though neither feline had ever shown much interest in hunting, a helpless, young bird in a box would be too great a temptation. Thus, my first task was to find a cool, quiet place to keep it. Second, I had to drive to Charleston and fetch the herring. The latter would take two hours at least, but the chick was already used to waiting long stretches of time for its parents to fly in from the ocean with food.

After my curious coworkers had looked at the murrelet and returned to their work, the district botanist had a suggestion.

"Why don't you take it to Sue's house?" Shane asked.

Our supervisor, Sue, had just left on vacation and I had volunteered to water her plants and generally keep an eye on her place. It was a somewhat dark home that stayed cool in the summer months. It would be quiet and safe and perfect. Additionally, this was the early 1990s. Cell phones, email, and constant communication were all things of the future. I didn't have to worry that Sue would send me a text wondering how things were going, and I wouldn't have to confess that there was now a murrelet living in her home and, oh yeah, sorry, the place currently smelled of herring.

"Murray," as the young bird was quickly dubbed, seemed to take easily to his new surroundings (I had no idea if the chick was a male or female, but as in the face of most gender uncertainty, at least at that time, the default was to a male identity). I found a larger box and placed some towels inside to replicate the mossy limb Murray had hatched on. The box went onto the kitchen table, and when I returned with the herring, he ate two whole fish in quick order. This would have been one more than he would have received from each of his parents as they alternated returning to the nest, but I figured he'd gone without food for some time and could use the extra nutrition. A few herring went into the fridge, the rest in the freezer. I breathed a sigh of relief. So far, so good.

*

The countdown to the federal listing of the marbled murrelet was in its final days during the summer of 1992. In response to a petition to list the species under the Endangered Species Act, the U.S. Fish & Wildlife Service had been gathering scientific evidence on the murrelet's conservation status. The greatest threat remained the loss of its nesting habitat—older, coniferous forest—through commercial timber harvest. This continued to be true despite the recent protection of large tracts of older forests on federal lands for northern spotted owl conservation. Even with vast amounts of the landscape no longer vulnerable to future harvest, most of the murrelet's habitat was already gone. Also, much of what remained existed in isolated patches, affected by changes in temperature and susceptible to weather events such as windstorms, insects, and disease.

Additionally, murrelets use the landscape in very different ways from spotted owls. Where owls live full time in the coniferous canopy, murrelets essentially use the forest as a summer home, traveling primarily before dawn and after sunset during the breeding season across great distances between their nest and food supply. Where owls move freely between upslope and riparian habitats, murrelets generally stick to river corridors. Murrelets must have adequate cover and protection along their travel routes, as well as in the stands where they settle for nesting. Edges of forest, where trees have been removed, are ideal places for avian predators such as ravens, crows, and jays to congregate, and these birds often prey upon murrelet eggs or chicks.

Yet loss and alteration of forested habitat wasn't, and still isn't, the murrelet's only challenge. At-sea risks included gillnetting, fluctuations in forage fish populations, pollution, and the risk of oil spills. From a practical standpoint, one must wonder if it might not have been better evolutionarily to become a nester on offshore islands, like other alcid birds. The commute for the murrelet would have been much shorter, the challenges limited to the sea, as opposed to both sea and land.

Watching Murray settle onto the towel after his meal and then close his eyes, my feelings of impatience vanished. It was a privilege to cross paths with this animal, at once so recognizable but also so mysterious. My life felt chaotic at the moment, but not so chaotic that I didn't have time to do what I could for the murrelet. I still didn't feel terribly hopeful about its chances. The current research in the early 1990s estimated a murrelet chick's probability of survival as very low. My only hope was that Murray's chances wouldn't be too much worse with me.

*

The days passed quickly. There's nothing like leaving on a plane to go somewhere for two years to instill a sense of urgency in every remaining moment. I advertised my Honda Civic in the local newspaper, while the small, manufactured home where I lived filled with boxes labeled "Mom's," "Guy's" (my boyfriend at the time), or "sell." Each evening, I waded through closets and the contents of long-forgotten drawers. In the field, I continued checking my marten and fisher camera stations. In the office, I wrote project reports, made lists of remaining tasks, and organized the paperwork involved with taking a leave of absence from the Forest Service.

Even as everything came together, I still felt nervous and overwhelmed. Consequently, visiting Murray several times each day became a welcome respite during this exciting but also stressful time. I would always feed him first, then clean out his box and sit in the quiet, dim room after and let my thoughts settle. Every time, I prepared for the worst—a dead or sick bird. Yet every time I found him bright-eyed, hungry, and growing bigger. An even larger box soon became necessary, as did more herring. Stories of my endeavors caring for the murrelet quickly traveled around the office. A few people came to Sue's house to see Murray. Many had similar comments.

> What a beautiful bird.
> Such a small thing for all the trouble it's caused.
> Smells a bit like fish.
> What will Sue say?

By August, most murrelet chicks have left the nest. Their apparent tendency to fly directly to the ocean might involve an inaugural flight of 1 mile, or it might involve 50 miles, a journey even more remarkable because it takes place at dusk. Presumably, Murray had been headed west toward the Pacific (as opposed to just slipping off the platform nest, which might have happened too) when something went awry. What his instincts were telling him right now was that he should be on the coast. He had the fish; where was the sea?

One evening, I filled Sue's bathtub with cold water. In went the murrelet. What had been an awkward creature in a box who moved around very little became a silky, swimming animal, full of confidence and purpose. He dove and surfaced and explored every part of the small space. Murray peeped and looked at me, perhaps wondering why I didn't join him (I'd taken no measures to prevent some level of imprinting, and he had surely assessed me as a care-taking figure even though his earliest memories would have been of the true parents). As I praised him and he dove back down, I thought how inadequate these tubs were for murrelets, lacking as they were in depth, salt, and fish. Still, my little charge seemed pleased. Tomorrow, I'd let him swim more and also add a herring or two for him to catch.

*

If the spotted owl in the early 1990s was the poster species for a cooperative study animal (i.e., coming when called and willingly leading surveyors to its nest), then the marbled murrelet was the complete opposite. That it lives both on the sea and high in the forest canopy creates enormous survey challenges, particularly since human beings are not naturally adept at navigating in either environment. Boats and diving equipment have made exploration of the under-water world possible. Climbing equipment has done the same in the treetops. Yet technology and human determination cannot overcome the difficulty in looking for a small bird that blends into gray-blue water and vanishes in the waves like a magician's assistant behind a curtain. Additionally, finding a murrelet nest is such a rare event that the discovery of the first one in the 1970s made it one of the last North American birds to have its nest described. Despite thousands of observations of flying murrelets by 2023, only a small number of tree nests have ever been documented in Oregon and Washington. In the species' range at higher latitudes where there are fewer or no trees, observations of ground nests are more prevalent.

Still, from the dedication and work of countless researchers and bird enthusiasts comes a clearer picture of a murrelet's inland life. In general, nests are in large, old trees that have developed hefty, flat branches with soft, mossy coverings. The nest platform needs to be inconspicuous enough to remain hidden from forest predators but also in an open enough area to allow the adult murrelet a safe landing. After the initial period when the chick is kept safe and warm by its parent, it's left alone for long periods of time. Alternat-ing visits by both adults bringing food is the only time the young animal has company in its high-canopy home. For this reason, the security of the nest site is of paramount importance.

The old-growth trees along the South Fork Coquille River on the Powers

Ranger District exist now in a relatively narrow band, having not been harvested to maintain habitat for fish rather than murrelets. Upland from the river corridor are forest stands of various ages. In the transition zones between forest types, edge-loving predators can be present in great numbers, searching for nests and vulnerable young. If you're a murrelet, it is much better to have your nest far from these places, tucked deeply into the protection of a continuous old-growth stand. Yet with substantially less of the Pacific Northwest landscape remaining in untouched, older forest ecosystems from just a century and a half ago, such options are not as plentiful as they once were.

*

After a week of caring for the murrelet, two things happened. One, I got a call from Free Flight saying they now had room for Murray. They would weigh him and continue to feed him until he reached a certain weight for release. I arranged to take him down the next day. The second event was that Sue returned home from her vacation.

"Looks like I didn't leave you enough to do," she said with a smile upon learning of her new roommate.

Her house didn't smell that much like the sea, and besides, Sue was a biologist too. The opportunity to see such an elusive animal up close thrilled her as much as it did me. I told her the whole story, emphasizing my daily monitoring of Murray and my attentiveness to keeping her house clean. I explained the added benefit of my having defrosted her freezer to make room for the herring. She also didn't mind sharing her bathtub with Murray, especially after I explained the thorough scrubbing I'd given it afterward.

We took Murray outside for pictures before his car ride to the coast (sadly, I never got photos of him swimming in the bathtub). He agreeably posed as if perched in his nest, the yellow, late-summer grasses providing a good contrast for his black-and-white plumage. Sue and I both held him to get pictures of his wings and feet while our coworkers gathered again to see him. Then we drove him to Free Flight in Bandon. It seemed likely that Murray was the first southern Oregon murrelet to arrive at his coastal habitat in a vehicle.

*

In the 30-plus years since my experience with Murray, I've only seen murrelets on the water and have only heard a few calling inland during surveys in the late 1990s on the Siskiyou National Forest or during other fieldwork and campouts in the Olympics. Yet much of my work, now as then, has been spent thinking about the many challenges land managers face trying to understand and conserve them and their habitats. Currently, for me, the murrelet exists as a dot on a map where a historic survey documented its presence. The murrelet might also be represented by a tree on the landscape, a proxy essentially, that in theory could serve at some future date as a nest site. The species is one of many I write about in Forest Service environmental assessments where impacts from human activities are predicted and quantified. In more than three decades of research, there are hundreds of reports, status reviews, and legal documents about the murrelet. The amount of information is staggering, yet the questions remain numerous too.

In the Olympic National Forest, there haven't been murrelet surveys since the late 1990s because the forest no longer harvests old growth. The primary method of supplying timber to local economies has transitioned to commercial thinning of second-growth stands, a habitat that is typically not used by murrelets. Yet there are still issues. Harvest operations are noisy, and noise can increase the levels of stress hormones in animals that may be using older forest nearby. People working and recreating in the woods sometimes leave garbage and this debris attracts ravens, jays, and crows, all predators of murrelets. The Forest Service works very closely with the U.S. Fish & Wildlife Service to minimize these threats to the species because the ultimate goal is to create long-term habitat for both marbled murrelets and spotted owls while minimizing short-term disturbance.

Commercial thinning work in second-growth forests is currently done with the intent of creating older forest structure and complexity faster than will occur naturally. Silvicultural techniques, such as removing some trees to let in more sunlight and maintaining a range of sizes and species of trees, are sound strategies, and vegetatively speaking, they produce expected results—that is, larger trees in a more diverse stand. However, wildlife responses to these efforts are far less straightforward and far less predictable. Will a tree selected for optimal growth actually be used by a murrelet? Will a forested stand that is thinned become protected enough at some later time to provide a safe haven for a growing murrelet chick? Only biologists and foresters decades from now, or maybe even centuries, will know the answers to these questions. And it's possible that even then they will not know for certain. It seems likely that marbled murrelets in the forest will still be as difficult to find in the future as they are in the present. Unless, of course, one happens to arrive on your doorstep in a cardboard box.

7

Northward Migration

Siskiyou/Olympic National Forests, 1998–2004

I don't remember exactly when I decided to resign from the Forest Service, but I know it was during the second trip I made to Africa in the fall of 1997. I hadn't gone this time to look for work but rather to see friends, travel, and get away for a few weeks. It had been just over a year since my mother had died and five and a half years since my father's passing. I'd inherited money from them and was beginning to think about what else I might do with my life. Though I loved Powers and the Siskiyou Mountains, I also felt restless. And uncertain about my goals. I'd served in the Peace Corps, but I wasn't continuing with international work. I loved the Forest Service, but I thought I might want to try something different. I thought I might want to be a writer.

The idea may have taken a fuller shape in the world of the Okavango Delta, a vast inland waterscape in northern Botswana and a highlight of my trip. I'd flown to the delta from Maun, the nearest town, with a handful of other tourists. During the half-hour trip, we saw the color-rich views of the African landscape. A trotting giraffe and various antelope made up most of our wildlife sightings until we came in sight of the airstrip. There, three elephants moved about slowly in the tall grass. Cape buffalo appeared next. Then tall, magnificent saddle-billed storks flew from a nearby pond. After a 20-minute walk, we arrived at the "Oddballs Camp," a remote outpost in the heart of the Okavango. Five tents for guests and a bar and restaurant all sat tucked beneath the canopy of forest on a small island.

From here I arranged a trip farther into the bush via *mokoro* dugout canoes with two Motswana guides named Ribs and X. As they poled us along the next day, a spectacle of bird life flew around the canoes: African jacanas, spur-winged geese, reed cormorants, African fish eagles, pied kingfishers, and more saddle-billed storks. There were also woodland kingfishers, gray louries, and golden weavers. My guidebook had explained that although southern Africa composes slightly less than 3 percent of Earth's surface, it contains over 10 percent of the

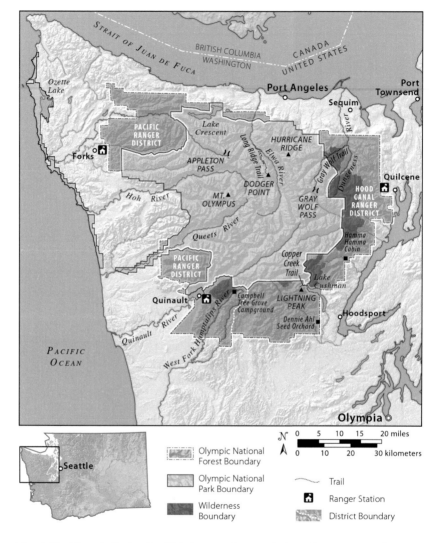

Map 4. The Olympic Peninsula of Washington State, including Olympic National Forest and Park.

world's bird species. I felt like I was seeing all these amazing, winged creatures at once.

As we arrived at the bush camp, a lone bull elephant fed nearby. Ribs and X stopped the *mokoros*, and the elephant turned our way. It flapped its ears and shook its head slightly. Later, after we'd gotten camp set up, I lay down outside my tent in the shade of a palm tree. It was blazing hot. We'd go on another outing in the canoes later, but now there was nothing to do but keep still. I knew I wouldn't sleep, but I closed my eyes anyway. After a few minutes, I opened them.

There stood the elephant! Not more than 40 feet away, it looked very large next to the palm tree. It had come into camp, as silent as a cat, to scratch its head and body on the tree. The big animal seemed wholly uninterested in us. It only wanted to rub against the tree. When it got on the other side of the palm from where I lay and began butting its massive head against the bole, the tree began to sway. At this, I sat up. Ribs and X also awoke. The elephant continued, rubbing its head and rump in happy pleasure. This continued for several minutes before it moved on.

*

The year of 1997 had been a hard one for me. In January, three months after my mother died, I stopped drinking. The 15-year-long stretch, beginning when I was 16, of experiences muddled by alcohol and rife with regrets and embarrassment was at an end, permanently, I hoped. I began to see a counselor and sort through the inheritance I'd received from my parents beyond the monetary one. Alcoholism, secrecy, and mental illness composed some of these legacies. So did bravery, strength, and generosity. How to understand the complex people my parents had been, and hence my own complexities, became an important goal of mine. Too late, I knew that many questions would never be answered. Too late, I realized much of what I had believed wasn't true. If I wanted to understand myself, I had to better understand them. I had little idea of how to do this, though the need for time to figure it out seemed apparent.

Since returning from the Peace Corps, my life had changed in other ways as well. Fully expecting to resume my relationship with my boyfriend Guy, I found instead that he wasn't interested. I'd been gone too long, and we'd both changed too much. Perhaps, too, he sensed something that I hadn't fully understood until some months after my return. I'd always had boyfriends, and I'd been very much in love with Guy; we had even discussed getting married at one point. Yet I'd still left him. I'd also never shared with him my secret, that I'd had many crushes on various women over the years, but looking back now, I'm sure he must have known. As the mid-1990s unfolded and Guy and I settled into a friendship, I decided to investigate these desires—not an easy exploration given where I lived. Between unresolved grief, the earlier fog of alcohol, and this drastic (as I saw it then) change in my perception of myself, those years felt challenging and dramatic. Still, I continued my pursuits, traveling far from Powers to meet other women who shared their stories and opened up my world.

When I got back from Africa in early 1998, I told my supervisor of my plans to resign. I didn't feel rushed, but I wanted to leave by the summer, so we settled on June 5 as my last day. There were projects that needed completion, including another camera survey effort for martens and fishers. Reports needed finishing, and preparations needed to be made for my replacement. The reactions to this plan from my remaining family members were not surprising. After finally being convinced a person could make a living as a biologist, they now couldn't believe that said biologist would abandon a well-paying, government job (with benefits!) to pursue a life as a writer. This seemed even more absurd to them.

Other things had changed in Powers too. My good friend and mentor, Dave Shea, had left the Forest Service the year before and returned to Glacier National Park. I missed him terribly, and when the agency didn't hire another botanist, I suddenly found myself responsible for his duties as well as mine. The doubled workload combined with my personal losses and desires to research my family and to commit to a new relationship that had developed with a woman over the past year made the decision to leave a simple one for me. I'm not sure what my parents would have thought, but they were no longer around to voice their opinions. I turned in my paperwork and made plans to move north to Portland.

In late May, the district hosted a going-away party for me. My old friend William from the Mt. Hood National Forest, now living in Bend, Oregon, attended, as did Lee, the forest biologist. Lee had been with the Forest Service for 23 years and was very devoted to the agency. He also could have been critical of my decision to leave, but he wasn't. At the party, he presented me with a cash award and made a speech praising my Forest Service work.

"You're doing what many of us would like to do but for whatever reason don't," he said. "We'll miss you, Betsy, but it's very important to listen to your heart. Good luck!"

In the time we'd worked together, I had come to appreciate Lee very much. The few days we'd spent in the field during different surveys had been filled with learning and enjoyment. He was an excellent role model, a passionate advocate for wildlife as well as a genuinely kind person. He was calm and measured in his responses to individuals and situations, both of which at times could be challenging. Once, when I made an utter fool of myself by criticizing our district ranger in front of a large group of people, and thereby incurring the wrath of this ranger, Lee later only said, "I do agree with you, Betsy." He didn't state the obvious, that I should have waited for a better time to make my point, leaving me to figure that part out myself. Consequently, perhaps, I've never forgotten that lesson.

After settling in Portland, I wrote in my journal that I was eager to begin my new life as a writer. I signed up for classes in travel, memoir, and environmental writing. As I learned more, I began a big project. I didn't have many personal items from my parents, but I did have two journals that had been written by my great-great-grandfather. During the American Civil War, this young man had been 18 years old when he signed up with an Illinois regiment in August 1862. During the next three years, he wrote of his experiences as a soldier, which included participating in the battles and ensuing siege of Vicksburg, Mississippi. I'd lived with these journals all my life as my dad proudly displayed them on the bookshelves in his den, yet I'd never read them. Now I had the time and, even more importantly, the interest to do so. I made plans to transcribe them that summer. I hoped that by going into the deep past I could learn something about the more recent past, about the people my parents had been before I was born and, by extension, the person I had become. My ancestor had been a soldier for three years; my father had been career military and participated in World War II and the Korean War. My childhood had been filled with my father's stories from these years as well as his drinking and withdrawal. I envisioned writing a memoir about both of these men's lives, our shared histories, and my personal connection to these consequential events in American history.

*

When I got my first article published in the *Oregonian* newspaper less than a year after resigning from the Forest Service, I thought, "This is easy!" The ensuing four-year publishing drought proved that assessment to be a bit hasty.

Still, I knew I'd made the right choice. In addition to the classes I was taking, I read numerous books on writing and I also worked on my ancestor's journals, which in turn led to researching more about the Civil War. In the spring of 1999, I took a three-month trip to the Midwest and the South to retrace his journey. Three months didn't prove to be long enough, so I returned in the fall of 2000 to finish exploring Mississippi and Alabama. I wasn't making any money from writing, but I loved the work. The research and creating something from nothing where words gave rise to images and ideas were what I had always wanted to do. In her 1989 book *The Writing Life*, Annie Dillard describes a well-known writer being asked by a university student, "Do you think I could be a writer?" The writer responded that he didn't know and then asked, "Do you like sentences?" (70).

I could see that after only a year there was no doubt for me: I liked sentences! And when I created one that captured what I felt and thought, in ways surprising and poetic, a great feeling of satisfaction flowed through me.

In between researching my family and the Civil War, as well as World War II, I kept my hand in the world of wildlife conservation. I volunteered with a nonprofit, environmental education organization in Portland and also assisted with Canada lynx surveys for the U.S. Fish & Wildlife Service. The lynx project involved fieldwork with noninvasive survey techniques, which I knew suited me very well from my efforts with remote cameras. As I worked on this memoir about my Civil War trips, father, and great-great-grandfather, I also began writing shorter pieces about wildlife and wildlife surveys. I enjoyed interviewing the people doing the crucial work of describing how the natural world functions and how humans impact it in both good ways and bad. The Civil War, however, would be my main focus for the next 10 years, as I finished my memoir and then began a novel about a woman soldier from the time. Consequently, it wasn't until 2012 at a wildlife conference, when I met a researcher studying the ensatina, a small, terrestrial salamander, that I returned to environmental journalism.

A challenge I hadn't expected being away from the federal government had to do with identity. For 12 years in the Mt. Hood and Siskiyou National Forests, I'd been a Forest Service biologist. Even while I served in the Peace Corps, I identified as such. It was how I introduced myself and explained my background. It was also how I described my future while living in South America, since I'd taken a leave of absence from the agency and planned to return to the Forest Service. But now I had left for good. It would always be a part of my past but not my future. My newly adopted title of writer was mostly aspirational, and despite the sense of possibility I felt with this new work, my life's path remained uncertain. Initially, I didn't miss the Forest Service at all. A few years later, this would change.

*

In the summer of 2001, I attended a memoir-writing class in Port Townsend, Washington. At the same time, my partner and I had just recently broken up, and I was searching for a new place to live. I'd also begun seeing someone new, Barbara, a writer and editor who lived in Seattle. I wanted to be closer to her, but I'd had enough of big cities. Though I had grown up just a little over an hour from Port Townsend, my parents and I had never visited. It was much smaller than Portland but much larger and far more liberal than Powers. Also, it was only two hours from Seattle. Barbara and I could easily visit each other on weekends.

That fall, I returned to Port Townsend, found an apartment, and continued writing. I made progress on my book, and in 2003, I had three essays published in a Northwest literary journal and an anthology of stories by biologists. I was improving as a writer, but I still wasn't making any money. This fact, universal to many in the writing profession, combined with the economic downturn of 2002 and the sinking of my investments, sent me back into the job market.

I spent the next two years working in seasonal positions with local environmental nonprofits and the Washington Department of Fish & Wildlife (WDFW). These jobs focused on marine life and involved working on the beaches and the inland waters of Admiralty Inlet and the Hood Canal, a natural fjord rather than a human-created waterway. For WDFW, our crew did population surveys of clams and oysters, as well as creel surveys documenting harvest. For the North Olympic Salmon Coalition, I headed out on a boat with the project manager to collect sand from different beaches and, later in the lab, to look for the eggs of forage fish species, including surf smelt, Pacific herring, and Pacific sand lance. These fish are crucial to the food chain, supporting salmon and thus many mammals, including orcas. The eggs are about the size of an eraser tip, and we had to search for them in the samples of sand with a microscope. It could be tedious, eye-straining work, but it felt immensely satisfying to find the little eggs.

These part-time jobs provided me time to write, but they didn't pay enough, so I contacted the Olympic National Forest. There I spoke with the forest wildlife biologist. Susan held the same position as Lee had on the Siskiyou and had just moved to the peninsula from eastern Washington. Similar to when I first began with the Forest Service, I had landed in the right place at the right time. The two district wildlife biologists on the Olympic had left recently for other jobs, and Susan was looking to hire two more. Based on recommendations from both Lee and Kim, my supervisor on the Siskiyou, Susan hired me on a temporary basis. For three months in late 2004 and early 2005, I found myself back in familiar and (now, after many years away) welcome work. Species inventories, habitat improvement projects, and participation on planning teams still made up the bulk of the duties of a Forest Service biologist. Though the Olympic Peninsula is different in many ways from the Cascade Range and the Siskiyou Mountains, many aspects are also similar. The Olympic is a westside temperate rainforest and has wildlife species such as spotted owls and marbled murrelets. The country is steep, and the temperatures mild. Several of the same species of amphibians and reptiles live here. This area is also within the range of fishers and martens, although none had been documented for many years on the peninsula.

*

The Olympic National Forest is shaped a bit like a ragged donut around Olympic National Park, and together these federal lands fill up a good portion of the peninsula. The highest peak on the peninsula was named Mt. Olympus by British explorer Captain John Meares after he claimed, "For truly it must be the home of the Gods."

Because there are no roads traversing the park, the drive times around the periphery can be long getting from one side of the forest to another. Small towns anchor the federal lands near the salt water: Sequim, Port Townsend, and Quilcene in the northeast; Hoodsport in the southeast along the Hood Canal, which is one of three water bodies enclosing the peninsula (the other two are the Strait of Juan de Fuca to the north and the Pacific Ocean to the west); Quinault, the wettest place on the peninsula, in the southwest; and Forks in the northwest. Radiating in all directions from Mt. Olympus are several great river systems with names derived from the Indigenous peoples' languages: Dungeness, Duckabush, Hamma Hamma, Skokomish, Wynoochee, Humptulips, Queets, and Hoh. It's a land of rivers and rain and dense forests and trees that don't require fire to regenerate. The landscape of the Olympic Peninsula is part of the largest area of temperate zone rainforest in the world, an ecoregion that stretches from Kodiak Island in Alaska to northern California and includes the west-facing coastal mountains along the Pacific coast.

While the landscape and species in the Olympics were familiar to me, much of the new technology to manage them wasn't at all. Desktop geographical information systems, or GIS, mapping had been developed, and anyone could make their own maps easily and quickly and without the chemicals of the blue-line printer of old. Facilitating this advance was the fact that the DG computer system had finally gone the way of the dinosaurs and been replaced with Microsoft Windows. When I contacted Kim about my hope to return to the agency and wondered if she had any suggestions, she said, "Learn GIS!" Digital cameras, PowerPoint, and pocket-sized GPS devices were all new as well. Though I'm generally a "late-adopter" and inherently suspicious of most technology, I saw great utility in all these developments. The ability to clearly convey information in map form is a powerful planning and educational tool.

Reflecting on both of my returns to the Forest Service, the first time after the Peace Corps and the second after pursuing a writing career, I realize that I missed some of the harder, recent transitions the agency had gone through in the Pacific Northwest. While I was in South America, the Powers Ranger District experienced an approximately 50 percent decrease in permanent, full-time employees. People's positions were eliminated due to declining timber harvest and corresponding budgets from selling timber, and many people I knew transferred, retired, or left the Forest Service. This was beginning before I departed in 1992 and continued while I was away. It wasn't an easy time, and I believe it was one reason my supervisor Sue decided to leave Powers and go to work for another agency. This opened up an opportunity for me, but I came back to a completely different environment, with far fewer employees and a very different management focus.

Transitions continued in the late 1990s and early 2000s. Forest Service offices closed, some national forests in the region combined, and personnel numbers continued to be affected during this time when the implementation of the Northwest Forest Plan was just beginning. By the time I started working for the Olympic National Forest in late 2004, the plan had turned 10 years old. It seemed to me that people had become more used to the changes that shifted the agency away from an emphasis on sustained timber volume to managing forests for biodiversity and conservation of endangered species. Yet not everyone was happy. Similar to when I first started with the Forest Service, I had to navigate conversations and respect others' opinions and feelings that were often quite different from my own.

Later that winter, Susan offered me a permanent job. I felt extraordinarily lucky, since I'd been out of the agency for six and a half years. I settled into my role as a member of planning teams for commercial thinning projects, road decommissionings, and trail construction. During that first year, I also worked on meadow restoration projects. I was assigned to the south end of the forest, and my office would be in Olympia, a two-hour drive south of Port Townsend along the Hood Canal. This commute would require me to stay part of the week in Olympia. Yet if one had to have a commute, two hours along the scenic fjord was a good one. I saw bald eagles on most trips and, during the winter, great congregations of waterfowl, including golden eyes, common loons, and buffleheads. Between traveling this route and going to project sites throughout the forest, I got to know the landscape well. The long hours spent in vehicles also gave me time to think about writing and my book projects. One of the reasons I had left the Forest Service was that I didn't think I could be a biologist for the agency *and* write. As I began working full time again on the Olympic, I saw that both were possible.

That first spring, longtime employees briefed me on coping with the rain. I told them not to worry; I'd grown up in the rain and had worked many years in western Oregon. They looked at me and laughed. They said that rain in the Olympics was like nowhere else, even in other parts of the Pacific Northwest. They explained that no less than three types of rain gear were needed here. A lighter coat and pants for the gentle rains or heavy mists that sometimes occurred in the mornings before the skies cleared. Next was medium wear that prevented rain from entering but remained breathable. This type could be used in cold and warm conditions and during rain that came and went. Finally, one must also have heavy gear, designed to be worn all day during enthusiastic downpours that never let up.

After providing this explanation of Olympic rain, one employee suggested I visit the Thriftway in Forks on the west side of the forest.

"That's where you'll find real rain gear," he said, a slight sneer curling his upper lip. "Not that lightweight stuff from REI."

At the Forks Thriftway, I purchased a heavy raincoat and bib overalls. This rubber suit, as I soon experienced, filled the bill for the enthusiastic, pouring-down kind of rain that never lets up, not even for one second, during many days on the west, or *wet*, side of the peninsula. What I also learned, however, is that this material, while keeping the rain out, also keeps everything else in. Consequently, a person ends up almost as wet on the inside from sweat due to exertion as on the outside from rain.

Despite the need for new gear and the steep learning curve I encountered around technology, I felt very glad to be back. The forests of the Pacific North-west, and the Forest Service, were where I belonged.

Part II
WASHINGTON

Ecosystem management requires us to think in three unusual ways: at landscape scale and across artificial boundaries, at expanded time frames, and with an underlying objective of maintaining biodiversity, which conceptually evolves into keeping every cog and wheel, which leads to the maintenance of ecosystem function.

—Jack Ward Thomas, *The Journals of a Forest Service Chief*

8

Field Biologist

Olympic National Forest, 2004–10

My supervisor, Susan, looked up from the notes she'd been writing during my performance review.

"Tell me about your career plans," she said.

"Career plans?"

"Yes," she nodded. "The next steps. Forest biologist? Staff officer? Maybe a ranger eventually? You'd be great at any of them, Betsy."

Discussing the future of one's career was usual for these reviews, but I didn't have any ambitious ideas to share with Susan. It was 2008, and I'd only been back with the Forest Service for a few years. A little more than two decades had passed since my first job with the agency as a spotted owl surveyor, and my career path had meandered and felt strangely unfocused at times. Diverse interests had pulled me away from biology, but now I was back—in my home state, not far from where I grew up, close to where my parents were buried, near some family and old friends. Rising in the Forest Service had never appealed to me. I told Susan only half-jokingly that if anything, I would prefer to go back *down* the ladder. My first job as a technician had meant I worked more in the forest and less in the office. However, I also enjoyed having more input into our wildlife management program. Developing projects and partnerships fit well with what most satisfied me as long as this also included fieldwork. I now had projects in most parts of the forest, and though it was a heavy workload, I wanted to keep getting to know the Olympic Mountains.

*

Southwest—Quinault

In 1993, President Bill Clinton directed an interagency team of scientists to create a new plan, "scientifically sound, ecologically credible, and legally responsible," for managing federal forest lands within the range of the northern spotted owl. The impetus for such a plan came from the president's wish to break the gridlock that had consumed the region since the late 1980s over the harvest of older forests. This document became known as the Northwest Forest Plan, and it vastly changed the way these forests were to be managed. Though the concern with old-growth harvest had initially been focused on spotted owls and marbled murrelets, the Northwest Forest Plan addressed the needs of a much broader range of aquatic and terrestrial species. It included an "aquatic conservation strategy" to maintain and restore habitats necessary for aquatic and riparian-dependent species as well as a "survey and manage" program to address lesser-known species.

The Northwest Forest Plan was awesome in geographic and scientific scope. It covered 24,500,000 acres of coniferous forests from Washington to northern California. It tiered to or superseded the individual national forest plans that had been written in the 1980s and early 1990s. Predictably, many people inside and outside of the Forest Service viewed the plan as either going too far or not far enough to protect species and habitats. I remember attending a wildlife conference after returning from the Peace Corps where Jack Ward Thomas, the lead scientist for the team assembling the plan, was the featured speaker. The audience of biologists asked Jack many questions, some quite pointed. One woman from eastern Oregon, who knew him personally and felt bolder than others, pressed Jack about the plan not doing enough for the conservation of imperiled species. He gave an answer I don't remember now, but when she wanted more, he grew impatient.

"God dammit, this is what you've got!" he told her, and indeed all of us. "Don't you get it? I go everywhere right now with two bodyguards. This is the best you're going to get. You've got to make it work!"

The pressure had been terrific upon Jack and the team to synthesize the information from five science assessments written between 1989 and 1994 that informed the Northwest Forest Plan. By 1995, he'd also been chief of the Forest Service for nearly two years, a position he'd taken reluctantly but that was a milestone as he became the first biologist in the job.

I, too, worried that the plan didn't go far enough to protect species. At the same time, an important change had occurred. When I first began working for the Forest Service, biologists needed to prove that management actions would be *harmful* to wildlife species in order to change those actions. This meant we often found ourselves in a defensive posture, having to provide burdens of proof and navigating arguments of "owls versus jobs" that spuriously simplified managing complex ecosystems.

The Northwest Forest Plan, however, put the onus on the agency to prove that actions would be *beneficial* to species dependent on older forests in order to implement those actions. This resulted in a tremendous shift in the intent of forest management. The objective of benefiting the ecosystem was particularly important in areas designated in the plan as "late-successional reserve," or lands reserved for the protection and restoration of old-growth forest habitat for associated species. In these reserves, timber harvest could occur, but only if such activity would enhance late-successional conditions and propel natural processes toward more diverse, complex, and healthy forests. Other land designations of the Northwest Forest Plan focused more on commodity extraction, though ecological restoration was still part of their management as well.

Because most of the Olympic National Forest had been designated late-successional reserve, the management emphasis was, and still is, on creating older forests. The employment of silvicultural techniques to achieve conditions such as a diversity of large trees, multiple canopies, and an intricate understory is a primary focus. It's work that is premised on current scientific understanding of how management can play a role in restoring and facilitating what occurs naturally in the successional process. It's also an effort that requires a very long view. Such benefits may not be realized for decades, or even centuries. After decades of harvesting older forests, the Olympic has many watersheds filled with young, second-growth stands that are now ready to commercially or precommercially thin, two of the main techniques employed to foster natural growth.

Matheny Creek, north of Lake Quinault on the west side of the Olympic Mountains, drains into the Queets River, an impressive waterway originating on the glaciers of Mt. Olympus and arriving at the Pacific Ocean after a winding, 52-mile path. In 2011, the Olympic National Forest received partnership money from Rocky Mountain Elk Foundation to precommercially thin 240 acres of young stands to improve forage habitat for big game. Matheny is home to a year-round herd of 300 Roosevelt elk, but the quantity and quality of forage has been an issue since the Olympic stopped clearcut harvesting in the 1990s. Opening up these dense stands to more sunlight stimulates the growth of the conifers that remain. It also fosters the growth of shrub and forb species, such as huckleberry and cascara, in the understory.

Because this thinning work took place on the wetter side of the Olympic Mountains, where trees grow fast and big, the material generated from the thinning process filled the stands with impenetrable slash. A second grant from the foundation helped fund efforts to cut and pile the slash. In 2014, I began working in partnership with the WDFW, the state agency responsible for managing wildlife populations, and Eyes in the Woods, a nonprofit organization dedicated to assisting state and federal agencies in protecting forest resources. For almost 10 years, we've hosted several weekend work parties each winter and spring where volunteers with chainsaws create travel paths for the animals, open up the ground for natural seeding, and provide shelter for different species of wildlife.

The benefits of this work to wildlife can be seen almost immediately. On a warm spring day when I visited one stand to install photo monitoring points, I found three snakes curled up next to the slash piles. Likewise, remote cameras in the Matheny stands have documented many of our smaller and larger carnivores on the peninsula, including black bears, cougars, coyotes, and bobcats, as well as the animals for which the work has been designed, Roosevelt elk and blacktail deer. Unlike remote cameras set out to specifically document carnivores, these cameras weren't baited, thus the animals that "happened to come by" had not been enticed into the area. We've recorded mother bears, deer, and elk, all with twins. Elk, an economically and culturally important species for the peninsula's tribes, as well as for recreational hunters, are able to take advantage of the new growth in the understory while also staying protected by the cover that remains.

*

Southeast—Skokomish

Lake Cushman, a reservoir created by the damming of the North Fork Skokomish River in the southeast corner of the forest, is a place I knew well from my childhood. In the early 1970s, my parents bought a small lot on a cul-de-sac near the lake. They had great plans to build a weekend getaway cabin, and we'd take our motor home and boat to camp adjacent to the lot and water-ski on the lake. Much to my disappointment, the cabin never came to fruition. Yet we still spent many weekends and summer holidays at the lake, the Olympics forming a wild background to my parents' ultimately unrealized dreams.

More than 30 years later, in July 2006, I returned to Lake Cushman and to wildland fire assignments. The Bear Gulch II Fire began that month when a campfire got away along the north shore of the lake. The Olympic Mountains, with copious rainfall and moderate temperatures, aren't known for wildfires, and the ones that do occur are often started by humans. The impressive Forks Fire of 1951 (33,000 acres) was started by a spark from a logging train; the first Bear Gulch Fire in 1979 (50 acres) began by fireworks; and the Big Hump Fire of 2011 (1,300 acres) grew from an escaped campfire. Commonly, fires in the Olympics burn along south-facing slopes, where conditions are the driest, with the flames moving upslope to the ridgelines. At the top, the fire encounters snow on the north-facing slope or at least moister and shadier conditions. Either way, it usually goes out. Larger fires here (*larger* being a relative term compared to other parts of Washington State and the West) can occur on the east side of the peninsula due to the rain shadow effect of the mountains and the drier conditions to be found.

The Bear Gulch II Fire provided me with my first assignment as a resource advisor. This position, also known as a READ, was then a relatively new job in the fire organization. Resource advising, as described in the 1996 "Resource Advisor's Guide for Wildland Fire," included responsibilities such as "identifying and evaluating potential impacts of fire operations on natural and cultural resources, promoting excellence in the integration of resource concerns, and identifying political concerns" (National Wildfire Coordinating Group 1996, 1). When a wildfire is raging, human life and property become the top priorities. At the same time, there are many other things to be concerned about, including habitats for threatened and endangered species, important archaeological sites, and historic structures. As fires began growing bigger and more destructive and fire seasons longer each year, the need for someone to represent these concerns had become critical.

The idea of being in this role appealed to me. It had been 10 years since I'd worked on wildfires, and the previous September, I'd turned 40 years old. Working on a 20-person hand crew digging fireline all day was not something I could do any longer.

In March 2006, I attended a three-day READ training at Mt. Rainier National Park where we learned important concepts such as the following:

To be a good resource advisor, you have to be a good firefighter.
In order to do a good job, you must prepare before an incident.
Firefighter and public safety are first priorities always; next are human communities and natural resources.
You are an advisor.

During role-playing exercises, we advised fire management teams, also known as "incident command teams," on resource protection. These games emphasized the challenges inherent in this position. Being a resource advisor would require knowledge, yes, but it would also require knowing and understanding people. The concept of putting a fire out at all costs stretches back decades to Smokey Bear and is deeply entrenched in the agency's mission. At the same time, fire suppression techniques can be damaging to the environment. Being prepared to interact with many types of personalities whose only goal is to extinguish flames would be key.

Because the resource advisor needs to know and understand the natural and cultural resources potentially impacted by a fire, it follows that READs will mostly work on their home forests. This didn't bode well for me receiving many READ assignments if they had to be on the Olympic. As it happened, however, the Bear Gulch II Fire began a few months after our training. With the fire impacting the habitat for spotted owls and marbled murrelets, as well as bull trout, a federally threatened fish species living in the North Fork Skokomish River, I got my first opportunity in this new position.

Bear Gulch II proved a good first assignment for me as a resource advisor. Though numerous houses and summer homes around Lake Cushman made for a touchy political situation, the fire also wasn't large or fast-moving. Additionally, the steep slopes of the Olympic Mountains don't lend themselves to building firelines, which, particularly if done with bulldozers, can be very damaging to soils and other resources. For this fire, the primary means of suppression involved water drops from helicopters. However, there were still impacts to consider. Noise disturbances to spotted owls and marbled murrelets possibly occupying nearby stands of old growth and the possibility of scooping up threatened bull trout, or invasive species and pathogens, in the buckets of water lifted from the lake to douse the fire all had to be considered.

*

Northeast—Gray Wolf

In January 2008, the first fishers, small members of the mustelid, or weasel, family, returned to Olympic National Park after a decades-long absence. The planning to bring the species back to the peninsula had involved many agencies and organizations and environmental analyses. The animals came from British Columbia, where a healthy population of fishers still thrived. Over three winters, 90 fishers were released, spreading across the peninsula with a speed that belied their small size and short legs. In the winter of 2008–9, I returned to the work of remote camera monitoring.

That fall, we didn't have money in our wildlife budget to purchase remote cameras, so I contacted the Powers Ranger District to see about borrowing the TrailMaster cameras I'd bought in the 1990s. Fortunately, no one there was using them, and soon I received a box in the mail of cameras and motion sensors (it was very odd to also find a sticky note I'd written in 1995 describing issues with one sensor). These systems weren't digital, of course, and I had to work to locate a drugstore that still developed rolls of film. I also contacted the WDFW to see about obtaining beavers that had been trapped on damage complaints. I installed the cameras on the east side of the Olympics where the telemetry data showed the new fishers to be.

The snow fell in great quantities that winter. I skied and snowshoed to the camera stations, wrangling a few coworkers to help occasionally. While it was fun and inspiring to be out in the forest doing this work again, it also wasn't efficient to be doing it all myself. The nonprofit organization Conservation Northwest, originally called Greater Ecosystem Alliance and then Northwest Ecosystem Alliance, had been particularly instrumental in bringing fishers back to Washington. In 2003, they had formed a partnership with WDFW and raised $25,000 to fund the initial feasibility study. During one of the releases, I'd met Dave Werntz, science and conservation director for Conservation Northwest. We both agreed that this wasn't going to be an easy experience for these "founder" animals, but the greater good for fishers and the Olympic Mountains had been realized. The fishers were back!

That summer, Dave and I organized a partnership program between the Olympic National Forest and Conservation Northwest. By the fall, we had volunteers selected to monitor three new digital cameras purchased with money my supervisor Susan had scraped together. With the telemetry data showing much fisher activity in the Gray Wolf River, a tributary to the Dungeness River in the northeast part of the forest, we focused our efforts there. When the memory card from one camera showed 3,100 photos had been taken, I couldn't believe it. Having just used the old cameras the winter before with rolls of film and also still clearly remembering the first line-trigger systems with only one photo taken per event, I was in awe.

So many photographs revealed a forest story. In late September, a few days after setting up the station, a Steller's jay appeared. Two days later, a fisher wearing a radio collar, a founder animal, showed up. Two days later, a different fisher without a collar arrived. This individual had either been born on the peninsula or its collar had broken off. The camera captured many photos of its white throat patch. This particular "blaze," relatively large and a bit like a parallelogram, didn't seem to resemble any of the photos on file from the released animals. Consequently, we concluded this fisher might have been born on the peninsula, a very encouraging development.

After the fisher with the large white throat patch left, the collared fisher returned but didn't stay long. The pattern of visitation repeated itself; the two animals traded off, carefully visiting the site when the other wasn't around. The fisher without the collar appeared larger so was likely a male. At times, he looked intently down the slope, opening his mouth and dashing back and forth on the log adjacent to the bait tree. A few weeks later, another uncollared animal came by, this one with almost no white throat patch. We now knew that there were at least two other animals in the area besides the founders.

In addition to fishers, I was also curious about peninsula martens, the smaller cousin of the fisher and the species I'd documented at Powers. In 2008, when the first fishers were returning, a dead juvenile marten had been discovered on Mt. Rose, just north of Lake Cushman. This animal was an extraordinary find. There hadn't been a marten observed on the peninsula since 1990 despite dozens of cameras having been installed across the landscape during that time. This young marten provided evidence of reproduction, and we supposed the parents to be close. But cameras subsequently installed on Mt. Rose got only coyotes, bobcats, and flying squirrels. Where were the martens?

Though the fishers now roamed across much of the peninsula, including at low elevations outside of the park and forest, the martens, many of us felt, must remain only in higher, more remote backcountry. To find them, we had to survey deeper into these wilderness areas. However, I also felt we'd asked all we could ask of our Conservation Northwest volunteers. Much to my good fortune, another opportunity for a new level of survey work presented itself in 2012. That's when I got a call out of the blue from a man named Gregg Treinish.

The year before, Gregg had founded his nonprofit organization Adventurers and Scientists for Conservation, later renamed Adventure Scientists.

"I've started this organization to help scientists collect important data," he told me in April of that year. "I'm part of a community that can get back into these remote areas, but we don't want to do it just for fun anymore. We want to do something useful as well."

From an early age, Gregg had found solace in spending time in the wilderness. This love had taken him on trips across the globe, including a nearly two-year expedition hiking the length of the Andes Mountains in South America. For this accomplishment, he'd been named the 2008 Adventurer of the Year by National Geographic. In time, however, Gregg realized he wanted to bring purpose to his adventures, and he knew there were others who felt the same. He began his organization with the objective to connect experienced, backcountry enthusiasts with researchers and managers that needed field data, which would help them make informed management decisions. On that spring day in 2012, Gregg had begun calling biologists with various agencies across the West to see if they had any projects that might fit with this mission. Of course, I immediately thought of the need to learn more about the martens.

After putting together another partnership agreement, Olympic National Forest and Adventure Scientists began remote camera surveys that would ultimately engage more than 30 volunteers and obtain approximately 36,000 photographs of different wildlife species. Gregg and his staff recruited people through a rigorous application process. Suddenly, I had volunteers who were rock climbers, mountain climbers, ultramarathon runners, and trail through-hikers. These participants didn't flinch at the distances involved in setting up the cameras or the weight that needed to be carried. Many had already done some type of wildlife survey work.

In January 2013, when we installed the first cameras, a reporter from the local National Public Radio station joined us for the all-day hike. That story and subsequent ones brought awareness of the new partnership and the continuing mystery of the marten, which in turn attracted more people to the project. During the winters of 2013 and 2014, volunteers from Adventure Scientists installed 41 camera stations on the east side of the forest near historic marten records. Gratifyingly, we obtained more important information on fishers, including confirmation through genetic analyses of the first second-generation animals born on the peninsula. In contrast, we didn't obtain a single photograph of a marten. While disappointing, this lack of evidence didn't mean the animals weren't there, only that we hadn't successfully detected them.

*

Northwest—Sol Duc

Having always been something of a loner, I found myself surprised to be enjoying working with large groups of people on wildlife projects. The camaraderie and the shared effort to learn and understand the natural world made me feel connected to people in a positive way. It felt a little like perhaps being part of a sports team, something I had never done growing up. Together we shared the triumphs and the disappointments. We also got a lot of work done.

Still, as I settled into my life in the Olympic National Forest, the best times for me were the ones I spent alone in the forest. As I surveyed second-growth stands for proposed commercial thinning activities, I returned to my roots doing surveys for amphibians. Closed roads, small meadows, and forested openings in swales provided pond habitat for breeding. In the springtime pools, I found egg masses laid by my old friend, the northwestern salamander. The Pacific chorus frog, a.k.a. treefrog (*Pseudacris regilla*), also frequented these areas. The Olympic torrent salamander (*Rhyacotriton olympicus*), a small stream amphibian, could be observed along the fast waters of rivers and creeks (in the Siskiyou, I had known the similar southern torrent salamander, *R. variegatus*). Torrents, with spots on their sides and tails and bright, yellow bellies, have very reduced lungs, which aid in their ability to live in fast-moving water without floating away (since lungs make an individual more buoyant). In these streams, I also occasionally observed the larvae of the coastal tailed frog (*Ascaphus truei*). These young animals, with flattened heads and streamlined bodies, attach themselves to rocks using their sucker-like mouths.

For reptiles, the Olympic National Forest has only five species, including three species of garter snakes (*Thamnophis* spp.), the rubber boa (*Charina bottae*), and the northern alligator lizard (*Elgaria coerulea*). I still haven't seen a rubber boa, but during the summer months, I frequently encounter the garter snakes sunning along paved or gravel roads. For each, I stop and coax them off the road with a gentle nudge of my toe.

My interest in amphibians and reptiles, collectively known as herptiles, led Susan to nominate me for the Region 6 (Washington and Oregon) Forest Service contact for all matters herp-related. Though flattered, I didn't feel at all qualified for this role. Enthusiasm for the different species didn't translate to expertise. However, much of the position involved managing and organizing information, something I was good at. The job also involved participating in the new national organization, Partners in Amphibian and Reptile Conservation, or PARC. In 2008, the Northwest Chapter of PARC was formed, and

I attended the inaugural meeting in Missoula, Montana. In time, I would become the treasurer and then, for three years, the cochair of NW PARC. Being a part of this group introduced me to biologists and ecologists who *are* experts in the field and filled with passion for animals that most people rarely think about or, if they do, view negatively. At the 2012 NW PARC meeting, I met Michael Best, a research scientist from California studying the role of ensatina salamanders in the process of forest carbon cycling. The following year, I contacted Michael to propose that I write an article about his work.

*

As the years unfolded on the Olympic Peninsula, my writing and biology worlds began to overlap. I also began to focus even more on amphibians and martens, the small mustelid I'd first searched for in 1991 and whose conservation status in the Olympic Mountains was proving to be a challenging question to answer.

9

Little Critter with Big Influence

King Range, California, 2012–13

The foundation for all life begins on the ground. And below the ground. In the temperate, coniferous rainforests of western Washington and Oregon, this is easily seen by the sheer amount of life emerging from the forest floor. From the many moss species that hug the earth to the trees that reach 300 feet into the heavens, none would exist but for the life-giving soil. It is a place taken too much for granted. We humans rarely notice the world we step over as we hurry from one place to the next, along one trail system to another, accessing that peak or taking water from that river. Generally, only those individuals who study this community's denizens, including the fungi, invertebrates, and terrestrial salamanders, can appreciate the complexity found out of sight.

The ensatina (*Ensatina eschscholtzii*) is one such salamander, with shoe-button eyes and orange and brown mottling. On a warm, rainy day, these amphibians will leave the saturated world belowground and come to the surface, taking shelter under pieces of bark. It wasn't until I began working with Dave Shea in Powers that I really started to notice salamanders. Dave didn't just admire grizzly bears and other large predators; he was interested in all wildlife, including the very small. We spent many days surveying ponds for egg masses and looking under bark and rocks for adult terrestrial salamanders. Since those early years, I have turned over dozens of pieces of bark to find only a few salamanders, but each observation is worth the many disappointments.

Ensatinas are about half the length of a pencil when fully grown and are completely terrestrial. Apart from their large eyes, they are easily identified by bright, yellow markings on the tops of their legs and a slight constriction at the base of their tails (*ensatina*, a Latin word meaning "swordlike" refers to the way the tail is held straight and displayed to predators). They are a "lungless" salamander, meaning that they absorb oxygen solely through their skin. This makes them extremely sensitive to changes in air temperature and humidity; however, they also seem to be an adaptable species. I have observed them in older forests, younger forests, and even sometimes on the edges of clearcuts, though it's possible ensatinas didn't "select" this last habitat but rather just found themselves there as the forest was removed. The ensatina also has an extensive geographic range, occurring along the West Coast of North America, from Baja California to southern British Columbia, Canada.

Because ensatinas live only on land, they don't lay their eggs in water as some salamanders do. Instead, their breeding cycle begins with an elaborate dance between the male and female. Eventually, the male will deposit a packet of sperm, known as a "spermatophore," on the forest floor. The female then picks up the packet with her cloaca and the sperm moves from this transport vessel into a part of her body called the spermatheca. When conditions are favorable, generally in the spring, the sperm is released inside her body. She will then deposit her fertilized eggs in rotten logs, underground burrows, or any location that is protected and contains adequate moisture. The new mother guards the eggs throughout the summer until they hatch as miniature adults in August or September.

For biologists, the life of the ensatina is fascinating. For the average person, it is less so. If I tried to describe this subterranean world at a social gathering, I would likely encounter polite boredom. If I tried to use the word *spermatophore* in general conversation, I would definitely regret it (I can just imagine my family's reaction if I had started my career studying ensatinas instead of owls; at least they knew what an owl was). I can hear people's questions already. What do ensatina salamanders have to do with me? What does it matter if they live in the forest or they don't live in the forest? In short, *Who cares?*

In the mid-1970s, studies conducted in New Hampshire determined that land-dwelling salamanders existed in tremendous numbers in eastern forests. In one hectare, an area the size of a football field, approximately 2,950 salamanders were counted. This biomass—that is, the total weight of all the salamanders, was double that of birds during the breeding season and equal to that of small mammals year-round. Most of these were the eastern red-backed salamander (*Plethodon cinereus*), a cousin of our western red-backed salamander species (*P. vehiculum*). In another study in New York, it was found that the eastern red-backed salamanders directly influenced the community of invertebrates that consume leaf litter. These amphibians were a kind of super predator on animals like beetles. Because ensatinas are the most common terrestrial salamander in western coastal forests, is it possible that they fulfill the same role? And if so, what is the significance, if any, of such an ecological job?

*

Michael Best sat behind a table at the 2012 PARC conference. A research scientist who had been studying ensatinas in northern California since 2006, Michael had come to the conference to present a paper on his work. His big smile conveyed his enthusiasm, and in just a few minutes, he had me riveted as he described the vital role of ensatinas in the carbon cycling of western forests. Though the research was intricate, particularly all that was involved in identifying invertebrates consumed by salamanders and measuring the carbon content of leaf litter, Michael's explanations made the work easy to understand. Over the next year, I thought more about how a tiny salamander few people ever think about is key to the health of forest ecosystems. I contacted Michael to see if I could write an article on his research. We began to correspond, and I learned more about ensatinas as well as what had propelled him into the field of wildlife science.

Now on the West Coast, he'd come a long way from his childhood in Queens, New York, where growing up in an urban environment didn't deter his inherent interest in the natural world. As a child, Michael explored vacant city lots, capturing insects and observing small animals. When only six years old, he started a "bug club." One accomplishment of this club included breeding praying mantises and populating one of the vacant lots with them. More than bugs, however, amphibians and reptiles became the animals that captured his imagination.

"The most significant salamander moment for me as a youth," Michael recalled, "was discovering the adorable, solitary tiny red efts [eastern newts] wandering through the forest, completely unafraid due to their deadly toxins."

Likewise, witnessing the migration of thousands of spotted salamanders and spring peepers (small chorus frogs), as well as observing a snapping turtle digging her nest in the Adirondacks, propelled Best toward a bachelor's degree in biology at State University of New York. After completing his undergraduate work, he read a 2004 scientific review by Robert Davis and Hartwell Welsh, two well-known herpetologists. "On the Ecological Roles of Salamanders" explains the abundance of salamanders in forest ecosystems and how they function as regulators of food webs, species diversity, and ecosystem processes. Despite much being known about these amphibians, however, there were still many questions. The mystery of how western forest salamanders affect invertebrate densities gave rise to a master's project for Michael. Soon, he was peering into the little-known world of the ensatina.

The King Range in southern Humboldt County, California, lies less than 10 miles from the Pacific Ocean. Michael's study area, shielded from maritime influence by a rugged landscape known as the Lost Coast, is dominated by a Mediterranean weather pattern, with hot/dry summers and cool/very wet winters. The forest here is mixed hardwood and conifer and includes such species as Douglas fir, tanoak, and madrone. Owing to private ownership that has allowed the trees to grow for many decades, the forest floor is largely open. There is no herbaceous layer except for tree seedlings, and the shrub component includes only huckleberry bushes. The leaves of deciduous tanoaks and madrones accumulate every year in deep, wide swaths on the ground, eventually curling and drying into brittle crackling forms.

Before Michael came along, Hartwell Welsh had been wanting to investigate the effect of salamanders on the forest litter invertebrate community. Yet the daunting task of sampling insects had frightened most people away. Fortunately, this was not an issue for Michael, whose early work in the bug club had only deepened his interest in the insect world. The project began with him building and transporting "salamander housing units" to his study area. Each unit was constructed from sheet metal sections 23 centimeters tall and 3 meters square. This 9-square-meter area was then further divided by interior walls to make four 1.5-square-meter salamander plots, with each plot containing three Douglas fir slabs as cover for the animals. One adult male ensatina was placed into half of the 12 total plots, while the other half were salamander-free.

"We used male ensatinas," Michael explained, "because it was possible that nesting females could exhibit specific behavior attributes that would have biased our results. After laying eggs, females might stay underground longer and feed less, or they might consume only certain kinds of invertebrates and not others. We wanted to be careful not to introduce that kind of bias." Though the salamanders in the treatment plots weren't marked, he could identify them by their length and weight, which he had measured at the beginning of the study.

Michael had constructed short, overhanging edges on the tops of the structure walls to prevent escape by the treatment salamanders as well as immigration by other salamanders. In the first few weeks of the project, he still encountered baby ensatinas and California slender salamanders within plots that had emerged from the leaf litter. These extra animals were carried to areas outside of the study.

Into every plot went three bags of forest leaf litter weighing exactly three grams each. Invertebrates consume leaf litter, and with that consumption, carbon is released into the atmosphere, similar to when trees are harvested or when peat moss is dug up. Since ensatinas consume invertebrates, and since fresh, dry leaf litter is 50 percent carbon by weight, the amount of leaf litter weighed later in the study would reflect changes in the amount of carbon remaining on the forest floor in areas with and without salamanders.

Michael then created a grid pattern of 100 points in each plot. From this grid, he randomly selected 5 sample points for invertebrate sampling. Firmly inserting a soup can with both ends removed through the leaf litter down to mineral soil, he extracted cores full of different species of insects. Samples were taken each month in each plot for four months. In the first year of the study, Michael documented a staggering 14,000 individual invertebrates from the plots. In the second year, owing to early spring rains and an increase in soil moisture, he found almost 33,000.

"This number," he said, "is conservatively less than 5 percent of the invertebrates actually on the plots in each year."

He also found, similar to earlier results obtained in the eastern U.S., that ensatina salamanders have enormous effects on their environment. The experimental plots that had a salamander showed a marked decrease in the number of large invertebrate leaf-litter shredders, such as beetles and fly larvae. This in turn resulted in 13 percent more leaf litter remaining in these plots than in the plots with no salamanders. More leaf litter means more carbon is stored in the ecosystem. Conversely, plots without salamanders had more invertebrates, which consumed the leaf litter, resulting in the release of carbon into the atmosphere through their respiration. The ensatina's removal of these large, competitive shredders also opened up food resources for tiny grazers, such as mites and barklice. These animals, which are crucial in the consumption of fungi and bacteria, could then increase in numbers.

Having ensatina salamanders doing their job means more leaf litter is retained on the forest floor, which means less carbon is released into the atmosphere. This retained material is then available for another forest process called humification. In contrast to decomposition, which is about decay, humification involves the creation of humus, the rich, organic matter that is the basis for all life in the forest.

"Each process is always happening simultaneously," Michael explained, "but the ratio of each to the other may increase or decrease based on weather patterns and trophic dynamics."

Measuring humification is difficult, so he doesn't know to what extent this process is happening, but he can definitively say that an ensatina salamander's presence in his study plots resulted in a smaller proportion of leaves being converted into carbon dioxide, thus making this organic material available for the creation of humus.

*

In a perfect world, every species would be valued and given ample space to simply *be* without needing to justify its existence. In the Forest Service, because it is virtually impossible to manage everything, we must prioritize species and habitats for conservation that are declining and most affected by human activities. At the same time, with so many creatures whose function we still don't fully understand, it also seems prudent to not make far-reaching judgments about which are, or are not, important.

Yet we don't live in a perfect world. Judgments, acknowledged or not, are made every day. Even the tendency for humans to conserve animals most like themselves doesn't always happen. Certain species—coyotes and crows, for example—with their tremendous adaptive capabilities, intelligence, and devotion to family (characteristics all much admired in the human realm), often inspire our greatest wrath. Yet prudent thinking, as well as sound research, shows again and again the wisdom of Aldo Leopold's words in *A Sand County Almanac, and Sketches Here and There* about maintaining all the pieces of an ecosystem: "A thing is right when it tends to preserve the integrity, stability, and beauty of the biotic community. It is wrong when it tends otherwise" (1989, 224–25). This is a moral and practical philosophy. Michael Best believes that woodland salamanders are the stewards of the forests, silently channeling invertebrate biomass into energy and maintaining productive ecosystems. Even if the ensatina's shoe-button eyes, interesting courtship rituals, or strange life underground aren't enough to get someone's attention, its effect on the storage of carbon in a world whose atmosphere is already overloaded with the chemical should be.

10

Searching for Snakes

Winthrop, Washington, 2018

Even before we had left the parking lot one spring day in 2018, someone had spotted a snake. Luke, 11 years old and the youngest student in the class, was looking through his binoculars at a tall shrub at the Methow Valley Ranger Station in Winthrop, Washington. When he announced, "There's one!" we all ran over. A western yellow-bellied racer (*Coluber constrictor mormon*), a common snake that lives up to its name, nearly disappeared but for the quick hands of another student. Scott Fitkin, a wildlife biologist with the WDFW, praised the move with a warning.

"That's great," he said, now holding the snake, "but you always want to make very sure of the species you're reaching for."

In a landscape where northern Pacific rattlesnakes (*Crotalus oreganus*), Washington's only venomous species, are also common, such words are sound advice. Still, even racers will bite. This one did just that, nipping Scott on the hand though the bite didn't break the skin. Even as the snake displayed its feistiness, Luke was eager to hold it. The racer is an attractive animal. Its solid coloration includes olive green above and lemon yellow below.

"Go slowly, go gently, and move with the scales," instructed Scott on the proper method for holding a snake that will keep moving forward as it's being held.

Gathering closer to admire the racer, we listened to Scott and John Rohrer, a biologist colleague of mine (now retired) who worked in the Okanogan-Wenatchee National Forest, talk about snakes. They were the instructors for the "2018 Spring Snake Search," a one-day environmental education class they still teach each spring and that my wife, Barbara, and I had traveled from the Olympic Peninsula to attend. The class has been the product of a unique partnership between Scott, John, and the North Cascades Institute (NCI), a northwest Washington nonprofit that fosters environmental stewardship through educational experiences in nature. The event is designed to show how fascinating and even personable snakes are, as well as to demonstrate their important roles in the ecosystem. It can be difficult for biologists to convey an appreciation for the species they study, and reptiles, especially snakes, often invoke such strong, negative reactions in humans that simply stating the facts isn't enough; a personal relationship needs to be established.

Though I've always appreciated snakes, I've never known them well because we have fewer species in western Oregon and Washington. My closest experiences with these animals before the Spring Snake Search had mostly included finding them sunning on the road (during my time in the Peace Corps in Argentina, we also had them come into our house occasionally). On one memorable encounter, as I swam in the Ozette River in Olympic National Park, I'd found myself in the company of a garter snake that was also cooling off with a swim. We both were equally startled by the meeting. While I yelped in surprise, the snake turned and swam the other way. Later, I learned garter snakes actually forage in the water and have seen them lying at the bottom of lakes and creek beds.

We took many photos of the racer. After it was returned to the shrub, Scott and John continued the class briefing. We would visit different nearby areas that were known to have snakes present, including racers, rattlesnakes, garter snakes, and the very secretive rubber boas. The focus would be on reptiles, but we'd also be near ponds, good places to find amphibians. While teaching the class, Scott and John planned to keep track of the snakes observed during the day. They'd send this information to the Center for Snake Conservation, a Colorado nonprofit organization that incorporates the numbers in its Snake Count program, an effort to map and track snake distributions across the world.

"Did you really see that snake in the binoculars?" I asked Luke as we dispersed to load up in the vehicles.

He shook his head, smiling. "I thought it looked like a good place for a snake, but I was really looking at something else. I just got lucky."

*

This May morning in the Methow Valley of eastern Washington had already grown warm. We didn't see many reptiles before a young woman spotted a Pacific gopher snake (*Pituophis catenifer*) in the shade of a sagebrush clump. Gopher snakes are constrictors, so they're not venomous and are safe to pick up. Scott, who has been a snake enthusiast since before he can remember, explained that they will, however, imitate a rattlesnake to appear more menacing to would-be predators.

"A gopher snake will vibrate its tail and hiss," he said as the snake twined around his hands and arms. "But they also settle pretty quickly and don't mind being handled for short periods."

The dark markings on the animal's back were ragged diamond shapes, further increasing its similarity to a rattlesnake. This individual had recently shed its skin, so it was particularly shiny and attractive. Many people wanted to hold the snake, and it was passed gently from person to person. Scott and John told us that gopher snakes are good "ambassador" animals. Because of their docility, they can be brought into classrooms and other venues for up-close, personal meetings.

As others held the snake, I thought about animals being ambassadors, a common phrase in wildlife education circles. The dictionary defines the word *ambassador* as an "official herald, messenger, or agent with a special mission." There was no way of knowing what this gopher snake thought of its current experience, or if it could fathom the idea that its species can function as a connector between humans and reptiles. Still, it didn't appear stressed. The handling, the strange beings all around it, and the foreign smells elicited only an occasional flick of its tongue. We returned the snake to the sagebrush, and it moved off silently into the shade.

The Spring Snake Search class began in 2012. Katie Roloson, then program manager for NCI's field classes, had met Scott and John when they taught a class on carnivores for the institute. Katie got to know both men and knew that they felt sharing their work was an important part of their jobs. At the same time, NCI, with its goal of educating and connecting people to the natural world, had a real interest in citizen science and getting more people to interact with biologists.

Working together was a "win-win," Katie told me some months after I'd taken the class. Scott and John agreed to provide the expertise and leadership for the class; NCI would manage funding and logistics, from advertising to transporting participants to the sites. Both biologists donated their time for the event, but it had also become an important component of their work. Katie said that some NCI staffers initially worried that a class with snakes as a theme wouldn't be popular, but after its first year, the concerns disappeared. Between the general public and NCI staff, approximately 140 people have attended since 2012, and John's and Scott's passion and in-depth knowledge are big reasons the snake class has been so successful. Additionally, their enthusiasm for finding snakes and their calmness around the animals instill the same in others. John, Scott, and Katie all have stories about people uncertain, even afraid, of snakes before signing up. One of Katie's coworkers at NCI was fearful, but when her mother wanted to take the class, she attended as well. "When she found a rattlesnake and got to hold it in the tube," Katie told me, "she was simultaneously horrified and elated."

*

The morning passed, and soon it was lunchtime. Though snakes are ectothermic, meaning they rely on warm surfaces or air temperatures to heat themselves, they can also find a sunny, spring day too hot. We'd observed only a handful of gophers as well as the racer so far. If the snakes had messages for us, they were keeping the communications to themselves.

The big challenge with this type of class is always the timing. "You have to be in the right place, at the right time, with the right weather to be able to find a lot of snakes," John said. During the first couple of years, they did both spring and fall classes, but a full season's worth of grass and forb growth made it hard to see the animals in the autumn. Even in the spring, environmental conditions might not be ideal. "Being able to flex the day or time of the snake search is important," John continued, "but that's not possible when NCI has to advertise and people are traveling from the west side of the Cascades to participate."

As a backup, the focus sometimes switches to amphibians, which are more active in warm, rainy conditions.

"We try to keep it fun," John told me, "and share our excitement, as well as expand people's knowledge about snakes and amphibians and reptiles."

I nodded. Before he retired, John worked with wolverines and lynx in addition to snakes, as well as other animals of eastern Washington. He reminded me a lot of my mentor, Dave Shea, naturally quiet and unassuming but with great knowledge, born of long years of experience working with many wildlife species.

Soon we were exploring a shadier area adjacent to a wetland. Robin, a young woman from western Washington, who was doing the class for the fourth time, found a small rattlesnake on top of a stump.

To observe rattlesnakes more closely and to, yes, even hold them, a different approach from reaching and grabbing must be used. As a venomous species, they can potentially inflict damage if they should bite. For this reason, both John and Scott carried "snake sticks." These long, aluminum poles have a clamp on the end that can be opened and closed to fit around a snake's body. Once a rattlesnake is held with the clamp, it can then be coaxed into a plastic tube where its mouth and head will remain safely out of reach while the lower parts of its body, including the tail and rattle, can be admired or measured for data collection.

Robin's snake was a young one, born late last summer. It measured less than two feet long and had only one segment, also called a button, composing its rattle. Though it vibrated its tail, without additional segments for the button to rub against, there was no sound. This individual had chocolate-colored markings on its back that alternated with a tan background. When placed back on the stump, the snake's uneven pattern blended in well with the chunks of decomposing wood. It remained coiled up and alert as we left it to continue with its day.

Seeing what can sometimes be "hidden in plain sight" is a skill referred to in wildlife biology as developing a search image. Wild animals depend on camouflage to keep themselves safe and unnoticed. Consequently, for those of us not used to searching for snakes every day, it took time to learn to see them. Many of us fanned out over the landscape and investigated every shrub or clump of cover we could find. Other students approached the endeavor in a more relaxed way. This worked too. Barbara hung back from the main group, enjoying the scenery, the dry air, and the smells of the valley. Soon she alerted everyone to a large gopher snake in the shade beneath a sagebrush. People were impressed with the animal's size.

"I just looked down," Barbara said, "and there it was."

*

John Rohrer, like Scott Fitkin, has always been interested in snakes. As a boy growing up in northwestern Arizona, he always kept a few lizards and snakes in cages, though his parents didn't allow him to keep rattlesnakes. Instilling similar curiosity in other people is what the Spring Snake Search is all about. The two men have been teaching the class since 2011, when it was advertised as a Field Herp class and included an evening in the classroom with PowerPoint presentations (the next year they modified it to a one-day event set only in the field and called it Spring Snake Search). Their goals with the class are simple:

to lessen fears around snakes, correct misperceptions, help people appreciate these important animals, and collect data. Often, someone will come who is apprehensive about snakes, yet usually by the end, she or he has gained a new perspective. In general, kids have less trepidation than adults, and if they do, they move past it more quickly. Scott says he watched two of his relatives go from complete fear to guarded fascination. While John knows people who can't understand why anyone would pay good money to search for snakes, he's also seen positive changes over the years.

"Education is the key," he said. "I definitely think there are fewer people, compared to 25 years ago, that kill rattlesnakes just to kill them."

Scott agreed, adding that changing people's minds is helped immensely if they can see the snakes up close in a controlled situation. Though some people in our group didn't want to hold the snakes, everyone at least touched the tail of the rattlesnake.

In addition to educating people about snakes, Scott and John work to find and protect winter den sites. Using tips from residents, as well as snakes they've implanted with small radio tags, they've documented 42 dens as of 2024 in the Methow Valley. This information, though not generally made public, is crucial for protecting both snakes and people. The discovery of one den at the base of a popular rock-climbing spot prompted a seasonal closure during the time the snakes would be leaving the shelter for the summer foraging and breeding season.

*

One place we visited was the 1,500-acre Golden Doe Wildlife Area managed by WDFW. It was acquired by the department in 1991 from a private individual, who had hoped to make a success of a working ranch but found the land to be too "snake-y." One of our stops on the property included the "concrete castle," a name ascribed by John to the abandoned cement foundations of a dwelling that was never finished.

"The building crew kept coming across so many rattlesnakes," he explained, "that they eventually refused to come back. It appears the workers dug into the hillside, and my guess is that they unknowingly excavated a communal den site during the summer. Then all the snakes started showing up in September looking for their winter home. The workers were likely killing rattlesnakes every day, but then more would turn up the next day."

This story, along with another from someone in the group whose friend rode her horse the previous week at Golden Doe and found "wall-to-wall snakes," attests to the animals' ubiquitous presence. Yet even after thoroughly searching among the concrete walls and piles of rubble, we found nothing beyond one black widow spider guarding her egg sac.

Still, it was hard to feel too disappointed. The spectacular view around the concrete castle encompassed a valley green with spring grasses and the sunflower-like petals of balsamroot flowers. Warm breezes spread the perfume of sage, while bitterbrush had just begun budding. The snake search day had been perfectly timed for us to witness the blooming bitter root, or rock rose, flower. This delicate plant with pale pink-white petals makes its living among dry, rocky soils and only blooms for a short period. Being from the tight, dark world of the Olympic rainforest, Barbara and I were greatly enjoying this sunny, open country.

As we began the hike back, John spotted an adult rattlesnake in the tall grasses of a shady, aspen grove. Though generally difficult to tell the gender of a snake, this one was thick with eggs and so clearly a female. With Scott's assistance, John coaxed her into the tube. I got to hold the snake, using one hand to support her body where it entered the tube and the other hand to keep track of the tail area. We counted six segments to her rattle, and the rattling sounded like a soft purr. Because she had eggs, people asked questions about snake reproduction.

"When a male rattlesnake gets the urge to mate," John explained, "he'll travel in a straight line that you could set a compass bearing to. He'll follow this direction until he finds where a female has crossed the path. Using his tongue to detect her scent, he can tell which direction she was going. Then he'll go that way."

"What's the territory of a rattlesnake?" someone asked.

"The territory of a male is basically the female. Sometimes, a male will find her and there will be another male already there. They will then interact to see which one is dominant."

John described how each male raises a portion of his body off the ground and then tries to knock the other back down.

Another question concerned what happens to snakes when wildfires occur, a common event in the Methow Valley. John told us that if the snakes are near rocks when the fire comes through, they can get to cover and survive in the cooler, protected area that also won't burn. If they're caught out in the open country, then they usually don't make it.

When all who wanted to had held the rattlesnake, we placed her and the tube on the ground. At first, she didn't move. Then when she tried to go forward, she seemed to get stuck. Her body was too big where the eggs were.

"What if she can't get through?" one woman asked, worried.

John nudged the snake's lower part while Scott said calmly, "Once she stretches out, she'll be able to move through."

A few moments passed where we all held our breath, but this is what happened. Through the tube she went, back into the tall grass, rattling occasionally, and finally away from view.

*

Contrary to popular mythology, human fear of snakes is not instinctual. In many cultures, snakes have been revered as symbols of transformation, rebirth, or fertility. They are wise and possess healing powers. They may act as messengers, either of cunning and trickery, as Christianity teaches, or of simple communication between worlds, notably the underworld and the upper world. The sheer "otherness" of these animals must be the catalyst behind both

Me with a gopher snake during the 2018 Spring Snake Search. Betsy L. Howell.

humanity's adoration and antagonism. Scott told me he's not entirely sure why he's so drawn to snakes, but "perhaps it's because they're so different from us and so accessible." This last point is important. Reptiles are easier to know than many groups of animals. That they can be found and caught readily and observed up close means that a relationship, based on respect and admiration rather than fear and dominance, is possible.

At the end of the day, I held a gopher snake. The animal flicked her tongue and explored along my forearm. With a dark stripe that extended across her forehead like a folded bandana and black, penetrating eyes, the snake couldn't be anything but wise. Her memory, usually described as *instinct*, stretched back millennia. Too, her ability to perceive the world through taste, and know of dangers and opportunities, is a skill that I would never have. Despite our shared moment together, this gopher snake's understanding of existence contrasted so greatly with mine that I wondered if her message was simply about the value of being different. And that by accepting this value, empathy and compassion necessarily grow, blossoming into a mindset that is less self-focused and more generous. It's a view that we all belong. That we all contribute. That we all ultimately help each other to survive, whether we are snakes, or humans, or one of the millions of other species living on the planet.

Making an Old-Growth Forest

Olympic National Forest, 2008–22

On a typical, wet, Pacific Northwest winter's day, I walk through a dark and dense second-growth forest. This particular stand is located high within the West Fork Humptulips River watershed on the west side of Olympic National Forest. Misty tendrils of low clouds have settled in the canopy above me. Streams where the land had been dry only the week before now flow enthusiastically with bubbling, white froth. My boots sink easily into the softened ground. I wear a hard hat that keeps the rain from sliding into my eyes, but my rain gear is now as wet on the inside as on the outside.

My task on this cool, damp day is to survey the young stand that my colleagues and I hope to encourage into old growth with commercial thinning. I'll be making note of the original stand's legacies, including the big trees and snags that weren't harvested as well as all that will contribute to a more diverse future: hardwood clumps, small wetlands, rocky outcrops. I move across the slope, sketching the stand and its unique features in my Rite in the Rain notebook. I make a list of bird species undeterred by the weather: chickadees, kinglets, nuthatches. Turning over pieces of bark, I look for salamanders escaping the saturated ground. Though I will eventually record only a small fraction of the stand's many residents, the information will still be useful in understanding what remains of the old-growth forest that once grew here. It will also help reveal what is still needed.

It has been more than a century since the first trees were harvested from the West Fork Humptulips. Now many decades later, the land is a spiderweb of roads that link together a quilt of stands of young trees. Many of these stands host remnants from the past. Ten-foot-diameter stumps, cracked and separating, are not uncommon and attest to the 1,000-year-old giant conifers that once blocked all trace of the sun; huckleberry bushes now grow from the top of these stumps like vegetative heads of hair. Springboard notches below the huckleberry display where the loggers stood above the trees' bulbous bases to saw the trunk. A six-foot diameter log nearby stretches out long, providing evidence of the bounty of the time. Impressive as this tree once was, for whatever reason, it was not worth the effort to bring to the mill.

At the edge of the harvested stand live the survivors of the crosscut saw and later the chainsaw. The presence of these remaining ancestral trees reassures me, though they are ever silent about the changes they have witnessed. As I return the notebook to my vest and move to another part of the stand, I am thinking about what once was. I am thinking about fragments.

*

One of the rooms in my childhood home in Tacoma was my father's den. Now such a room would be called a library, or maybe a study or an office, but in the 1970s, these were dens. My father, a career army soldier who'd participated in two wars, built a bookcase for his den and filled it with his many tomes on military history and combat. As a child, I loved the feeling of the den. On a sunny afternoon, I would sit on the couch and open books such as *How to Make War* or *A Stillness at Appomattox*. The evocative titles stoked my curiosity, though I usually lost interest after a few pages. Not having, or so I believed then, a personal connection to the topic couldn't compete with my real love: nature and wild animals.

In addition to the many books were two small, very old journals from the 19th century. These had belonged to my father's great-grandfather, James Darsie Heath, a Union Civil War veteran and a man my dad had known briefly before Darsie, as he was known, died in 1930. They had a dry, slightly musty smell, and a timeless feel. My father often presented them proudly to our dinner or weekend guests. The small, delicate script seemed daunting to read when I was a child; however, during the summer after I resigned from the Forest Service, I read and transcribed them in just a few days. A few words proved tricky to decipher, and sometimes the phrases didn't always make sense to me. Yet mostly, it was as if a curtain had been removed from a part of my past.

Accompanied by Darsie Heath's writings from 1862 to 1865, I embarked on two trips in 1999 and 2000, retracing his wartime travels from western Illinois through Kentucky, Tennessee, Mississippi, and Alabama. I went to every town he did, visiting museums and historical societies. I read newspapers of the time and looked for the landscapes he would have seen. I took a two-week canoe trip traveling down the Yazoo Pass and the Coldwater and Tallahatchie rivers in northwest Mississippi that the Union army had also traversed trying to dislodge the Confederates from Vicksburg. Unsurprisingly, some towns and landscapes had changed completely, unrecognizable from photos I had found from the 1860s. Others seemed suspended in time. In these, I experienced a world I had always longed for, where some of the natural world, at least, was less impacted by humans, and the pain of my own life, including my mother's accident, my parents' deaths, and my own struggles with alcohol, had yet to happen. In one library, I found a memoir written after the war by an officer in my ancestor's regiment. In this chronicle, the lieutenant mentioned my great-great-grandfather, giving me important insight into the young man 18-year-old Darsie Heath had been.

In Vicksburg, Mississippi, I learned of the USS *Cairo*, the first ship ever to be sunk by an electrically detonated torpedo. After a brief exchange of gunfire with Confederate forces in December 1862, the ironclad settled to the bottom of the Yazoo River north of Vicksburg in only 12 minutes. After the war, time quickly passed. *Cairo*'s survivors began to die, and soon the ship's whereabouts were forgotten.

Not until the 1950s did noted Civil War historian Edwin Bearss and two colleagues set out to find *Cairo*. By using historical information and contemporary maps, they at last located her. *Cairo* lay buried under almost 40 feet of water and a thick layer of Mississippi mud that the fast-flowing Yazoo River had deposited over the decades. The ship was a perfect time capsule. It would reveal many secrets if it could be lifted intact to the surface.

*

As the Civil War unfolded in the eastern part of the United States, across the continent the old-growth coniferous forests of the Pacific Northwest teetered on the edge of an era. In 1862, only a handful of European Americans had ever penetrated their darkened interiors, though for thousands of years, Indigenous peoples had known the deep forests, winding rivers, and high meadow country as well as the bountiful, saltwater shorelines. Trees had been growing across the landscape for 1,000 years or more and stood 300 feet tall.

Yet the time was rapidly approaching when the societies of the newcomers, hungry for the giant trees, would begin to nibble away at the forests. At first, this work was necessarily slow and laborious. Men used crosscut saws and axes. Donkeys, horses, and oxen pulled the logs out of the woods. The sheer size and density of trees made the work a tedious, and at times life-threatening, process.

In fact, early harvest techniques, more dependent on men than machinery, must have made it seem as if the forests would last forever.

They didn't.

In only a few decades, the technology outstripped by orders of magnitude the ability of the forests to replace themselves. Without specific protection from Congress, the temperate ecosystems of the Olympic Peninsula and other landscapes vanished as if they had never been anything except the walls of homes and businesses and the frames of carriages and ships and boardwalks. If society hadn't slowed the rate of old-growth harvest when it did, these ecosystems would now exist only in national parks.

Beginning in the late 20th century, management of the remaining old growth in the national forests of the Pacific Northwest changed drastically. No longer did the American people want all the ancient trees cut down. The federal listing of the northern spotted owl in 1990 as a threatened species spurred a rethinking of the concept of ecosystem management. Likewise, the listing of the marbled murrelet in 1992 further required managers to consider the far-reaching consequences of forest conversion. In response to these listings, President Bill Clinton's 1994 Northwest Forest Plan designated vast tracts of land in western Oregon and Washington as "late-successional reserve." The primary management objective for these areas would be the maintenance and enhancement of habitat for animals and plants dependent on older forests. Timber harvest could still occur, but only if such activity could be shown to benefit these species. Thus began the work of restoring younger, homogenous stands of trees to the intricate, historic ecosystems that had once been so numerous.

This restoration task, however, isn't a simple one. Some landscapes are missing many parts that compose an older forest. Managed second-growth forests are more like agricultural fields than the complex temperate rainforests of earlier centuries. When mechanization brought rapidity and efficiency to the logging industry, nearly everything standing on a piece of ground was removed. Immediately postharvest, the land was burned and replanted with Douglas fir seedlings, the favored wood for building and other uses. Subsequent management focused solely on the new trees. The Forest Service sprayed invasive weeds with herbicides, pruned back other species, and thinned the fir to let a few individuals gain more growth. Everyone knew what the land was capable of. It had grown trees 10 feet or more in diameter once; it could do so again. One problem remained, however. The forest operates under a very different timeline from the one instituted by humans. It experiences no sense of urgency stemming from economic climates. Nor does it much care if some people, now mourning the loss of the giants, wished the big trees back again in their own lifetimes.

Those days of clearcut harvest, at least for now, are a management technique of the past on the Olympic National Forest, as well as in parts of other national forests in the Pacific Northwest. We better understand that the intrinsic health of any system is dependent on the maintenance of all the parts. We now know that a landscape may look intact from a distance, but with even the smallest resident missing, the ecosystem will remain vulnerable. A homogenous stand of one species of tree and one age group may be eradicated by any number of physical or biological insults, including windstorms, fire, diseases, or insects. Consequently, one premise of rebuilding an old-growth forest is that diversity within will aid in surviving the elements that come from outside. To do that, it is imperative to understand what is still there and what is still needed.

*

Nearly a century after its sinking, divers recovered *Cairo*'s armored port covers, one cannon, and the pilothouse. The cannon's white oak carriage had also resisted time's erasing effect and came to the surface, bright and shiny. Ephemera such as toothbrush handles, combs, mirrors, and leather shoes had all been preserved, buried by the mud that had encased the ship like a tight-fitting glove.

However, when the salvage team tried to lift the ship in its entirety, the three-inch cables cut deeply into its hull. The men had to divide *Cairo* into three sections, bringing up only what the river agreed to relinquish. After collecting all they could, they loaded everything onto a barge for transport to Pascagoula, Mississippi, where restoration began. This process, called "ghosting," combined what had been salvaged with replica pieces. The result was then transported back to the Vicksburg Military Park. Open views of the ship now stand in stark contrast to a vessel that once was enclosed by two-and-a-half-inch thick metal plating and two-foot thick white oak timbers. *Cairo* is an amalgam of the past and present, a vessel not worthy of water travel yet quite recognizable for what it once had been.

Like the divers searching the opaque waters of the Yazoo River for what remained of *Cairo*, my colleagues and I are somewhat "ecological historians," combing through the second-growth forests, essentially old-growth kindergartens, documenting the remnants as well as the immigrants. In order to plan future activities, we must understand what was once and what remains.

The fisheries biologist surveys the streams for salmonid species. The botanist searches for rare plants in meadows and wetlands. The archaeologist combs the site for evidence of Indigenous people's presence. It's a team effort, with everyone seeing the landscape through a different lens.

For many years, I've worked with Mark, a forester on the Olympic National Forest and a fellow Washingtonian. Because we must use silvicultural techniques to achieve our goals of a more diverse forest, Mark plays a crucial role in developing prescriptions for how to harvest the stands. He has a keen eye not only for imagining the future but also for seeing into the past. He also has an encyclopedic memory for everything he finds on the landscape.

"It's kind of like being a detective," he told me recently. "It's about looking for clues, things that can give us insight. We know some things from the official records, but then it's important to see what we can find on the ground."

Mark traverses each stand proposed for thinning, examining the remnants of the past and identifying the species of trees that once grew here. In this way, he knows what the historical stand looked like as well as events it experienced long ago, such as fires, indicated by char still visible on stumps and logs.

"The type of fire a stand experiences, for example, a light burn or a more severe one, can affect what will grow after," he explains. "Also, the current understory of shrubs and forbs can tell us a lot about what to expect after we've thinned and let in more sunlight. Legacy components, such as snags, that remain from the original stand, will also make a difference in how the forest will function in the future."

Sometimes Mark and I look at stands together after they've been commercially thinned. I'm interested in finding salamanders and other wildlife species in residence; he examines the stumps of the trees that have been thinned. Apart from just showing the age of the tree, the stump has a now-exposed history. The stump of one tree that we examine shows an inner part that looks distinct from the rest.

"My guess here," he says, using his hands to encompass the spot in the center, "is that this was the tree that stayed after the original harvest. But see this mark?" He points to a darker area where the even, concentric lines have been broken up. "This is where the tree got wounded, maybe hit by another tree or a piece of equipment during the harvest. But it still continued to grow."

The growth rings before the original harvest and the wound are tight, evidence of being shaded and in competition with its old-growth superiors.

After harvest, the rings are wider, indicating the tree grew quickly. Just understanding a small bit of this tree's history makes me feel sad. I tell Mark I'm sorry the tree was cut during the commercial thin, the second harvest of this stand.

He nods. "Yes, but they can't all stay."

This kind of history is something we're all looking for. I envy that Mark is able to study beings that don't move or hide. Back in the office, we all share our data and impressions and begin looking into the future. Envisioning and planning for what could be once again is both science and art, necessarily dependent on the mind and the heart working together. This is what the restorers of the *Cairo* did. The "ghosted" parts of the ship now on display include the chimneys, the gun deck, and the laminate wood framing. Early photographs helped historians reconstruct the ship. Notes and other documents from that time recreated life aboard the ship. Without this information, the work of connecting the pieces today would have been much more difficult. Maybe even impossible.

*

The utility of my rain gear seems more and more questionable. The hard hat, however, continues to prove its worth by keeping my head dry. Fortunately, the temperature is not cold. Despite early forest management that desired only the presence of Douglas fir, other tree species have made their way into this forest. Vine maple grows in dense thickets, bending in arches above me. A bigleaf maple is nearly as tall as the fir, with a thick trunk clothed in a mossy sweater. There are also groves of red alder, individual cascara and western red cedar trees, an occasional white pine, and very rarely a yew tree. Part of the thinning prescription will include the protection of all of these. They are considered "minor" species due to being less abundant, yet all are important. Cedar waxwings and band-tailed pigeons will forage on the berries of cascara trees. When truffles are no longer available, northern flying squirrels, an important prey species for spotted owls, will seek the protein-rich seeds of the vine maple. Hardwood trees and their fall leaf litter provide a suite of insects for foraging birds and amphibians; mollusks are also associated with deciduous trees. High in the canopy, golden-crowned kinglets, chickadees, and red-breasted nuthatches all confirm that despite the drastic changes to this ecosystem, the land continues to provide.

Across one creek, I find another stream, and another. This stand, narrow and situated crosswise on the slope, is sandwiched above and below by two areas of old growth that weren't harvested. Animal paths are braided throughout, illustrating the connection this younger stand provides between the older forest fragments. I follow one path. Clumps of sword fern and deer fern grow along the trail. Banana slugs, some nearly white and others deep green with single black spots on their mantles, move slowly upon the less soggy pieces of earth. Along with the mollusks, the most common animals I observe on the forest floor are a type of black ground beetle that always seems to be in a hurry, as well as slower "flat-backed" millipedes, dark in color with yellow spots. When picked up and placed in my palm, the millipede emits a toxin smelling of almonds. This toxin, hydrogen cyanide gas, is not harmful to humans in such a small quantity but is a powerful deterrent to predators. Such an adaptation allows the millipede to focus on its forest job, that of macroshredder. It's responsible for breaking down litter and beginning the nutrient-cycling process.

One of the factors preventing the growth of more diversity in a second-growth stand is a lack of sunlight. With an annual rainfall of approximately 90 inches per year, the soil of the West Fork Humptulips is some of the best tree-growing ground in the world. It shows, too, in the crowd of trees around me and the tight roof of branches over me. By removing some individual trees, more sunlight can combine with the already plentiful rain. Midstory trees, such as cascara and vine maple, will continue to thrive instead of dying in a world that is only growing darker. So too will huckleberry and blueberry bushes, willows, salmonberry, and sword fern. Herbaceous plants, such as trailing blackberry, wild ginger, and twinflower, will multiply and spread. Simply making space for natural processes to occur is one of the best techniques managers can employ.

After opening the stand to sunlight, we may ghost in essential forest pieces that we know will be decades in the making. By topping, girdling, and inoculating fungal spores into select trees, we can create snags, important refugia for many wildlife species, in only a few years. By removing more trees on the south side of certain individuals, we can "release" the tree and encourage greater branch growth for murrelets. In one area, Mark and I select such a tree that has a patch of mistletoe fungus about 40 feet up.

"My guess here," Mark says, "is that this tree's growth was suppressed in the dense stand that followed the original harvest. Also, the bigger trees were 'raining down' mistletoe seed on this tree. Mistletoe seeds pop and then fall and infect trees below them. The infestation doesn't generally travel up the tree, though it can, but it will do so more slowly, and if the tree is growing well, then it can outgrow the mistletoe. In this example here, with the stand opened up after harvest, the tree began to grow well and wasn't infected further with mistletoe."

For our purposes now, to provide suitable platforms for murrelet nests, this mistletoe is not a bad thing. That the tree can grow taller and bigger, and quickly, is also important.

Additionally, by arranging together parts of felled trees not removed during the thinning process, we will create cover piles as well as "log pyramids," which replicate the six-foot, old-growth log I observed earlier. Even as crews are still constructing these piles, juncos and song sparrows already exhibit great interest in them. Snakes may be curled up at the entrances as soon as the next day, taking some sun before retreating into their new, protected home.

*

In an old-growth stand, one steps easily into the past. To stand next to a tree that has been growing for eight or nine centuries is awesome to contemplate. There is something precious in that moment, not easily defined yet filled for me with bits of humility and connection to this individual, its history, and our shared moment. Certain places, towns and cities and rivers, have made me feel more connected to members of my family. Likewise, the natural world has made me feel more connected to everything. The tree beside me, one of the "standing people" as Robin Wall Kimmerer describes trees in *Braiding Sweetgrass*; the slug at my feet, chomping on an oxalis leaf; the marten and cougar that see me but never let me see them; the salamander I happen to meet only because the rain has begun to fall.

*

I don't know if it's hubris or hopefulness that causes foresters and biologists to believe we're capable of creating something that first evolved over many, many centuries. It's one thing to piece together an inanimate object for display in a museum. It's another endeavor entirely to bring a complex, dynamic world into being. It's also difficult to reconstruct something that we still do not fully understand. And we will never know in our lifetimes, let alone our careers, if what we have done has completely achieved what we have desired. My coworker Mark acknowledges this too. "It's humbling," he says. "We know a lot, but there's also a lot we do *not* know. All we can do is work toward creating legacies and nudging forest processes forward."

Fortunately, some results are gratifyingly more immediate. Mark can measure the growth and diameter of trees as they respond to thinning and more sunlight. Likewise, I've walked through stands commercially thinned in the 1990s, a very short time ago in the life of a forest, and other growth is impressive as well. Carpets full of ferns and mosses support a range of tree species and sizes. A dense canopy is interspersed with openings. Log pyramids and messy conglomerations of sticks and branches fill the land and provide cover for different wildlife species. Studies examining bird and amphibian presence in these areas show that the work of thinning and adding in certain habitat components is beneficial; habitat complexity is improved, as are species abundances, richness, and diversity. As for the two species, the spotted owl and marbled murrelet, for which much of this restorative work originated, only the forest managers of the future will know if we in this time have succeeded in our restoration aims. If we haven't, these fragments we're puzzling together may become nothing more than the ghosts of the past. If we have, then the work of filling in the rest may continue.

12

The Young Naturalist

Olympic National Forest, 2006

In the summer of 2006, Jace (not his real name) was 18 years old and had just graduated from high school. By contrast, I was 40 that summer and had finished college before he was born. We'd hired Jace as a seasonal wildlife intern to help with various field inventories in the Olympic National Forest, including surveying for bats, deer, and elk. During my years with the Forest Service, I had rarely seen precollege people hired for summer work. It wasn't that there was a policy on being a specific age; it had more to do with needing certain qualifications, and college students usually filled these better. Yet Jace was special. He came highly recommended by his supervisors at the wildlife rehabilitation center where he'd volunteered, and he'd taken week-long field courses studying wolves and other predators. He showed initiative and enthusiasm, and his grades were excellent.

In August, Jace and I traveled to the West Fork Humptulips River watershed for a week of surveys. One might have thought we were headed for Antarctica with the many Rubbermaid tubs and stuff sacks full of food, camping gear, reference materials, field equipment, and rain gear. As I drove the vehicle four hours to our field site, Jace read and initially didn't say much. He occasionally looked up from his book and out the window at the hawks and vultures soaring above the highway. After a time, he broke the silence.

"What do you think of when I say 'pigeon-toed'?" he asked.

"What?"

"Do you think of toes inward or outward?"

"Oh. Inward, I think."

"That's right!" Jace shouted, impressed. He held up his track book. "And it's the same with the term, 'duck-foot'!"

"Why do you ask?" I glanced at him and the page in his book with drawings of the webbed feet of waterfowl.

He shrugged. "For some reason, I always think of toes outward with the term 'pigeon-toed.'" It was clear he had thought about this a lot.

Jace began drawing in a journal while studying his bird book. When I asked about his sketches, he said they were part of an online naturalist course he was taking. As he continued to draw in silence, I felt slightly envious of his focus. At 18, I knew I wanted to be a wildlife biologist, but I was still very distracted with partying and boyfriends.

Our task for the week was to look at second-growth stands that the Forest Service wanted to commercially thin in the West Fork Humptulips. Though I generally did these assessments by myself, the work often went faster with two of us covering the larger stands. I explained to Jace the process of taking notes on tree, shrub, and forb species; current wildlife use; remnant snags and logs that had been left from the previous harvest activities; and any unique habitats present, such as wetlands or areas of vine maple. Jace listened attentively and copied this information into his notebook. At our first stop, I suggested we split up. We'd each cover a different part of the stand and communicate by handheld radio if needed.

"I can also let you know where I am with my raven call," Jace said. He then turned his mouth into an oval, took a deep breath, and emitted what sounded like the gulpy caw of the common raven.

I smiled. "That's great. I don't do bird calls very well though, so I'll just yell."

He seemed disappointed. "OK."

We went our respective ways into a second generation of Northwest temperate rainforest. Though to many, a forest is a forest, and having trees on the landscape is enough, no matter what size, age class, or species, we had to be more discerning. The Forest Service had harvested centuries-old, diverse stands for most of the 20th century with the goal of then growing single-species plantations back that could be harvested again in only a few decades. There were many reasons why this happened: society's desire and need for lumber, a belief that such vast forests could never end (even though the demise of forests in the eastern and midwestern United States had already happened), and a belief that older forests weren't healthy and should be removed to make room for vigorous, young growth. In the 21st century, however, we understand so much more about the complexity of forests and the values they provide beyond supplying timber to mills: carbon storage, habitats for threatened and endangered species, clean water, temperature regulation, solace and comfort, protection from the elements. The list of the values forests provide to people and other species is long, and we are still learning more every year. This work of finding ways to jump-start the successional process to re-create the grandeur and biodiversity of the ancient forests in the Pacific Northwest is a big focus of the Forest Service's mission now.

Jace may have been young, but he was also smart and observant. He took many notes, as I would later see when looking at his survey sheets. He found everything of interest, from small fungi to shed bird feathers to stray pieces of animal bone. Toward the end of the afternoon, he called me excitedly on the radio.

"I've found an egg!" he shouted.

"What kind of egg?" I asked.

"It looks like a blue grouse. The others on the nest have hatched but this one seems to have rolled out."

I asked Jace to give his raven call and then hurried across the slope toward him.

The nest had been at the upper end of a log leftover from the original harvest. It was little more than a mass of sticks and feathers and moss with various shapes of broken shell scattered within. The egg Jace found was at the base of the other end of the log and had apparently, as he said, just rolled out. Without the warmth of its parent, it never hatched. Jace handed the egg to me. It was heavy, its contents still inside. The shell was an off-white color without any blemishes. We took several photos, then Jace put the egg in a Ziploc bag and into his surveyor's vest.

"Let's look at the other shells," he said. "I think a predator got them." We examined these and concluded that the very uniform way in which the shells had separated, and fit back together, indicated that most of the chicks in this clutch had hatched instead of being predated.

On the way back to the truck, Jace walked behind me. A sudden loud popping noise stopped us. I turned around, startled. Jace's eyes, initially round in puzzlement, quickly narrowed with suspicion. He reached into the back pocket of his vest and pulled out the Ziploc bag. The egg had exploded into a snotty mess of yolk and shell fragments. An odor of putrefaction enveloped us when he opened the bag.

"It exploded because it was rotten!" he said excitedly.

"Yes," I agreed. "Maybe the gases that built up in the confined space helped too."

"No," he shook his head. "It had nothing to do with gases. The egg was just rotten."

Surprised and a little annoyed, I said, "OK," but didn't feel convinced. Yet I didn't have much experience with why an egg would explode, so maybe he was right.

*

That night we camped at Campbell Tree Grove campground along the West Fork Humptulips River. This little-visited campground is a jewel of 200-foot-tall spruce and fir trees. Other universes of life exist in the canopies several stories off the ground, and I expected to hear marbled murrelets the following dawn. Jace didn't seem quite as impressed with the old stand or the possibility of hearing murrelets. He did, however, become captivated by the dozens of horseflies that immediately descended on our white Forest Service vehicle. After we set up our tents, he returned to the blazer. Suddenly, Jace shouted.

"A bald-faced hornet is eating a horsefly!"

A vigorous buzzing sound coming from the ground indeed involved a hornet devouring the head of the fly. The horsefly's brethren glued to our vehicle seemed oblivious. In the next moment, the hornet snapped off the fly's head. Jace squealed again, utterly delighted. Perhaps growing tired of an audience, the hornet flew to the top of a red elderberry bush. A little while later, we watched the same event. Though gruesome, I felt grateful to the bald-faced hornets. The horseflies were pests and bit us at every opportunity, causing me to have little sympathy for any unfortunate end they met.

Our tents set up, Jace and I made dinner. I had one entire Rubbermaid box devoted to food, including granola, soy milk, fruit, dried soup, and sandwich makings. Jace seemed to have packed only a partial loaf of bread and a jar of peanut butter.

"Is that all you have for dinner?" I asked. For all that Jace had brought along, including field guides, notebooks, camping equipment, and gear, enough food for a week in the field didn't seem to be among the items.

"Yeah," he said, looking sheepish. "I didn't have time to shop."

"I have some extra soup if you'd like."

"OK."

After dinner, Jace brought out a foot-long dowel and a square piece of plywood from his pack. He looked at me seriously and asked, "Do you know what a fire board is?"

Without waiting for my reply, he explained that the idea was to rub the dowel quickly between your palms while one end of the dowel sat in a hole in the plywood. With enough friction in the hole, he said, it would produce flame. After several minutes, Jace had produced nothing beyond a lot of panting and sweating. I left him and his fire board and went down to the West Fork Humptulips.

At Campbell Tree Grove, the West Fork is a soft glide this time of year. It flows quietly above smooth rocks of many shades, rust brown, deep gray, and blue. A log bridge crosses the river, and just downstream, a jutting rock the size of a chair breaks up the flow. As I came to the bridge, I saw the outline of an American dipper resting on the rock. The dipper, also known as a "water ouzel" is the only truly aquatic songbird in North America. This individual remained very still, its profile dark in the waning light. It was unusual to see a dipper so stationary, and my reward was to observe the tiny white feathers on its eyelid as the bird blinked.

When I got back to the campsite, Jace still worked at his fire board. He had a few small piles of ash but no flame yet. I went into the tent to escape the bugs. Both of us hoped to hear owls that night, but in fact, the campground was utterly silent. We didn't even hear the scuffling of a raccoon in search of leftover crumbs. The peace continued until around midnight. That's when a yell from Jace split the blackness like a chisel.

"The egg!" he shouted. "The egg!"

My heart raced, and I scrambled to find my headlamp. I am typically very comfortable in the woods, more so than in the city, and I never worry about wild animals, but the possibility of encounters with other people always keeps me alert. "Jace, what is it?" I yelled.

He mumbled something but said no more. I lay back and took a deep breath. After a few minutes, I was almost asleep again when he shouted, "What did you say?!"

"What?" I sat up again. "Nothing!"

Two hours later, Jace woke me up a third time, asking what I had said.

"Jace! It's the middle of the night! I didn't say anything! Go to sleep!"

I now lay in the dark, completely rattled. I waited for him to shout more, however, all remained quiet. I eventually got back to sleep, but it was an uneasy rest. At six o'clock the next morning I crawled out of my tent groggy. Jace was kneeling by the fire board.

"You slept in," he said smugly, no doubt referring to my comment the previous day that I usually got up at five.

"Listen, buddy," I snapped, "I slept in because you kept me awake talking in your sleep."

"Really? What did I say?"

"You were shouting about the egg."

Jace found this quite amusing because, of course, he remembered nothing. It wasn't until after drinking a strong cup of coffee that I began to feel kindly toward him again.

*

We left Campbell Tree Grove to investigate more stands. The drive took about 40 minutes, and along the way, we discussed Jace's upcoming move to college. He was going to Washington State, where I'd graduated in 1987 with a degree in wildlife management. I told him I'd really liked it and that it seemed like the university had a good program for biologists.

"Oh, I'm just going there because they gave me a full scholarship," Jace said. "I'll do my first two years at WSU, but then I really want to go to the University of Washington."

"Why's that?"

"They have a better program."

As we got closer to our destination, a snowshoe hare appeared on the road in front of us. It ran back and forth, leaping high into the air. I stopped the vehicle, and we watched with our binoculars. It didn't seem to be running from a predator.

"I think it's playing," said Jace. He looked up hares in his mammal book while I slowly drove past the animal, which had hopped off into the bush. The hare apparently just felt full of vigor on this warm, summer morning.

Our stands today grew on the steeper slopes above the West Fork. Small openings filled with salmonberry and red elderberry bushes broke up the dark interiors, and here we found more birds. Feeding groups of kinglets, chickadees, nuthatches, and juncos flew excitedly above us. A giant snag with oblong cavities made by pileated woodpeckers added diversity to this area along with lime-green patches of vine maple bending high over our heads. Sword fern, deer fern, and oxalis grew on the forest floor. One stand had a small meadow where Jace and I saw several large garter snakes sunning in the grass. Other stands weren't as interesting, but there was always the *possibility* of finding something.

That afternoon, we found ourselves in a drainage with a long hike up the other side to the truck. Before beginning, we splashed water on our faces and looked in the stream for amphibians. Atop one smooth stone, stretched out long with the current, was a larval tailed frog. Jace had never seen this species before. We watched the small creature as its tail swayed gently with the current. After it dashed out of sight, we had no more excuses; we had to begin up the slope. Devil's club plants grabbed at us with their thorny branches in the wet bottoms, but after some careful stepping, we were above them. Arriving in a less steep area, I noticed dozens of vanilla leaf plants.

"Do you know why they call it 'vanilla' leaf?" Jace asked after I'd pointed them out. His tone told me he wasn't asking because he didn't know but wanted to see if *I* knew.

"Yes," I said, trying not to sound angry that I felt in competition with an 18-year-old. "Because when the plant is dried, the leaves smell like vanilla." Jace seemed surprised that I knew the answer. He confessed to only having just learned about the vanilla leaf after reading Pojar and MacKinnon's *Plants of the Northwest*.

Later that day, we found a stump 20 feet high and 10 feet across. Jace stood next to it, looking a bit like a forest elf, with his yellow hard hat and orange vest. Darkened entrances where the old stump had begun to separate were worn smooth, indicating some animals called this spot home. Huckleberry and salal grew out of the top. I tried to conjure the ancient tree in my mind. My gaze moved slowly from the stump into the space above it, imagining the massive form that had once been, with its thick bark, tangle of limbs, and shady canopy. These young stands now flourished with growth, and at the same time, I felt as if I walked through a graveyard. A few ghosts remained, and their memories surrounded their descendants.

During the day, Jace had used up the last of his bread and peanut butter, so that evening we drove to Quinault. At the mercantile, he bought a bag of peanuts and a supersized can of Campbell's Chunky Beef Stew. This didn't seem like enough food, but when I suggested getting more, he said it was fine. At camp, I asked him if he wanted me to start up the stove to heat his stew.

"Nah, I like it cold. That's the way my mother makes it."

Upon returning from the store, we'd found other tents at Campbell Tree Grove. After dinner, I went to meet the new people. As I approached, a jacked-up blue truck pulled in. Two guys wearing plaid shirts and ball caps emerged, the driver holding a rifle. He smiled and said that bear season had opened the day before and that they'd been out scouting.

"See any?" I asked.

"No, but we had fun hiking around."

His friendly demeanor eased my concern somewhat about having men with guns nearby. I returned to camp, where Jace was working on his fireboard. The conflict between horseflies and hornets continued and provided an occasional diversion.

That evening, Jace went down to the river and smoothed out a patch of sand. In the morning, he planned to see what had passed by in the night. This is a good way to capture clear tracks of different mammals and birds; however, it's hit or miss that something will come by if a site isn't baited with an attractant. Still, rivers and streams are natural travelways, so it seemed possible. Sure enough, the next morning, while I collected thimbleberries to put on my cereal, Jace returned from the river very excited.

"C'mon!" he yelled. "I've found mouse and vole tracks!"

By the log bridge where I'd seen the dipper, Jace showed me his sandy area and where there were now small depressions. He knelt and pointed.

"This part here is from the vole, and this part over here is the mouse," he explained. "These are great, though I will say, I don't know which vole and which mouse species walked here."

I looked closely. "I don't know, Jace," I said doubtfully. "They don't look very distinct to me." I was trying not to be too critical, but I was sure the depressions he pointed to had simply been made by the night damp.

He looked up at me, indignant. "No, this is definitely what they are. Can't you see? Come to this side. You'll get a better angle." I moved as he suggested but remained unconvinced. Jace, however, entertained no doubts. He nodded his head, pleased. "This is the best tracking I've ever seen."

*

The days passed. At times, I wished I were by myself, as Jace could be tiring to be around. On the other hand, he had no trouble entertaining himself in the evenings, and during the day we were largely apart except when we met up to compare notes. I continued to be alternately amused and irritated at the certainty of his observations. My experience had shown me the value of being doubtful. Sometimes a track or a birdsong could be clearly identified. Many times they couldn't. For tracks, the substrate could alter the size and shape of palms and toes, which could make all the difference in species identification.

For songs, variation or a bird singing only a couple of notes could make deter-mining the singer harder.

When Jace found a pile of feathers, he explained at length that since the shaft had been chewed on and there was a small drop of poop on a nearby leaf, the bird must have been predated. This seemed reasonable, though just to be contrary, I mused that the animal could have also died and then been scav-enged. When I found the remains of a dead blue grouse and he thought it was a band-tailed pigeon, I disagreed. Truthfully, it wasn't bad to have someone to debate about what the stories were. And I admired his enthusiasm. After discussing the grouse/pigeon, he brought out his very large knife and cut off the head. "I'm going to take this home and clean it," he said happily.

Maybe Jace was right in his assessments, which again demonstrates my own questioning nature. Even when something looks sure, I always consider other possibilities. This seems best to me and was something I had learned from Dave Shea and other experienced biologists—that is, it's best to be cautious in making conclusions. What seems true may not be, and it's important to stay open to other possibilities, especially with regard to dynamic ecosystems that are being affected by the presence and movement of different species as well as multiple environmental events, often happening at the same time. Of course, Jace had to find his own way of investigation. Confidence is a great thing, and if it's accompanied by a willingness to change one's mind, all the better.

*

On our last day, Jace and I worked in a rectangular, mostly flat unit with an old logging road bisecting it. This was a stand I'd visited before and was partic-ularly fond of. One winter, after a snowfall, I had walked the old logging road and found mountain lion tracks. The cat had recently passed by, providing clear impressions that, given the remote location, four smaller toes, and large palm, couldn't be confused with dog prints.

We each took a side of the old road and began zigzagging back and forth through the stand. I hadn't seen anything dramatic though the small mush-rooms and different colored fungus and lichen were interesting. Jace and I had been separated for close to an hour when he called me on the radio.

"Betsy, there's a hunter in blaze orange due north of me!"

Given the men camping at Campbell Tree Grove, I wasn't surprised to hear this. Still, it concerned me to be so close to someone with a gun. Jace and

I both wore our safety vests and yellow hard hats, but a person who only heard us might not realize we weren't bears.

I radioed back, "Call out, Jace, and let him know you're there."

Immediately I heard a whoop right behind me. I turned around to find Jace standing about 50 yards away on the road. He waved in my direction, and I looked all around but saw no one else. Relieved, I pressed the mike again. "It's OK, Jace, it's not a hunter. You're just seeing me."

*

It's been nearly 20 years since Jace worked on the Olympic National Forest. After that summer when he'd left for college, we didn't hear any more from him. In the modern way of finding out about people, I recently looked him up on the internet. Unsurprisingly, he has had an adventurous and productive career in wildlife conservation. With both a bachelor's and a master's degree, and an array of experiences around the globe working primarily with birds, but also with mammals and in environmental education, Jace has undoubtedly made great contributions. He had a fire in him that summer we worked together, and it looked to be a long-burning one.

Mt. Hood and Salmon River Meadows, 1987. USDA Forest Service by Betsy L. Howell.

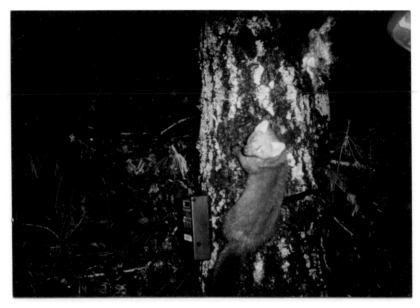

Pacific marten, Siskiyou National Forest, December 1996. USDA Forest Service, Rogue River-Siskiyou National Forest.

Murray, the marbled murrelet I cared for in August 1992. USDA Forest Service by Betsy L. Howell.

The feet of a murrelet are made for diving and swimming in the ocean.
USDA Forest Service by Betsy L. Howell.

Ensatinas are fully terrestrial salamanders. Alan St. John.

Northwestern salamanders spend their lives in both aquatic and terrestrial habitats. Alan St. John.

Michael Best with ensatinas during his master's research. Michael Best.

Juvenile rough-skinned newt found during a summer migration event, 2014. USDA Forest Service by Betsy L. Howell.

Rough-skinned newts are found in both aquatic and terrestrial habitats and are a commonly seen salamander in the Pacific Northwest. Alan St. John.

Second-growth stand prior to commercial thinning. USDA Forest Service by Betsy L. Howell.

Second-growth stand after commercial thinning. USDA Forest Service by Betsy L. Howell.

An old-growth coniferous forest is characterized by large trees, large snags, and large logs. USDA Forest Service by Betsy L. Howell.

Mountain goat, blindfolded and with horn guards, being delivered by helicopter, 2019. USDA Forest Service by Betsy L. Howell.

Northern spotted owl, Olympic National Forest, 2014. USDA Forest Service by Betsy L. Howell.

Barred owls are slightly larger than spotted owls and have vertical brown bars on their bellies. Philip Brown, Unsplash.

Goat Lake, Olympic National Forest, 2020. USDA Forest Service by Marc McHenry.

The Christmas Salamander

Olympic National Forest, 1999, 2014

During the holiday season of 1999, a salamander in a Styrofoam cup arrived on JD Kleopfer's desk. Dark brown without any markings, it had been driven to the Virginia Living Museum in Newport News, Virginia, where JD worked at that time as curator of herpetology. Only hours before, the salamander had been residing in a noble fir tree in a local Lowe's parking lot. Laurel Glasco, a master gardener, had just purchased the tree when the funny creature fell from the branches onto the floor. Her son thought it was a pile of animal poop. Fortunately, she looked closer. JD knew instantly that the animal wasn't native to Virginia. Upon calling Lowe's, he learned the Christmas trees had come from Oregon, and from that he determined the animal was a northwestern salamander, a species found only on the West Coast of North America.

The *Daily Press* of Newport News quoted JD in a December article about the new arrival: "My theory is some trees were cut and stacked overnight, and [the salamander] climbed in, and the next morning they were picked up and away he went. The next thing he knows, he's in Virginia" (Di Vincenzo 1999).

While he kept the salamander comfortable and fed it crickets, JD also arranged for the Oregon Zoo in Portland to take in the traveler. The *Daily Press* article, as well as one by the Associated Press, explained how the salamander would return home via FedEx in a plastic box full of wet cloths and crickets. The media attention resulted in Northwest Airlines offering to transport the celebrity back home in more style.

"The salamander didn't just fly First Class," JD told me in 2014 when I interviewed him for a PARC newsletter. "It flew in the cockpit alongside the pilot."

*

The northwestern salamander is a member of the family of "mole" salamanders, species that spend most of their lives underground. Because northwestern salamanders only leave their burrows to travel to breeding ponds in the late winter and early spring or during heavy, warm rains, they are rarely seen. There are two subspecies of *Ambystoma gracile*: a spotted subspecies, *A. g. decorticatum*, which lives in British Columbia, and *A. g. gracile*, which displays a solid, chocolate color and resides in Washington, Oregon, and northern California. Despite the plain appearance of the subspecies where I've worked in Oregon and Washington, there is no mistaking a northwestern for anything else.

During one of my autumn field days working in the West Fork Humptulips River watershed, it had been raining the entire day. The nearness to the winter solstice meant the days were short. Inside the dense world of the younger forest, the environment stayed dark and quiet. Because the temperature remained fairly warm, I'd been looking under pieces of bark for salamanders. In the Olympic Mountains, the two species most often observed with this technique are the ensatina and the western red-backed salamander, both fully terrestrial amphibians.

Much to my surprise, upon lifting one large piece of bark beside a rushing creek, I found a northwestern salamander. The animal moved slightly, otherwise it might have gone unnoticed against the dark soil. The large eyes and parotid glands behind the eyes are diagnostic for this species. They give them a rather determined look, and in fact, the salamanders may release toxins from these glands and the sides of their tails when they feel threatened. The rain continued falling while the salamander and I regarded each other. Finally, I reached into my field vest. That's when I realized that I didn't have my camera with me. I *always* have my camera, but this stand had been my last stop of the day. It was raining awfully hard, and it would be too dark to take photos, *and* I hadn't imagined finding much anyway. So I'd left it behind.

It would take me less than five minutes to return to the vehicle and get the camera. I replaced the bark and made note of the arrangement of rocks and trees nearby in order to find the same spot again. Unlike my surprise at finding the northwestern salamander, I wasn't at all surprised to find it gone upon my return. Back down it had traveled, into its underground home, away from curious giants and picture-takers.

*

When the traveling salamander arrived at the Oregon Zoo, it was "in good body condition" and "fed readily when offered meal worms [*sic*]." Additional medical notes provided the assessment and comment "alert but lethargic (tough call in a salamander)" (Oregon Zoo 2000).

It's true that salamanders, being ectotherms and deriving heat from their environment, can appear less than active in cooler conditions. In warmer temperatures, however, I've seen an adult northwestern salamander out of the water and moving quickly. The time of year was late summer, and low clouds and wet weather had been constant during that August week in Matheny Creek. A crew from Northwest Youth Corps, an organization that provides youth and young adults education and experience in conservation, had been working for the Forest Service piling slash left over from precommercial thinning activities. The group of boys, ranging in age from 15 to 18 years old, had been trying hard to maintain their spirits through sodden days of creating travel corridors and habitat structures for different wildlife species.

One morning, as I drove to the project site, I saw a rough-skinned newt (*Taricha granulosa*) crossing the road. Though this road, compared to many in the forest, wasn't heavily used, the newt was still in danger of being smashed by unaware drivers. I pulled over to help the animal across. As I picked it up to carry it to the other side, I noticed a small, red-brown object nearby. After placing the newt safely in the grass, I looked more closely. This tiny thing turned out to be a juvenile newt! As I glanced around, I saw another juvenile. And another. A second adult appeared as well, then two. More little ones became obvious. They popped into view like buttons scattered across the road. It was a migration from a nearby wetland to upland habitats, an event I had never seen before.

I took several photos of the more than 40 juvenile and adult newts I carried to safety. During this process, I came across a northwestern salamander, dark and shiny, who had joined the exodus. Unlike the newts, it didn't dawdle. I attempted to pick it up, but it wanted no help. The northwestern fairly jogged to the other side.

Later, I told the crew what I'd seen. A photo of one juvenile in my palm with a quarter for scale was of special interest. The boys had been finding frogs all week, and we agreed the rainy weather was good for amphibians at least. When I left them at the end of the day, I again stopped at the migration site. Again, there were many young newts, with a few adults scattered in the mix. Once more, I carried them across the road, wishing them well on their journeys.

*

The story of the northwestern salamander that traveled from Oregon to Virginia and back again is amusing and extraordinary, but it's not unusual. In today's world of global transit, species are constantly being transported, intentionally or unintentionally. It's been this way for thousands of years, ever since humans began sailing the seas and traversing the continents. Cats, rats, and even snakes have stowed away on ships, birds and plants were brought to new lands as reminders of home, and domestic animals have accompanied migrating people in order to sustain livelihoods. The examples are numerous and the reasons many. Yet at no point in world history has the rate and reach of species displacement been as high as it is currently. Sadly, too, the consequences are not always amusing. In 2013, a scientific report of a massive die-off of the brilliant yellow and black European fire salamanders revealed the presence of a novel pathogenic chytrid fungus believed to have come from Asian salamanders exported to various countries for the pet trade. This fungus, scientific name *Batrachochytrium salamandrivorans*, or more simply *Bsal*, will infect and eat away at a salamander's skin, causing lesions, loss of appetite in the animal, and eventually death. Based on the presence of the fungus in a 19th-century museum specimen of the Japanese sword-tailed newt, it appears that Asian salamanders may have evolved with the fungus to become asymptomatic hosts.

With the advent of new genetic techniques, the *Bsal* finding was later followed up with a study supporting an Asian origin of a related chytrid fungus, *Batrachochytrium dendrobatidis* (or *Bd*), another pathogen infecting amphibian skin. *Bd* has been cited as the most devastating wildlife disease due to its infection of hundreds of amphibian species across the world—many with lethal consequences. Globalization ties *Bd* to emerging diseases on every continent with amphibians (a paper published in 2022 also links introduction events to the emerging snake fungal disease in North America, as well as a snake lung parasite currently spreading in Florida apparently from invasive Burmese pythons set loose there). In addition, and to make matters more complicated, both *Bsal* and *Bd* are complex, with some species not being infected, and often becoming carriers, and some dying from the disease. While *Bsal* currently causes the greatest losses in caudates, or salamanders and newts, it has recently been found to infect anurans, frogs and toads. Conversely, *Bd* is predominantly fatal to frogs and toads, but it also can infect salamanders and newts.

If it's true that connection and interdependence make a biological system more resilient, it's also true that evolution follows laws of fitness and adaptation. When someone tells me that animal species have always been undergoing processes of extinction, I can't disagree. However, it's a question in current times of the *rate* at which this is happening. Survival requires time for adapting and increasing resiliency, both of which are difficult, if not impossible, when the pace of change is so fast. No one alive today has ever seen such a rapid loss of biodiversity and species richness, primarily caused by human activities, that we are now documenting in nearly every corner of the globe. We can observe some consequences of these losses, and we can project others. Yet the true reach of the impacts may remain unknowable.

*

In contrast to the little-seen adults, northwestern salamander egg masses are readily visible. The size of a softball, they can be found in small waterbodies, generally attached to grass stems, twigs, or small branches. The masses are firm and may contain as many as 200 individual eggs. I had first seen these in the Siskiyou National Forest when Dave Shea and I surveyed small ponds and lakes. I've also often found them in the Olympics in pools along closed or decommissioned roads. This gathering of water isn't always good for the roadway, as it can contribute to structural failure and sediment pouring into streams. But for a salamander looking for water that will remain for some months, it's a great place. Especially if the road has no vehicle traffic.

On one occasion, I found a smaller mass, bluish in color. The female had just recently laid these eggs, hence the blue color, and the mass itself had not had time to absorb the water that would eventually give it the larger size. I picked it up gently, taking photos with my hand for scale. Northwestern salamanders, like ensatina salamanders, have an interesting reproductive cycle that involves a type of package delivery. In the late winter and early spring, male and female northwesterns travel from their underground burrows in upland forests to breeding ponds. After the male finds a potential mate, he will mount and stimulate her with his chin and tail. After this interaction, the male swims off a short distance and deposits a spermatophore for the female. A clear, gelatinous pedicel attaches the spermatophore to the bottom of the pool, while the sperm, a white, opaque, round packet, sits on top. If the female finds this suitor acceptable, she will then collect this packet into her cloaca by walking over the top of it. The sperm may be combined immediately with the ova to start the fertilization process, or this may not occur until a few days later. With terrestrial salamanders, female ensatinas and western red-backed salamanders may store sperm for weeks or months before beginning the egg-laying process.

*

Two five-gallon buckets filled with water are heavy buckets. The northwestern salamander egg masses in the buckets contributed a negligible amount to the weight, but the water, at eight pounds per gallon, was the main challenge. My arms felt a few inches longer as I carried the buckets down the logging road toward the Wynoochee River, a waterway on the south end of the forest that eventually pours into the Chehalis River. I could only go about 50 feet before needing to stop and rest.

It was April, and earlier in the week, I had come out here to look for the bald eagles that nest along this stretch of the river. I hadn't found the eagles, but I had seen many egg masses in puddles behind the gated road. I'd also seen tire tracks. Upon calling the timber company that owned the road that accessed Olympic National Forest land, I'd learned there would be more activity on the road soon. This traffic would destroy the eggs, already developed into recognizable salamanders with gills and legs. A large, deep pool closer to the river and on a closed road of the national forest would provide a quiet area free from vehicle traffic and human activity. Thus I began the amphibian egg mass translocation project.

After the massive die-off of fire salamanders in Europe, research began in earnest to determine the cause, as well as other potential victims, of such an event. In the United States, different salamander species were part of a series of "challenge experiments" to test for resilience to the fungus. Though the sample sizes were small, the results were still sobering. For some, including the rough-skinned newt, all the tested animals died. Other species appeared to be resistant to the fungus or at least tolerant. For now, *Bsal* is not known to exist in the wild in North America; however, most experts believe it's only a matter of time before it appears. The salamander trade is a vast, industrial machine that makes money and fills the demand for exotic pets. In 2016, an "interim rule," still currently in effect, was enacted by the U.S. Fish & Wildlife Service to ban imports of 201 salamander species determined to be susceptible to *Bsal*. This ban has greatly reduced the potential of *Bsal* arriving via salamander imports. Daniel Grear, a wildlife disease ecologist, and his coauthors published a scientific paper in 2021 describing an evaluation of the ban's success and the reduction of legal imports by several orders of magnitude of the 201 species, from approximately 139,000 animals imported per year between 2010 and 2015 to less than 400 individuals per year following the ban. However, the threat remains from both the release of captive animals with undetected *Bsal* and also from some frog and toad species, now known to be carriers of the fungus, which continue to be imported. Alarmingly, since 2021, three Cuban tree frogs, a species that can die from *Bsal* infection, have been found on tropical plants sold at local nurseries in Oregon.

The egg masses moved around as we trudged together down the road. The spring air was cool, but I still sweated profusely. During rest breaks, I captured the effort with my digital camera: the tiny salamanders inside their eggs, still growing; the buckets at different points along the road; the buckets atop a massive wind-felled, old-growth Douglas fir that I had to climb over. Later, a coworker said the buckets reminded her of Dr. Seuss characters. Like the brown Bar-ba-loots or the Swomee-Swans from *The Lorax*, the buckets and their passengers were searching for a better habitat.

Beyond the downed fir tree, the road dipped to its lowest point. During most spring seasons, I had found this natural depression full of water, and this year was no exception. The previous autumn's leaves from alder, bigleaf maple, and willow trees bordered the dark pool. I couldn't see the bottom, but it had to be deeper than the puddles on the road. In any case, this site was the only option. The next stop was the Wynoochee River. Northwestern salamanders are pond breeders and don't lay their eggs in fast-moving water like creeks or rivers; it was here or nowhere. After catching my breath, I carefully placed the egg masses into the water. They rolled a bit before settling into the soft bottom.

*

Sadly, the Christmas salamander didn't live long after arriving back on the West Coast. This isn't too surprising, given its adventures and perhaps the many days or weeks where it didn't eat much. It also may have been an older animal and possibly not in the best shape for such travels. Its story helps to show how, due to the tremendous ways that humans and international commerce are now moving around the planet, wildlife species can be connected to places far outside their natural ranges. These introduced animals can then impact those novel environments and species already present as well as potentially be affected themselves.

14

Wetlands Surveys

Olympic National Forest, 2011

I looked out of my tent with a sinking feeling. The rain continued vigorously this September morning, and puddles now surrounded where my coworker Cheryl and I had made our camp. Not that we were surprised. Campbell Tree Grove campground, in the upper West Fork Humptulips watershed, is tucked beneath ancient Douglas fir and Sitka spruce trees and can be a wet place. We knew this because this was our second campout here this summer and the second time we'd gotten drenched. Our objective was to complete a survey at a nearby wetland. The first attempt in July had been aborted. The steady, heavy rain that day had worried us. Though the wetland was only a quarter mile straight-line distance from the road, it involved a steep climb up a forest stand thick with blueberry bushes and then a steep drop to the site. We knew it would be slippery and had decided to opt for a better, drier day. Unfortunately, this was not that day.

*

Cheryl and I had started setting aside "Wetland Wednesdays" during summer 2011 to do our inventories gathering basic information about these habitats. She'd done her master's thesis on wetlands in California and was thrilled to get back to this kind of work. Tall with long hair corralled into a braid or a bandana, or both, Cheryl has a booming laugh and for many years kept a sticky note above the desk in her cubicle that read, "Volume Control!" Our coworker Robin, an ecologist who had been studying whitebark pine, an important high-elevation species (listed under the Endangered Species Act in 2022), accompanied us when she could. Robin's dry sense of humor and appreciation of irony brought lightness to our endeavors. We all felt grateful for a good field project that would yield important information.

Each of us had our assignments during a wetland survey. Cheryl would do a walk-through, noting all plant species, including invasives, and would also set up a 10-by-10-meter plot to record the presence and abundance of each species within that plot. Robin's job was to take notes on water levels and inlet and outlet locations. She would also determine if a road or a plugged culvert had been involved in the creation of the wetland.

My tasks included making notes on all wildlife observations and signs, including tracks and other evidence (dropped feathers, scats, bones). I also captured as many frogs and toads as I could. This last was part of an effort to test anurans, the phylogenetic order of "no tail" amphibians, or frogs and toads, for the chytrid fungus, *Bd*. This fungus, first discovered in 1998 and in the same genera as the *Bsal* fungus, causes the disease *Bd* chytridiomycosis. Both *Bd* and *Bsal* chytridiomycosis, now believed to each have Asian origins, infect and thicken the skin of individual animals and impede their ability to absorb water and important electrolytes, such as sodium and potassium, from the environment. With abnormal levels of electrolytes, the animal's heart stops beating, and it will die of cardiac arrest. *Bd* spores move around in the environment via water or moist or wet materials, including the animals themselves, field equipment, and soil. Knowing which drainages have *Bd* can lead to important precautions to prevent its human-mediated spread. These may include encouraging people to disinfect their rubber boots and nets when moving between watersheds, discouraging the use of certain infected lakes and ponds as sources for fire suppression efforts, and being aware of which areas could see die-offs of animals. Unlike *Bsal*, which is not yet known to be in the wild in North America, *Bd* has been documented in many watersheds throughout the country. In 2011, we didn't know if it was present or not in Olympic National Forest.

Unfortunately, I had not grown up catching frogs and toads. Cheryl and Robin laughed at my leaping around the wetlands like a fairy trying to catch the lightning-fast northern red-legged frogs (*Rana aurora*), and Cascades frogs (*R. cascadae*), that didn't want to be held and rubbed with a Q-tip to swab their skin for later *Bd* testing. The western toads (*Anaxyrus boreas*), more hoppers than leapers, were easier to catch and fairly agreeable to the process, though I still felt guilty when they squeaked softly in protest.

After our respective efforts at each wetland, we'd come back together to fill out the Collective Assessment Data Form. Besides notes on plant and wildlife species, this form summarized information on signs of human presence and major natural disturbances. After rating the ecological integrity of the wetland, we answered the all-important, bottom-line question: Is this wetland a candidate for (a) restoration, (b) conservation, or (c) enhancement? If the answer was anything besides conservation, we provided recommendations.

*

On this day in the Humptulips, it was just Cheryl and me. We discussed the weather situation while drinking our coffee in the drizzle. The rain didn't particularly bother us, but walking up and down slippery slopes was a safety concern. Still, the long drive up here meant it wouldn't be so easy to reschedule. We'd been thwarted once but weren't much in the mood to give in today. The wetland we sought was in the headwaters of the East Fork Humptulips, less than one mile from the ridge separating the two watersheds. Given the higher elevation of the area and the lateness of the season, we knew this might be our last chance.

"Let's just do it!" Cheryl said. "We've got rain gear, and we can go slow. How hard can it be?"

I agreed. After having completed several surveys this summer, we had our wetlands legs, and we were both very curious about this site. We finished breakfast, packed up our wet tents, and drove north to the end of the road.

*

During my years working in the Olympic National Forest, I've spent many good field days along both the West and East Forks of the Humptulips River. While conducting surveys for various projects, I've monitored bald eagle nests, found hundreds of western toadlets in quiet side channels of the West Fork, and watched the tributaries and two forks turn deep brown as the land and water blended after days of intense rain. The watershed never ceases to impress. Trees 500 to 1,000 years old can't help but awe. Even if I live to be 100 years old, I will never witness all that these trees and this land have witnessed. I will never play such an important role in the world. My life will always be of little importance compared with the forces that have shaped this landscape and left the small wetlands and vast expanses of trees and tremendous numbers of species, all working to create the fabric of life.

Being in the forest reminds me of my insignificance, and I like that. In fact, the more inconsequential I feel, the more relaxed I am. Sometimes I've wondered if this reassurance is an echo of what I felt so many years ago as a child. When I left the inexplicable silence and anger of my home for the forests nearby, I found mystery but no pain. I found other beings that were steady, predictable. The trees did not play games. They didn't care about my presence, but they also didn't leave me. They were always just there. As a child, I didn't analyze all this. I just knew the forest was an easier place to be, rain or shine. I didn't feel like I always had to be among the trees and the wild things, but when I wasn't, I continued thinking about them.

*

The steep cutbank above the road looked intimidating. As did the thicket of tall blueberries beyond the cutbank. The vegetation, the ground, were all soaked, and the rain continued to fall lightly. Cheryl and I gathered our equipment. My pack had everything for testing the frogs and toads, including aquarium nets, cotton swabs, small vials of ethanol to store the samples, vial labels, nitrile gloves, and Ziploc bags. Additionally, I had my camera, binoculars, notebook, and lunch. I also decided to bring a long net with a wooden handle for the deeper ponds. It would likely get tangled in the blueberries, but it could also serve as a walking stick. Cheryl was similarly laden with what she needed to collect botanical specimens and do her plot.

At last, we were ready. As we donned our rain gear, I thought Cheryl's rain pants looked a little flimsy.

"Yes, they are light," she agreed. "But they're also not too hot. I can move in them more easily."

The blueberries, growing above our heads and heavy with moisture, grabbed at us enthusiastically. The plants' wet embraces were compensated for by the large, ripe berries they offered. We gobbled as we went, warm from our exertions and damp from the rain.

This would be our 14th wetland survey. For my part, I had documented nine amphibian species in total, including the first record of the American bullfrog in the forest. This wasn't good news, but it was very important to know. The bullfrog (*Lithobates catesbeianus*) isn't native to the Pacific Northwest and had been shown to be an asymptomatic host for *Bd* (this individual was later captured and removed). Though wetlands are not a predominant ecosystem in Olympic National Forest, their numbers are inversely proportional to their importance. They provide open habitats for numerous species of birds and mammals as well as still, or slow-moving, water for amphibians and reptiles.

We didn't see the latter often, although I had observed garter snakes swimming across the surface of several pools. On one occasion, I'd inadvertently broken up an encounter between a garter snake and a western red-backed salamander. This interaction, had it progressed, would likely not have gone well for the salamander.

Nothing is more important to biologists working in land management than getting to the field and making observations. Trying to understand the complex web of ecosystem processes that are always in motion takes time and attention. Sometimes what we observed was expected. At other times, it was a complete surprise. This was true with the bullfrog, as well as a few years before, when we'd observed a garter snake eating a rough-skinned newt at a wetland in the South Fork Skokomish River watershed. Newts are highly toxic; however, some lineages of garter snakes have evolved to be able to withstand the toxins. Sometimes, our observations led to specific management recommendations, such as removing the bullfrog or treating invasive plant species with herbicides.

Upon arriving at the ridge, Cheryl and I began our descent into the headwaters of the East Fork Humptulips. The rain had let up, though cloud fingers remained twined through the trees. We zigzagged our way downward. Glad to be done with the blueberry forest, we appreciated the open understory beneath the ancient trees. The old-growth forests of the Pacific Northwest can vary greatly in accessibility. Sometimes the dense canopy precludes much understory growth. In other areas, with more sunlight, the ground erupts with vegetation. There also may be several centuries' worth of material on the ground. A person climbing over eight-foot-diameter logs and sinking into soft duff while navigating paths through the salmonberry, Devil's club, and salal will feel greatly tested. And heaven help her if she ends up in a blowdown patch of such material where *everything* has come down. At those times, I have wished I were a marten, small and low to the ground, for whom tight spaces are not an issue.

For now, however, we appreciated our good fortune and moved ever toward the wetland. And a long way down it seemed! Finally, a different view appeared below us: a lime-green pocket within the darker green and brown of the old-growth trees. Cheryl and I mused on the likelihood that few people had ever been here. In our current world of hypertransmittal of massive amounts of information and documentation of wilderness landscapes, anywhere that is at least somewhat unknown is like a precious jewel. We looked forward to finding no evidence of humans, including trash.

"And no weeds either!" sang Cheryl happily.

A big part of her job included managing the forest's invasive weed program, a great effort to document and treat noxious plant species including Scot's broom, Japanese knotweed, Himalayan blackberry, and tansy ragwort. Some eradication is done through mechanical methods and some by using approved herbicides. If nothing else, there is job security in this work. As long as people can access areas, by foot or vehicle, the likelihood of unwanted species traveling with them will always exist. But here that wouldn't be a problem.

*

By the time we arrived at the wetland, Cheryl and I were thoroughly soaked. I sweated in my too-heavy rain gear; Cheryl appeared to be molting, her rain pants shredded from the blueberry plants. Yet our personal discomfort didn't detract from our triumph. The wetland, even cloaked in fog, met all expectations. The sedges and grasses and marsh marigolds formed a neat carpet beside a stream flowing into a large pool. Small dime-sized frogs and toads leapt as we walked by. In a 1962 aerial photograph, some parts of the wetland had been more open, but normal successional processes had been in motion for the last 50 years. Conifers had begun creeping in from the edges where the ground wasn't too wet.

After a quick break, Cheryl set off to do her walk-through and look for a good location for her plot. I headed for the pool. On the way, a large western toad presented herself (female frogs and toads are larger than males) by taking a couple of hops. She then sat among the glistening marsh marigolds, the white stripe down her back prominent among her otherwise brown and gray coloration. Adult western toads also contain toxins, emitted from their skin. This deters some would-be predators, though not all. Garter snakes, raccoons, coyotes, and ravens are among those with strong constitutions for a perhaps slightly bitter meal.

The toad stayed still while I got out a Q-tip and vial. The protocol directed rubbing the cotton swab approximately 25 times across the animal's belly, groin, and undersides of the legs. This work gathers skin mucous and cells that can then be tested in the lab for the chytrid fungus. Though I had to catch the animals to do the swabbing, I appreciated the minimal impact the overall procedure caused and the short amount of time required to hold them. Some quick work of swabbing ensued, and I let the toad go. She took a few more hops and then sat, quiet again.

I continued through the wetland, noting bird and amphibian species and mammal tracks in the damp ground. The elk clearly visited here frequently. Many hoofprints had filled with water from rain the previous night. When I came upon another very fast Cascades frog, the animal leapt away and took refuge in one of these minipools. With the frog feeling protected, I was able to get quite close. After taking several photos, I placed the net over the top of the track and captured it. Cheryl, nearby, came over to help with the swabbing. She also had some news.

"I found tansy," she announced, looking a bit glum about an invasive weed in the otherwise pristine-looking wetland.

"What? How?"

"The elk, of course," she said, then shrugged and laughed. "It happens!"

*

There's nothing like being in the natural world to experience the truth of change and impermanence. It's at once reassuring as well as unsettling. Life on this planet is premised on everything transforming all the time. Yet most humans work hard to create security and an environment that we hope will be the same, or better, day after day. The idea that it can all disappear in a moment is highly disturbing.

However, in the forest, along rivers and streams, besides wetlands and rocky outcrops, and meadows, from the smallest species to the largest, from the individual to the ecosystem, life and death are constantly happening. Seasons pass, animals and plants grow, then they all die. The system is altered, beginning again and ending, over and over. Even the words *beginning* and *ending* are misleading because there is never a moment when life isn't in motion. As a person who grew up with much uncertainty and craved predictability, I can feel very sorry when something changes. For example, when the old, giant snag that I've walked by and regarded many times finally falls over. Or when a spectacular hillside of centuries-old trees is flattened by a windstorm. But then, after a few years, mushroom cities grow on the now supine log, and young, exuberant trees pop up in the blowdown to make a new forest. More time passes, and more changes occur. Soon, the fallen snag and the transformed hillside are the new normal. The natural world is the consummate example of a dynamic, changing force.

As I researched my family's history in the early 2000s, I began to see how my relatives had resisted change in all its many quotidian, as well as dramatic, forms. Such resistance resulted in taking refuge in anger and alcohol from what they couldn't control. My mother, possibly as a result of the accident and the head injuries she suffered, or possibly because of her own childhood experiences, or maybe just because of genetic makeup, was one of the most rigid of all. Something like my father wanting to retire from his job at the post office (employment he'd taken after retiring from the military) and go to cooking school prompted as much opposition as the local bank changing ownerships. Her resistance to the inescapable vicissitudes of life caused my mother to suffer greatly. It followed that the rest of her family also suffered.

Still, trying to untangle my mother and her motivations more than two decades after her death is itself a lesson in impermanence. Most of the time now, I experience forgiveness, some level of understanding, and even compassion for her. My mother's injuries undoubtedly affected her in ways over which she had no control. Additionally, there is much more about her life that I don't know than that I do know, and her behavior may have had other origins. At other times, though, I am still haunted by memories of abandonment. In those moments, I feel only resentment that hasn't been assuaged by time. Yet I've lived long enough now to know how complex people are. That they are, in fact, maybe as complex as old-growth forests. Both species, nonhuman and human, and ecosystems are biological systems. One could say that there is more that is unknown about them than that is known about them. My parents have been gone for many years now, but our relationship continues. Acceptance of the past comes when the peace of the forest surrounds me. When the sounds and smells and what I observe remind me that life is short, but connection is long.

*

In the main pool, I observed several rough-skinned newts and two hatched-out egg masses from either the northwestern or another species of mole salamander, the long-toed salamander (*Ambystoma macrodactylum*). Two neotenic northwestern salamanders also sat on the bottom. These individuals were the size of adults but continued to retain juvenile characteristics, including feathery gills on either side of their heads. Around the pool's edge, an overhang of sedges and grasses provided great hiding places for the newts and smaller frogs and toads that didn't want to be seen. After leaving the pool, I walked up the wetland's steeper slope, finding a smaller pool filled with tadpoles that I believed to be those of Cascades frogs. It seemed odd that I hadn't observed or heard any Pacific chorus frogs at this wetland, though not hearing them didn't mean they weren't there.

Cheryl had finished her botanical survey, so we returned to our starting point. Apart from the presence of tansy ragwort and the natural encroachment of conifers, this wetland probably hadn't changed dramatically in the last century. Still, general conclusions were best made cautiously. We had just spent four hours of one day at a specific time of year here; our few observations were mere snapshots. To really understand a place, one must come back repeatedly. Still, one snapshot was much better than none.

Cheryl finished writing up our recommendations and looked up. "Well?"

I nodded. "We better start back. It might take awhile."

By the time we arrived at the vehicle two hours later, Cheryl's rain pants had disintegrated. We were both soaked and exhausted but also triumphant. We'd finally made it!

*

The East Fork Humptulips wetland was our last survey site for the year. All the animals we swabbed here tested negative for *Bd*. Across all the wetlands we visited, we swabbed a total of 82 animals of five different species: Cascades frog, northern red-legged frog, Pacific chorus frog, western toad, and rough-skinned newt. Of these, three red-legged frogs, one chorus frog, and several toads tested positive for carrying the fungus, though none appeared to have symptoms of the disease, *Bd* chytridiomycosis. Only one animal during our surveys showed any abnormality. A skinny northern red-legged frog had a prolapsed cloaca, perhaps the result of being grabbed by a predator. None of the Cascades frogs tested positive, and neither did any of the red-legged frogs at the wetland where we'd found the bullfrog, a known carrier of *Bd*.

15

Silent Survivor

Olympic National Forest, 2014

It was June 2014. A medium-sized owl with a spotted breast and big, chocolate eyes had just arrived on a branch above us without a sound. I felt thrilled to see this individual, as I hadn't seen a spotted owl in almost 20 years. This female, now perched above me and Debaran Kelso, a researcher with a long-term owl demography study on Olympic National Forest, had come immediately to Kelso's soft hoots.

"Last week," Debaran told me as she grabbed a mouse she had brought to feed the bird, "I found the female and two owlets. One owlet was dead at the base of the nest tree, likely from accidentally being bumped off the too-small nest platform. The other owlet was still perched in the branches of the nest tree." She looked around. "I don't see the survivor yet."

The female ate the first mouse immediately. During the next half hour, the bird cached another two proffered mice in the upper canopy for later meals. She made no attempt to call to her remaining young or to take the mice to it. None of these were good signs, Debaran said, yet she'd been fooled before.

"If she has just fed the owlet, it may not be interested in any more mice from me, so it might not call to be fed. However, generally, she makes at least some attempt to show the prey to her young."

Sunlight filtered through the forest above us in a kaleidoscope of shapes and yellowish hues. This stand in the Big Quilcene River watershed on the east side of Olympic National Forest was almost 300 years old. A fire had burned through it more than a century ago. The trees were not classically large, being on average 30 to 40 inches in diameter and fairly uniform in appearance. Consequently, the owls' nest was in an unlikely tree, an even smaller 23-inch diameter Douglas fir that supported a small shelf where the top broke out. It wasn't a very protected residence against predators or the Olympic Peninsula's rainy spring weather.

We spent the next few hours searching for the owlet yet found nothing to indicate its demise or continued survival. The female followed us for a while, perhaps expecting more mice, then vanished back into the forest. She never hooted, and her departure was as undramatic as her arrival. In the early days of spotted owl research, and when I first did the work in the mid-1980s, the birds' willingness to answer human vocalizations, in addition to their lack of wariness, made them a relatively easy animal to study. However, nearly three decades later, the game had changed. In Debaran's study area, the birds had become quieter over the years, their comings and goings during surveys less predictable. This has possibly occurred in response to them now having to share space with their more aggressive cousin, the barred owl.

"Sometimes," said Debaran, "I'll see sign, either pellets or prey remains, and I'll know they're here, yet I'll call and call without any answer. I can search all around their nest tree and roost trees but won't see them anywhere. Eventually, I have to wait for them to either fly in or call and give their location away."

*

Debaran Kelso began studying northern spotted owls on the Olympic Peninsula in 1987. Many biologists, including myself, began careers with the U.S. Forest Service on spotted owl survey teams, though few of us continued with the rigorous night work year after year. In the late 1980s, the conflict over how to manage Pacific Northwest forests was at its peak. Consequently, tensions ran high between the environmental community, the timber industry, and land managers.

"It was a bit unnerving," Debaran recalled of her early work on the Olympic Peninsula. "We'd be leaving the woods at three o'clock in the morning after a night of surveying, and the log trucks would be going in. They all knew, of course, why we were out there. I never told anyone what I did."

The stories of antagonism against owls are well known in the Pacific Northwest. One year on the Powers Ranger District in Oregon, we found a rubber chicken tied to a gate post with "spotted owl" written across its body. Bumper stickers that read "I love spotted owls . . . fried" were ubiquitous. So were boxes of "Spotted Owl Helper" for sale in the restaurants of small logging towns (sadly, still on display in some places). In 1989, in Forks, Washington, one of the communities on the Olympic Peninsula that had been heavily dependent on harvesting timber from the national forest, a cross had been erected with numerous papier-mâché spotted owls sitting on top; below the cross, a mock grave had been designed, and above it was a billboard sign that read "Here lie the hopes and dreams of our children." Yet despite all this vitriol toward the species, Debaran wasn't deterred.

"I took the job initially," she said, "because that's where the funding was. However, I quickly fell in love with the owls. There aren't many wildlife species that are so curious about humans and aren't actively distressed in our presence. There also was an element of urgency in finding the birds and protecting them and their habitat that wasn't there with other species."

As the seasons passed, her affection grew. In 1990, the owl was listed as a federally threatened species, and in 1992, after having been on other owl crews, Debaran began working on the demography study. This effort focused on monitoring population trends of the species on federal lands. The demography work has taken place in 11 study areas across the owl's range, including three in Washington State: the Olympic Mountains, Mt. Rainier National Park, and the Cascade Range near Cle Elum, a small, but growing city along Interstate 90.

Throughout the '90s, Debaran, in conjunction with other researchers working on the study, found and banded birds in the Olympic National Forest. As she became more a part of the owls' world, the 1994 Northwest Forest Plan came into existence. With the adoption of the plan, most of the Olympic National Forest was designated "late-successional reserve," where the emphases would be on the maintenance and protection of older forest habitats as well as the acceleration of development in overstocked young plantations into stands with older forest characteristics (e.g., large trees, snags, and logs, multiple canopies, a diversity of species). This change replaced old-growth timber harvest on the Olympic with the commercial thinning of the second-growth stands that had been clearcut 40 to 60 years earlier. In terms of previous habitat loss due to harvest, the spotted owl has been helped tremendously by this change. However, the scientific and management communities didn't initially foresee the dramatic role that the increased presence of barred owls would play in the recovery of spotted owls, nor the impact that large, stand-replacing fires would have in the years after the plan was adopted.

Finding a barred owl in the 1980s was considered a novelty. They would respond to a surveyor's hoots just as readily as spotted owls. They also look quite similar, the main differences being a slightly larger size, striped breast, and white barring on the back of the head. However, behaviorally, they are quite distinct. Barred owls are far more wary of humans. I remember that they almost never came down closer to us from high in the canopy. Once a resident of only the eastern United States, the barred owl has expanded its range west-ward in numbers and speed matched only by the similar movements of European migrants in the 19th and early 20th centuries.

"Barred owls are cool birds," Debaran said, "and it is a wondrous thing to see them. But they are having a devastating impact on spotted owls."

*

Debaran Kelso is a bit owl-like herself. She admits to having become rather reclusive over the years and has often remained largely nocturnal even when she isn't surveying. Her home is a "tree house for adults," as she describes the four-story cedar building nestled in a second-growth stand of Douglas fir, madrone, and western hemlock. On the top floor, one is eye level with canopy residents, robins, warblers, and kinglets that fly, nest, and forage all a few feet away. Debaran has lived in many places, including Alaska, Chile, Mexico, England, and Namibia. She did her undergraduate work at the University of Colorado, where she began as a psychology major before switching to ecology.

"I'm really intrigued by people," she said, "but I also love animals and love being outdoors. The question was could I make a living in the environmental field? In the end, I just decided to do what I loved best."

That end took her to Alaska, with research projects studying wolves and wolverines, as well as Pilanesberg National Park in South Africa, where she completed a master's degree looking at resource partitioning in eland and kudu. Yet by 1986, Debaran was tired of having her life tucked away in boxes. With friends in Washington State, she made her way to the Olympic Peninsula in the spring of 1987 hoping to find a home.

*

Apart from Eric Forsman, a well-known U.S. Forest Service research biologist (now retired) who began studying spotted owls in the 1960s and served as the research lead for four of the northern spotted owl demography studies for many years, few have worked with the species as long as Debaran. She has seen many changes over the years and has come to know individual owls well. She's captured and marked each bird she's found with a unique set of leg bands for later identification. At a different territory I visited with her, we searched for a pair originally banded in 1996. This female, now more than 18 years old in 2014, was very reliable. If around, she would come when Debaran called. The male, a new mate for the female and only just banded in 2014, had been more wary.

We didn't find either bird on this day.

In another area, Debaran found a pair in 2005 and banded both the female and male. The next year, she didn't find them, and the following year was the same. Not until 2013 did both of the same birds reappear. In 2014, the pair successfully fledged two owlets. For eight years, the owls had disappeared, or so it seemed. In wildlife research, not finding an animal doesn't prove its absence. Obviously, these birds were not entirely gone; however, where they were during that period was anybody's guess. Given Debaran's familiarity with the species and the landscape, she would have the best insight of anyone.

"Where were they?" she shrugged. "I have no idea."

*

The U.S. Fish & Wildlife Service began reviewing a petition to upgrade the spotted owl's federal listing status from threatened to endangered in 2012. The petition came from a nonprofit organization called the Environmental Protection Information Center. The purpose of the review is to consider new scientific information that's been gathered about the species, most notably in this case, the huge effect of barred owls on spotted owls. In December 2020, the service published a notice in the Federal Register that upgrading the listing was "warranted but precluded by higher priority actions to amend the Lists of Endangered and Threatened Wildlife and Plants" (as of 2023, the northern spotted owl is a priority level three in the National Listing Workplan, which is a prioritization of workload associated with federal listing decisions; the agency's decision to reclassify the owl as endangered is estimated for completion in 2027).

In addition to the demographic data and the effects of the barred owl, the long-term demography studies yielded new insights into how long spotted owls live. Earlier estimates placed an owl's lifespan in the wild at approximately 15 years or less; now it's known they can live over 20 years. The oldest animal Debaran knew was a male she banded in 1991 as a juvenile. She found this bird most years in his territory, but the last time she saw him was in 2012. The following season, the female was alone. In 2014, the old female was gone as well, and a new pair had arrived in the area.

"The new birds were much sneakier than the old pair," she told me. "There was a lot of evidence they were around, but they wouldn't respond to my calls. Finally, I saw the male flying. After catching him later in the season, he turned out to be a juvenile I'd banded in 2004 at a site four miles to the north. I hadn't seen him in 10 years."

Debaran Kelso acknowledged the general, grim consensus that researchers are documenting the demise of the northern spotted owl subspecies. Yet she also remains hopeful. The birds are doing better in some parts of the Olympic National Forest, and perhaps they can survive in certain refugia. Additionally, she's seen the owls return to sites and observed their behavior change in ways that may be aiding their survival. In other areas within the range of the northern spotted owl where barred owls have been experimentally removed, spotted owls have returned to historic nest trees and territories. Whether a multifaceted management strategy of barred owl removal (the Draft Environmental Impact Statement for the removal of barred owls from certain areas was released on November 17, 2023), older forest preservation, and older forest creation through commercial thinning can buy enough time for spotted owls to recover is uncertain.

"There are many questions," Debaran admitted to me, "and the landscape is vast. When I can't find the birds, I search their favorite places, but if they aren't vocalizing . . ." She shook her head. "Well, they melt right into the trees and you never see them."

Debaran returned twice more in 2014 to the site where we had searched for the owlet but found nothing. Either it had died like its sibling, or it was already learning that survival depended on a silence as deep and as old as the forest itself.

16

The Whistle Pig

Olympic National Park, 2010–15

In July 1997, in the high country of Olympic National Park, Nina Pitts and Steve Zenovic watched two plump, furry marmots sliding down a snowfield.

"They slid fast on their bellies down the steep slope," recalled Nina in spring 2018 when I interviewed her for an article I was writing on Olympic marmots (*Marmota olympus*). "When they got to the bottom, they scrambled up to do it again. We rolled a snowball or two down to them, and they chased those too."

Nina, a library supervisor at Peninsula College in Port Angeles, Washington, and Steve, her husband and an engineer, had been hiking and backpacking in the national park since 1976. "We've appreciated seeing the marmots over the years," she told me. "They've often provided us with a welcome distraction from hiking up steep switchbacks. In later years, when we didn't see their burrows where we'd seen them before, we wondered where the animals had gone."

Since 2010, the couple has joined more than 80 other volunteers most summers to participate in a marmot citizen-science monitoring program. The goal is to document the presence of the animals in select areas throughout the species' range, 90 percent of which is in Olympic National Park. For six to eight months each year, Olympic marmots, large, burrowing members of the squirrel family with small ears and big, stubby muzzles, go into a state of deep hibernation. During this time, each animal's body temperature and heart rate drop so that it can conserve energy during the seasons when food is unavailable. In the spring, the animals emerge from their winter sleep. As the snow melts and the lupine and glacier lilies begin to bloom, the marmots are easily visible. They feed and scamper about in the alpine meadows of the Olympic Mountains, breathtaking landscapes that people trek to every summer. Citizen scientists like Nina and Steve are ready each year when the marmots emerge. They're eager to connect more deeply with the park and its residents. They also want to give back in the process.

*

In 2009, one year before the monitoring program began, the Olympic marmot, affectionately known as the "whistle pig" for its high-pitched alarm calls, was designated Washington's State Endemic Mammal. The proposal for this distinction came from elementary school students in Seattle. Their goal: to bring attention to a declining species found only on Washington's Olympic Peninsula. This recognition couldn't have come at a better time.

Beginning in the 1990s, Olympic National Park rangers and visitors began noticing an absence of marmots from historically occupied areas. The same year Steve and Nina observed the sledding marmots, Patti Happe, wildlife branch chief for the park, attended a public meeting on wolf reintroduction. During a break, a longtime park visitor approached her to talk about marmots. He had spent a lot of time in the high country and had observed that the animals seemed to be disappearing from the southeast and southwest parts of the park.

"The man was a credible observer," Patti told me. "I grew concerned after talking to him. When the Vancouver Island marmot population started crashing in the late 1990s, these concerns were elevated."

Approximately 2,600,000 years ago, the Olympic marmot diverged from other marmot species in Washington and British Columbia and began to evolve in isolation on the peninsula. The nearby Vancouver Island marmot population is only 125 miles to the north, but it's separated from the peninsula by a vast waterway, the Strait of Juan de Fuca. Because of this geographic isolation, which made natural recruitment unlikely, investigating the status of the Olympic marmots became a high priority in Olympic National Park's 1998 resource management plan.

*

In the early 2000s, Sue Griffin was a student at the University of Montana. "I had just finished my undergraduate degree," she said, "and was becoming quite interested in the effects of climate change on high-elevation species."

While working in western Montana and researching a subspecies of sparrow that breeds in *krummholz*, the stunted, twisted trees that grow at timberline, Sue had had the opportunity to watch marmots. She grew curious as to how this mountaintop-dwelling rodent might be affected by the reduced size and connectivity of habitat patches. She began formulating questions on this topic as well as an approach to answering them. Dr. Scott Mills, Sue's advisor and a population biologist at the University of Montana, had been an employee at Olympic National Park many years before. He contacted Patti Happe to see how the university could help gather data on marmots. In addition to gaining access to research that would turn into a PhD dissertation for Sue, Patti was also interested in a long-term monitoring program.

"From 1998 to 2002, I was doing a lot of hands-on work with Roosevelt elk and black bears," Patti explained. "At the same time, I was also getting a lot of questions from the public about volunteering in the park. Yet the projects with bears and elk weren't good fits for volunteers. Marmots, however, are easy to see and live in places people love to visit. Studying them *would* be a good fit if we could get robust and reliable data. Early on I asked Scott [Mills] for help designing a monitoring program that could be done by volunteers."

In 2002, Sue began using different methods to assess the park's marmot population as part of her PhD thesis. These included making visual observations of marmots and marmot burrows at sites the animals were known to have occupied historically, surveying high-elevation meadows throughout the park for the rodents, and intensively studying three different groups of animals using radio telemetry to estimate birth, death, movement rates, and population trends over four to five years. The results of these efforts were sobering.

Of the 25 historic colonies Sue monitored between 2002 and 2006, 60 percent were not occupied, including 3 that went extinct during the study. No recolonizations were detected, and no new areas were colonized by marmots. Additionally, large regional differences became clear. A higher proportion of abandoned sites existed in the southwest and southeast portions of the park. Finally, of 101 animals that she'd marked, 33 died during the study and another 11 disappeared—neither their bodies nor transmitters were ever found. At least one-third of these confirmed and presumed mortalities were due to predation by coyotes.

After analyzing the data, Sue concluded that the spatial patterns of Olympic marmot site extinctions were not like the long-term patterns observed in other, apparently stable marmot populations. For example, in Colorado, yellow-bellied marmot *(Marmota flaviventris)* populations, studied in the early 2000s, had larger colonies that were able to supply animals to reoccupy sites that became vacant. By contrast, Olympic marmot sites were "winking out" regardless of colony size or proximity to other sites. Sue also documented that Olympic marmots, particularly females, appeared to have limited dispersal capability. She observed that mortality rates for females closely resembled those of the declining Vancouver Island marmot.

Sue Griffin's dissertation research showed statistically what a decade before people had been observing anecdotally: the Olympic marmot was disappearing from certain locations in Olympic National Park. While Griffin finished her degree, Julia Witczuk, another graduate student, began working with Patti to design a citizen-based monitoring program with the goal of determining changes in marmot colony occupancy over time. After Julia's University of Montana dissertation committee reviewed the plan to make sure it had scientific rigor, Patti hired Sue to turn the thesis project into an implementable program.

"She organized a pilot year in 2009," said Patti, "and I took over for the first full season of surveys in 2010."

*

In the spring of 2010, Nina Pitts and Steve Zenovic saw the request in the Port Angeles daily newspaper for volunteers for the marmot monitoring program.

Olympic marmot in Grand Valley, Olympic National Park, 2009. Betsy L. Howell.

The opportunity to find out more about marmots, as well as contribute to the ongoing research, appealed to them. As of 2018, they have since participated in every year of the program. They prefer to survey a new place each season, though they will also go wherever the park needs them most. Kelsie Donleycott, a web/graphic designer from Bremerton, Washington, has also participated in the program since the beginning. She appreciates getting to know new places and loves the park landscapes, but the best part, she told me, is being able to do the surveys with her father, Ken. The Donleycotts' perseverance has paid off. After not seeing a single marmot for the first five seasons, during their sixth season, they visited Upper Grand Valley, 14 miles south of Port Angeles. Here they at last saw several animals.

"It's a lovely place," Kelsie said. "And it's amazing how much faster surveying goes once you find a marmot!"

The citizen-science monitoring program is designed to simply document whether marmots are present in a given area, not to count their actual numbers. Volunteers systematically walk survey areas to look for the animals. They also use binoculars to scan steeper slopes. If a marmot is observed, the area is classified as "occupied" and the survey is done. If none are spotted, then a more thorough investigation of the area is completed to look for other evidence indicating presence. Trampled vegetation; fresh digging, flies, marmot feces, and clipped and compacted vegetation around burrow entrances; and trails between burrows are all indications of marmot presence. If burrows are found without any of these indicators, then the area is classified as "abandoned." Finally, if there is nothing to show that marmots are, or have been, living at a site, then the area is given a "no sign" designation.

My early involvement in the program had been to coordinate volunteers in the national forest where there is a small portion of marmot habitat. In 2015, however, I also did my first survey. That year, my backpacking buddy, Carrie, and I went to Lake of the Angels in Olympic National Park, and in 2017, we did Appleton Pass, also in the park. From my own experience having citizen scientists help with remote camera surveys, I knew that the foundations of the marmot program were solid. People love this work because of where it is, the appeal of the animals, and the desire to participate in a scientific study.

Patti puts on a mandatory, day-long training for the marmot volunteers every August. Instruction begins in the classroom in Port Angeles, where she gives an overview of marmot biology and history. Copies of the data form are provided to volunteers, as well as explanations on the kind of information to record besides the indicators of marmot presence: weather conditions, start/ end times for the survey, and other wildlife observed. After lunch, the class continues at Hurricane Hill, an easy-to-get-to part of the park where marmots are observed regularly. Patti shows everyone how to use a GPS device to record burrow locations and survey routes.

It's not uncommon to see young marmots during the training at Hurricane Hill. In contrast to the browner adults, the young animals' gray fur stands out amid the late-summer yellow and brown grasses. On a sunny, warm day there can be much marmot activity. The young and adults darting from burrow to burrow, some individuals whistling, others sitting atop rocks or on the porches of their burrows. All are watching the people below, who are watching the marmots above.

*

Between 2010 and 2015, an average of 87 volunteers worked each year gathering data on marmots at 45 sites. Some areas involve day hikes, others week-long backpack adventures. Steve and Jackie Thompson, a retired construction worker and a retired teacher, respectively, live in Redmond, Washington, just east of Seattle. Jackie heard about the program on the local National Public Radio station.

"We thought doing this would be a fun way to combine our love of hiking and backpacking with a real purpose," she said. The Thompsons have enjoyed returning to the same site every year. They say that Royal Basin, at the headwaters of the Dungeness River in the northeast part of the park, has become an old friend.

"We like to see the changes that have occurred," explained Steve. "As the snowpack has varied, the vegetation has responded, and the marmot activity has adapted. We were told that marmots didn't travel long distances, but one evening we observed a marmot run from our side of the tarn at Upper Royal Basin, around the tarn, and up the hill to another survey unit."

Vivian Bedford and Aeryk Bjork, yoga instructors from Olympia, south of Seattle, also appreciate seeing the changes that occur over time. "It's dramatic to witness how a poor winter can lead to a poor berry season," said Vivian, "which then results in our not seeing wildlife during the survey. We wouldn't know the impacts of weather as intimately if we went to different places. This way, we are starting to know the range of 'normal.'"

In addition to recording marmot sightings, volunteers also document other wildlife, including coyotes, the species Sue Griffin's research showed to be the marmots' dominant predator. The Donleycotts and Thompsons have not observed coyotes during their marmot surveys. Neither have Steve Zenovic and Nina Pitts; however, they have noticed their scats on trails. Vivian Bedford and Aeryk Bjork heard them for the first time in 2017 during their survey.

By contrast, Sue Griffin recalled seeing the predators frequently. "On many occasions," she said, "my crew and I watched a coyote attempting to stalk marmots. While I never witnessed a predation, members of my crew did. In the spring, when we monitored sites known to be occupied by hibernating marmots, I was struck by tracks of coyotes 'trap-lining' the snow-covered burrows. The coyotes clearly remembered the precise location of every hibernaculum, even without the help of radio telemetry."

Coyotes are a common, visible presence on the Olympic Peninsula. They are regularly observed in the national park and forest, as well as in the surrounding towns and cities. Yet it wasn't always this way. Prior to the 20th century, these small canines didn't live on the peninsula due to the presence of wolves. While wolves may have occasionally preyed upon marmots, they generally hunt larger animals, such as deer and elk, in areas below the tree line and away from marmot habitat. However, after the last wolf on the peninsula was killed in the 1920s, an opportunity appeared for the extremely adaptable coyotes, for whom a 15-pound marmot makes a perfect meal. Still, their presence at the highest elevations was less common until just recently. With changes in the climate causing lower snowpack some years, coyotes can easily move into alpine landscapes inhabited by marmots. Additionally, as Sue Griffin points out in her dissertation, since Olympic marmots have evolved with little predation pressure from other carnivores, they may be predisposed to population declines in the presence of an effective mammalian predator.

*

Olympic marmots have been observed and studied in the national park since the late 1950s, with four different monitoring efforts taking place between 1957 and 1989. With Sue Griffin's work in the early 2000s and the citizen-science effort beginning in 2010, there's a good understanding of population changes that have taken place in the park in the last 60 years.

Across the marmot's range, occupancy has remained relatively stable. There are regional differences, as shown by Sue's research and the observations by the citizen scientists; the south part of the park has a far lower percentage of recent marmot signs than the north part. Though they have limited dispersal capabilities, marmots have been documented during the citizen-science surveys at 8 of 13 sites that Sue had found to be extinct during her research. Additionally, none of her occupied areas have since become unoccupied. Finally, changes in snowpack, even with coyote presence, don't appear to directly relate to changes in marmot occupancy. However, snow levels had been less variable until 2015, when there was almost no snow that winter in the high country.

This news is encouraging, yet the stressors on Olympic marmot populations remain. Snow level, as a mechanism for preventing coyote pressure when marmots first emerge from hibernation, as well as for facilitating the growth of quality forage, must be considered in future analyses. Habitat changes, including increasing conifer encroachment on meadows as the climate warms, will affect marmots in the coming years. And range contraction, particularly in the south part of the park, must be further investigated to understand the potential isolation of some colonies. As far as using management actions to address stressors, Olympic National Park is starting to consider controlled burning to maintain meadow habitats and reduce conifer encroachment. And the need for wolves is apparent too.

"I can't do anything about coyotes," Patti told me, referring to the National Park Service policy of letting natural processes unfold without human interference. "But wolves can."

*

After taking a break to analyze data in 2016, Patti again gathered the citizen scientists for the summer surveys.

"I plan to keep the program going long term," she said, "with a year off every five years or so to analyze the information" (the program did take another gap year in 2023 after a six-year period of doing surveys from 2017–22).

Nina Pitts, Steve Zenovic, the Thompsons, the Donleycotts, and Vivian Bedford and Aeryk Bjork also plan to keep surveying for the whistle pig in the years to come. They agree that the species, apart from being endemic, is important ecologically for the park, and that it serves as a bellwether for climate change.

"There are so many things we don't understand about how all the pieces of an ecosystem enhance each other, that the arrogance of undervaluing any part is unwise," said Jackie Thompson.

Vivian Bedford agreed, adding, "Individuals need to begin taking responsibility as members of the planet. We need to learn about and care for the environment."

Many questions remain about how the Olympic marmots are faring and will fare in the future. Being able to contribute to a greater understanding of their status brings the volunteers back year after year. The people come from different places, different backgrounds, and have, or have had, very different careers. Yet what they all share are observant natures and curiosity about how species and ecosystems work to support life on Earth. For all the many ways that national parks can seem frozen in time with seemingly static habitats, they really are dynamic. The changes can be subtle, even imperceptible, to the casual visitor. Only when people spend more time in nature do those shifts in habitats and species presence become clearer. In an era of a rapidly evolving climate and mounting pressures on the environment, paying attention is more important than ever.

17

The Fisher

Olympic National Forest, 2010

The Gray Wolf River in the northeastern Olympic Mountains begins near Gray Wolf Pass at almost 6,500 feet elevation. In only 15 short river miles, it flows into the Dungeness River at an elevation of 830 feet. On a topographic map, the contour lines nearly touch. On the ground, the slope is often greater than a 45-degree angle. Sheer cliff walls line numerous places above the Gray Wolf. The only formal hiking trail lies along the river itself. The breathtaking views must be enjoyed from this path; the details of side canyons and the bat and bird residents of the rocky cliffs remain a mystery. It seems likely that there's much ground throughout the watershed that has never been trod by humans.

It was into this majestic but daunting landscape that I journeyed on a rainy late April morning in 2010 with my colleague Dave, an employee of Olympic National Park. We had been trying for some days to locate the den of a radio-collared fisher (*Pekania pennanti*), one of the animals that had recently been reintroduced to the Olympic Peninsula. During the weekly flights tracking the animals, Dave consistently heard this animal's signals from one area of the Gray Wolf. This likely meant that Female 001, an approximately four-pound adult, was settling down to have her kits. If Dave and I could pick up her signal in this tight canyon and follow the beeps to her den tree, then we could install remote cameras nearby and perhaps obtain photographs of her with her young. The process was simple in theory.

Yet Dave and I had been in the Gray Wolf before. There was nothing simple about moving around this watershed. Earlier attempts to find Female 001 from the riverside trail had all proved unsuccessful. The steep canyon walls caused the radio signal to bounce, making it difficult to pinpoint her location. On this day, however, Dave had devised another plan. We would start hiking from the end of a road at the top of the watershed's northern ridge. Moving south, we'd eventually drop down to the river and onto the trail. By being close to the river but above the interference caused by the canyon, we hoped to obtain clearer signals. Hopefully, the fisher would not have decided to den too close to the rock walls or other impassable sections above the river.

*

The work to bring fishers back to the Olympic Peninsula began in 1998 with the publication of the *Washington State Status Report for the Fisher*. From a lack of detections during remote camera surveys, less than four sightings per year since 1980, and few incidental captures by trappers, the report concluded that there likely wasn't a viable population of fishers in the state. It further recommended that the Washington Fish and Wildlife Commission list the species as endangered. Following this listing, conservation efforts began. Both the status report and a recovery plan developed in 2006 identified the need for reintroductions. Three areas were selected based on habitat quality: the Olympic Mountains, the northwestern Cascade Range, and the southwestern Cascade Range. Of these, the Olympics were selected to receive the first animals. Between 2008 and 2010, 90 fishers were transported to Olympic National Park from the nearest self-sustaining population in British Columbia.

When the fishers arrived in the Olympics, they scattered like wind-driven fire. The animals traversed the vertical slopes and reached elevations of approximately 4,700 feet. They navigated snow-covered ridgelines in midwinter with an ease surely envied by seasoned mountaineers and also moved along the region's many sinewy river corridors and down to the salt waters along the Pacific Ocean and Strait of Juan de Fuca (one biologist joked that maybe they were trying to return to Canada). Telemetry points plotted on a map, with a different color for each animal, resembled a Jackson Pollock painting. Though not unexpected, the fishers' movements still inspired awe. How could an animal weighing only 4 to 15 pounds (males can be three times as large as females) with 6-inch legs move so quickly over such terrain?

One answer is that fishers, like their smaller marten cousins, make up for their lack of height and long strides with jaw-dropping energy and stamina. Additional incentives for these 90 animals included the need to establish a new life and a new territory. I had attended many fisher releases, and the feeling among the people at these events was always one of triumph. Many years of planning and investment were finally paying off. Yet the animals must have felt something very different. They were trailblazers, or "founders," the ones chosen to begin a new era for their species on the peninsula. Danger and uncertainty

Fisher release at Whiskey Bend trailhead in Olympic National Park, December 2009. Coke Smith.

abounded for them. This was not a day of celebration, though leaving behind the confinement of their transport boxes must have made it seem so.

My career with the Forest Service has been spent trying to understand the habitat needs of wild animals and their responses to human activity on the landscape. Scientific studies as well as anecdotal observations provide the basis for what scientists and managers know. This information contributes to making sound management decisions. Yet all the knowledge in the world can't bridge the vast space between my perception of the world and an animal's perception. The theory of *umwelt*, developed by Baltic German biologist Jakob von Uexküll, attempts to explain this difference. *Umwelt* essentially is the world as it's experienced by an individual. This experience is shaped by the mind of an individual because the mind interprets the world for that individual. Put simply, each person or animal has their own outlook on any given situation. To complicate matters further in terms of study, another reality also exists. This is the "objective" environment, a world without any specific definition, or everything simply as it is. No one knows exactly what this objective world is like because we are each necessarily experiencing our own individual *umwelt*. In the case of the fisher, it resides next to my assessment of a coniferous Eden as well as her determination of a new and dangerous land.

*

As Dave and I began our expedition above the Gray Wolf River, quintessential Northwest weather enveloped us. The air and ground were moist; the vegetation dripped. Thin clouds hung in ragged forms throughout the treetops. Though it was spring, birdsong did not fill the air as it would have on a brilliant sunny morning. Still, we started the hike full of hope. The immediate loud, clear beeps on the telemetry receiver reinforced our optimism. Canyon or no canyon, sheer rock walls or river bottoms, we would not be bested today. Carefully but confidently, we moved down the slope.

Even with radio telemetry, trying to find a fisher in a landscape like the Olympic Mountains is akin to the proverbial needle-in-a-haystack search. Terrain and weather are the biggest challenges, with both intercepting radio waves and causing interference. So too are aspects of the animals' existence, including a mostly solitary lifestyle and long journeys either around established territories or in search of them. From a fisher's viewpoint, there is always much to do. Food and mates must be found and trouble avoided. Several Northwest predators, including bobcats, cougars, coyotes, and bears, are all much larger than a fisher. It is true that fishers and these other species have evolved together, but the founder fishers did not know where the specific dangers resided in this landscape. It would be to Female 001's benefit to be denning in a very inaccessible place along the Gray Wolf. Of course, this wouldn't make Dave's and my job today any easier.

We made a few changes in our direction of travel, but the signal remained strong. At one point, it came in so loud that we believed the fisher to be very close. We began searching the forest stand for suitable dens, either dead snags or green trees with blown-out tops. Then something happened: the signal abruptly turned muddled. I spun the antenna around and adjusted the "gain," the amplification of the signal, but the beeps remained vague in all directions. Dave took the antenna and stretched it into the sky. He is 6' 8", and the extra altitude, as well as his many years of telemetry experience, would help. After a few moments, a good signal returned. We descended farther down the mountain. Finding answers in the misty Gray Wolf would not be easy no matter how determined we were.

For all the hours I have spent searching for fisher dens in the Olympics, and for all the days I have labored transporting and installing remote cameras to document fishers, I have never seen one in the wild. On only one occasion that I know of did our paths cross within minutes of each other, though I never saw that animal either. That day had been a cold, brittle one in March the year before. I'd been checking two remote camera stations (using the TrailMaster cameras I'd borrowed from Powers, systems that required film to be developed) on the slopes above Lena Lake, 23 miles south of the Gray Wolf River. Here, Female 043 had been residing, and for several snowy weeks, I'd enjoyed skiing and snowshoeing to check the cameras, though neither had yet photographed any animal species. A light snowfall on the day I would remove the cameras had left an inch of snow on the trail. Vole, snowshoe hare, and Douglas's squirrel tracks crisscrossed the path in front of me. Reading this "morning news" of overnight animal activities cheered me even as I felt disappointed over the lack of fisher detections so far.

After packing up the second camera, I headed back down the trail. Not but one-quarter mile from the station and just minutes after I'd come through, a fisher had followed. Prints with five toes and large palms shaped like chevrons were clearly visible in the new snow. The animal seemed to "dance" around on the path, moving this way and that, looking in all directions, no doubt gathering my scent and assessing potential danger. Then it had continued on its way. I followed the tracks before losing them in patches of bare ground. By the time I returned to the trail, the evidence of the fisher was already fading in the melting snow.

A few days later, when I picked up the photos, the fisher was confirmed.

*

As Dave and I arrived at the *truly* steep and cliff-laden area of the Gray Wolf canyon, Female 001's signal went wobbly again. We walked around to find a better angle without success. Sitting down to eat lunch and consider the situation, Dave looked thoughtful.

"You know, if it were sunny and warm," he said, "I'd get out the cribbage board."

I nodded. "Yes, but it's neither sunny nor warm. Plus, you didn't bring the cribbage board."

"Right."

For most of my career, I have worked alone in the forest, and I generally like it that way. But I have also enjoyed being out with different coworkers, including Dave. He had much experience with telemetry, and I always learned a lot from him. He had an easygoing manner and a good sense of humor, and he always shared food that I rarely ate, like beef jerky or candy (I generally contributed the bags of Kettle Chips on our trips). Dave was also an incorrigible teaser. One time, this became downright annoying, perhaps because he was razzing me in front of another person. Finally, I said in a huff, "You're just like the brother I never had!"

Dave wasn't chastened in the least. "You're welcome," he replied.

Perhaps the low clouds and mist were contributing to the signal's bounce. We had also been counting on Female 001 to be stationary in a den tree. If, however, she hadn't mated last season, then she wouldn't be denning. Instead, she could be out hunting or maintaining her territory or, at this time of year, looking for a male to breed with. Any such activities would have her moving around the landscape with speed and agility that we would never be able to match. It was also possible that this fisher had traveled to somewhere on the slopes south of the river. If that were the case, we would do well to go home now. That country was even more inaccessible than the north side.

Dave and I finished eating and made a few more attempts at spinning the antenna around. Though the spring days were growing longer, the low clouds canceled any extra daylight we might have enjoyed. We decided to head for the trail by the river, where we would still have a three-mile walk out. My worst fear was having to climb back up the mountainside again after running into something we wouldn't be able to get around. With the slope's increasing angle, we glided over small loose rocks and last year's leaf fall. When we finally reached the path, we looked back to where we'd been. Such is the lushness of the Olympic forests that we'd been wholly unaware of the two vertical rock faces we'd just navigated between. For fun, Dave turned the receiver on again. The fisher still seemed to be along the Gray Wolf somewhere. Beyond that, we had learned little about this animal apart from confirming one very important fact: she was wholly adapted to this rugged world, and we were not.

*

Somewhere between human sentimentality and scientific assessment is the reality of a wild animal's life. The truth encompasses the inexorable urge to simply *be* as well as the many forces working against that state, including the interface with the landscape in which such existence unfolds. The theory of the *umwelt* helps relieve the pressure for humans to know everything because it is virtually impossible to do so. Yet information and the truth, as near as we can deduce them, are critical when decisions must be made regarding priorities for land management and species conservation. Finding Female 001's den in the Gray Wolf would have added to our understanding of what microhabitats for denning are important to fishers and what specific features they select for, including things like the sizes and species of den trees, slope, aspect, and canopy cover. However, such was not to be learned on this day of the fisher research project. Dave and I hiked to the trailhead that afternoon under a sinking sky and increasing drizzle. Wherever the fisher was in the Gray Wolf, her secrets would remain there.

*

Three months after our attempts to find Female 001, her radio collar began sending out the "mortality mode" signal. This rapid, higher-pitch series of beeps indicated the collar had become stationary, meaning it had either come loose (the radio collars used on the fisher project were not designed to fall off after a preset amount of time) or the fisher had died. The last point Dave had mapped for her from a telemetry flight was high on the rocky slopes south of the Gray Wolf River. For our own safety, we didn't attempt to find her or her collar. We simply hoped she had shed this piece of human contrivance and was still living her new life in the Olympic Mountains.

18

The Fire's Edge

Colville National Forest, 2015

One hundred miles east of Winthrop, where Barbara and I attended the Spring Snake Search, sits the town of Republic, Washington. Built around the mining and logging industries with a population of approximately 1,000, Republic is located near the headwaters of the Sanpoil River in a long valley bordered by the Okanogan Highlands to the west and the Kettle Range to the east. In the greater area surrounding Republic is the Colville National Forest. Unlike in the Okanogan-Wenatchee National Forest, where people regularly dealt with wildfire, the Colville had not been so burdened. Here, there have been far fewer wildfires and less dramatic ones when they do occur. However, the summer of 2015 saw Washington experience its largest wildfire season to date. More than one million acres burned from June through September across the state, and thousands of firefighters were engaged to fight the massive conflagrations, known as complexes. It was a season like no other, coming on the heels of another record-breaking wildfire year in 2014.

*

Four days before I arrived in Republic in August 2015 to begin an assignment as a resource advisor on the North Star Fire, the town had been ready to evacuate. That Saturday evening, firefighters watched from the Forest Service Ranger Station as flames moved down Copper Mountain just south of town. Many of the residents had packed their cars and loaded up their pets. They, too, watched from porches and the highest point in town, the cemetery. The evacuation plan called for heading east along State Route 20, up to the Kettle Crest, a long north-south ridge separating the Sanpoil River from the Kettle River.

However, the ultimate call never arrived. At the last minute, bulldozer lines, along with a shift in wind and a drop in temperature, encouraged the flames to settle and even fade out along the fire's leading edge. I arrived the following Wednesday. A gentle, north wind had pushed much of North Star's smoke south down the Sanpoil River Valley. On this day, I found Republic's residents going about their business in a hopeful manner. Still, when we spoke, their eyes turned nervously toward the south.

North Star was one of the 2015 "mega" wildfires burning in northeastern Washington. Ultimately determined to be human-caused, it had grown to more than 200,000 acres by early September, a mere two weeks after it began. The bulk of the fire burned on the Colville Indian Reservation south of Republic, while fewer acres, though by no means small amounts, were burning on portions of both the Okanogan-Wenatchee and Colville National Forests.

This was my second trip to eastern Washington that year. During my first tour, I had been assigned to two different fires, 300 and 500 acres in size, respectively. That was the end of July. The situations were serious, as fire threatened towns and municipal watersheds as well as habitat for federally listed species. Yet the blazes were also manageable, and very importantly, they responded in predictable ways to fire suppression efforts. By mid-August, however, everything had changed. A lightning storm had ignited dozens more fires across Washington and Oregon. Northern California had also erupted with fire behavior that didn't conform to either computer fire models or to the experience of many seasoned firefighters. Descriptions of wild and urban areas being consumed in only hours and fires jumping major highways and large lakes became quotidian reporting. Forests were being lost, and so were people. After returning from my first fire assignment that summer to my regular job on the Olympic, three firefighters were killed in eastern Washington. Members of an engine crew, they'd become trapped when the fire suddenly changed direction and triggered a series of catastrophic events.

A week and a half after this tragedy, I once again drove east over the Cascade Range. The nation now stood at a Wildfire Preparedness Level 5. This is the highest designation possible and one that reflects the number of major incidents and people, equipment, and aircraft committed to suppression. Firefighters had begun arriving from Canada, Australia, and New Zealand to help.

*

Every business in Republic had a sign in the window that read, "Thank You, Firefighters!" A generous coffee fund had been arranged for fire personnel at Java Joy's right before the turnoff to the Sanpoil River. One woman at Anderson's Grocery, keying in immediately on my yellow fire shirt and green pants, said, "Having you people here has really calmed everyone." Another person on the street thanked me for all I'd done. When I explained that this was only my second day in town and that I hadn't even seen the fire, she smiled. "Doesn't matter. You're here now."

At the Republic Drug Store, I asked the pharmacist for something to help me sleep. I was glad to be there and to help however I could, but worry had kept me awake for several nights. Most years it seems, records are being broken somewhere in the West, for the largest fires and for devastation to people, towns, and ecosystems. As of 2023, we have passed through more tremendous seasons with entire towns or parts of towns being consumed, including Santa Rosa, California, in 2017; Paradise, California, in 2018; and Lahaina, Hawaii, in 2023. The Labor Day Fires in Oregon and Washington in 2020 burned entire watersheds in the space of only hours. The 2021 Bootleg Fire in southern Oregon, started by lightning, was so big and powerful that it created its own weather, including enormous pyrocumulus clouds above the fire.

The pharmacist nodded at my request, looking tired himself, and suggested melatonin. The cashier, handing me a souvenir key chain, thanked me for coming to Republic.

The last large fire near Republic was the White Mountain Fire of 1988, a sizable event for the time of approximately 20,000 acres. Bleached snags still stood east of town along State Highway 20, while an enthusiastic, green understory grew beneath. Unlike the Okanogan-Wenatchee National Forest, this part of eastern Washington had not had the annual experience of a shutdown tourism industry, closed roads, and seemingly endless, smoke-filled weeks. Republic had been stunned by North Star's vitality. The start of school was delayed, the county fair canceled altogether. A mural along Main Street conveyed the making of Republic through the growth of the local hydroelectric industry and the taming of the region's rivers. It seemed clear that this western town, like so many others, struggled with reminders of how little humans at times can control their environments.

Without question, those most affected by wildfires are the people who have died and their grieving families, as well as those who have lost their homes or seen their businesses and livelihoods collapse. Yet the environmental and economic consequences of fires today affect us all. The loss of forests, the degradation of water quality, the destruction of fish and wildlife habitat that we will not see replaced in our lifetimes. Politically, the situation is also very complex. Some land managers feel more timber harvest is the answer. Others think naturally caused fires should be allowed to run their course. Neither of these extreme options is practical in modern times or beneficial to the majority of people and wildlife species. Thus, the answer must be found somewhere in the middle.

In my short 30+ years of working on wildfires, I've seen astonishing changes. In the fall of 1987, the Silver Complex on the Siskiyou National Forest, begun by lightning on August 30 that year, was not declared controlled until November 9. A tally board in the fire camp marking the fire's growth was updated each day, documenting Silver's approach to the 100,000-acre mark (the final number for this fire was 96,540 acres). Today, six-figure-acre fires that last for months are still noteworthy, but they're no longer uncommon. "Big" simply does not adequately describe anymore what is happening on the landscape.

*

Succeeding as a resource advisor and protecting natural resources during fire suppression is more easily done when a fire is moving at a pace that offers some possibility of stopping it. When it doesn't, and it's all hands on deck just to contain and control the blaze, the emphasis of resource advising turns to creating a repair plan for afterward. This plan may include fixing damaged livestock fences, returning fire lines to more natural appearances, reclosing roads (or reopening them, depending on their status prior to the fire), and restoring streams and wetlands. There's a crucial distinction when assessing this workload between that which was caused by the fire itself and that caused by fire suppression activities. It's a question of who can be billed, with Mother Nature being notoriously difficult to collect from.

My task one cool morning on the North Star Fire was to map a bulldozer line off a road that led to Deep Creek, a tributary of the Sanpoil River. The word *Sanpoil* comes from the Indigenous Okanagan language and means "gray as far as one can see," an apt description during the fire.

I had not driven more than a 10th of a mile along the road before encountering a fallen tree. Though there was little active fire now in this area, trees weakened by intense heat around their roots would be coming down for months. Within a few minutes after requesting assistance from an engine crew, Michael Cramer from Chewack Wildfire, a private company that provides forestry and wildland fire services, arrived with two assistants and several chainsaws. Michael, who went by the nickname Cosmo, had a bright, smiling face and an enthusiastic handshake. Shortly after cutting out the first tree and continuing along the road, we met a fallen 40-inch Ponderosa pine, broken in two and still burning. Yellow and orange flames licked furiously at the tree's core as Cosmo's chainsaw cut out the burning part.

As we moved farther toward Deep Creek, we found more trees down. Most were mature pines, and all had snapped at their bases. While the crew cut the trees into pieces, I took photos and made notes. Unlike other parts of North Star, the forest around Deep Creek had burned only patchily; overall, it appeared less a victim of fire and more a cooperator in the dynamic forces shaping wildland ecosystems. Chipmunks and squirrels scurried about collecting seeds and mushrooms in the unburned portions of the ground. Overhead, songbirds and ravens took advantage of insects displaced by the fire and smoke.

When we finally reached Deep Creek, we encountered a small herd of cattle. A few animals grazed while others rested along the stream. Some had blue ear tags, others green, and still others red or white. This rainbow of colors indicated individuals from different herds and reflected the mixing that had occurred during the fire's zenith. I felt immensely relieved to see these cows and calves looking healthy and uninjured.

*

Mackenzie Wilson grew up in Curlew, Washington, 15 miles north of Republic. In 2015, she was 25 years old, had the sturdy build of one who works outside all day, and had been an engine foreman at her previous job. She left the east side of the Cascade Range to attend Western Washington University in Bellingham. After returning home, she'd begun working as a forestry technician in the Colville National Forest. Mackenzie was not given to unnecessary smiling and maintained a practical, efficient manner.

Before going to Deep Creek, I had been with Mackenzie in the Scatter Creek watershed, just west of the Sanpoil River. We had an engine crew with us that day as well, to cut out trees that had fallen across the road. Injured cattle had been reported in the area and we found them, all lying down. While the crew filled containers of water for the animals, Mackenzie said that they would likely have to be put down. One large black-and-white cow, burned on her stomach and her eyes bloodshot, appeared in especially bad shape and had not moved since the previous day. Others lay about listlessly. A calf, still mobile but bleeding and jumpy, wouldn't let anyone get close.

The rancher who owned these animals had been notified, but a more active part of North Star was threatening his home 20 miles to the south. This was the situation I encountered day after day for many residents affected by North Star: homes being threatened or destroyed; livestock scattered and injured; crops and hay lost. Choosing between saving your home and caring for your animals seemed an awful decision to have to make.

*

"Where did you eat last night?" Mackenzie asked me one morning as we were headed to the Cornell Butte Lookout, which had reportedly been burned up by the fire.

"Freckles Barbecue. They gave us all souvenir magnets and massive portions."

She shrugged. "It's a logging and ranching town."

The fire camp in Republic was what is known as a "spike camp." The main camp was in Omak, almost two hours away and on the fire's western edge. With a megafire like North Star, spike camps are crucial; otherwise, crews can be driving half the day just to reach their work areas. Unfortunately, these satellite camps sometimes don't have all the amenities. Ours, for example, lacked showers, handwashing stations, and an on-site caterer. Though hot food was being transported to the camp in boxes, a number of people had chosen to eat in town.

"It's good for the businesses," Mackenzie added approvingly when I mentioned the crowds at the restaurants.

A few hours later, we were glad to find the lookout still standing. The structure was largely metal, so this was partially the reason for its survival. Yet why it wasn't more damaged with blackened moonscapes all around remained a mystery.

*

Within the North Star Fire area, a lake system is home to common loons, a state-listed sensitive species. Swan, Ferry, and Long lakes are 3 of only 13 sites in Washington where the birds are known to nest. The area is also popular for recreation, with campgrounds, hiking trails, and fishing. On the morning I visited the lakes, however, they all were eerily deserted by both birds and people. Informational signs leading to the lake had been encased in protective, aluminum wrap, and an outdoor kitchen, built by Civilian Conservation Corps crews in the 1930s, had a sprinkler system installed around it. Across the lake, the fire still burned, though in an undramatic way, with more smoke visible than flame. Still, the heavy thuds of trees crashing to the ground at regular intervals belied the calm.

The mix of impressions continued everywhere I went on North Star. Forest stands changed beyond recognition existed beside mosaic patterns of burned and unburned patches. I didn't feel surprised by the strange, unpredictable work of fire and thought again of the many benefits it brings in terms of ecosystem renewal. But I knew, too, that modern human society keeps a decidedly uneasy relationship with one of the main elements of life on the planet. We *are* living with fire, but we resist enormously the power it wields. We are very uncomfortable with the uncertainty it creates, and there is no place in the societal systems we've built for the kinds of far-reaching socioeconomic and ecological losses that result from catastrophic megafires. As I left the lakes and continued with my day of mapping firelines, I knew I had to focus on my small role in the fire suppression effort: documenting repair needs after the fire was fully out. If I didn't and continued thinking about the many challenges of managing fire, most beyond my influence, there would once again be no sleep that night.

*

The morning I left Republic in early September, the temperature sat in the low 30s, and a light frost covered the late-summer grasses. Smoke lay heavy in the Sanpoil River Valley, the result of controlled burns designed to help keep the uncontrolled areas of the wildfire in check. I met with my replacement, a Forest Service fisheries biologist from Alaska, who would serve, with the assistance of Mackenzie, as the resource advisor for the next two weeks. On the way out of town, I stopped at Java Joy's.

"You're a firefighter, right?" the young woman asked as she handed me my drink.

"Yes," I said, "but I'll pay today."

I traveled 30 miles west on Highway 20 to Tonasket before turning south on State Route 97 toward Omak, another 25 miles away. Two full hours passed before I finally stopped seeing parts of the North Star Fire.

19

Copper Creek Diary

Olympic National Forest, 2013

August 22, 2013

High in the forest canopy above me, golden-crowned kinglets send down parachutes of late-summer song. Below me, Copper Creek tumbles with a roar along its steep, narrow corridor. I am surprised there's so much water up here, since closer to the trailhead, three footbridges below me, the forest was quiet. The creek goes underground at that point, and the rocky streambed is empty save for moss and smooth stones. I listen now to this mountain music while catching my breath. The path before me presents yet another series of tall steps, each one a link in the climb to a ridge below Lightning Peak in the southwest corner of Olympic National Forest. Copper Creek is new territory for me. I don't know what I will find, but I'm hoping that the top of the drainage will provide suitable locations for installing remote cameras.

It's now more than 20 years since I started working with remote cameras as a wildlife survey method. The line-trigger systems that I first used on the Siskiyou National Forest have become antiques and objects of amazement for the next generation of biologists ("You only got *one* photo per event?" they ask me in disbelief). The TrailMaster cameras, which I used in the mid-to-late 1990s and early in the fisher project in the Olympic National Forest, used rolls of 35 mm film and infrared detection. In 2013, we now have digital cameras that record photographs on memory cards so large that they can store up to *40,000* pictures. Four years earlier, in 2009, I had purchased digital setups and, working with volunteers from Conservation Northwest, installed them along the Gray Wolf River, where we documented the two fishers without radio collars, some of the first animals to have been born on the peninsula. Looking through thousands of photos from those stations would have been unimaginable just two decades ago.

Now we are using the cameras to try to document Pacific martens. Copper Creek is only three air miles from Mt. Rose, where the most recent individual was detected, a juvenile female that was found dead (of apparent starvation) along a trail in 2008. Though this young animal's presence indicated that martens were reproducing on the peninsula, the number of verified records by that year totaled just six, all from different locations. From 2001 to 2003, Patti Happe and her National Park Service colleagues installed TrailMaster cameras in Olympic, North Cascades, and Mt. Rainier National Parks to survey for forest carnivores of conservation concern in Washington State. Fishers weren't detected in any of the three national parks, and although martens were commonly detected in both parks in the Cascade Range, they weren't detected at all in Olympic National Park. This greatly elevated concerns for the fishers and helped establish a program for their reintroduction to the state. However, questions had also been growing about the Pacific marten's status in the Olympics.

Two hours after setting out, I reach the peak above Copper Creek. Here, a loop trail encircles a half-mile-long ridge that is very narrow in places. There is a small opening overlooking the adjacent drainage where I eat lunch. Though the trail's linear distance is only 2.2 miles from start to finish, the elevation gain of 2,400 feet is a challenge for one who now spends too much time in the office.

Yet the hike has been worth it. The sky is a deep, clear blue, and the breezes are warm. A Douglas's squirrel appears at the top of a tree (level with my gaze due to the vertical drop), scolding me before going about its business. For many reasons, I am glad to see this squirrel. It's a spunky creature, approximately 12 inches long, which includes 5 to 7 inches of tail, and has one of the biggest personalities in the forest. It's also beautiful, with its gray-brown coat and orange belly. And finally, from a purely ecosystem perspective, the squirrel is an important prey species for many smaller carnivores. For martens to find this old-growth forest suitable, there must be things for them to eat. Cover and den sites, in the form of snags and downed wood, are numerous along the trail. Of water, there is also plenty. Now there is the confirmed presence of food as well. All things being equal, and if I ignore the sobering fact that there have been only six verifiable marten detections on the peninsula since the late 1960s, and a five-year goose egg for our survey efforts since 2008, then I can legitimately proclaim, "There should be martens here." The steep slopes will prove challenging for the installation of the cameras, but they can be navigated safely.

I begin back down the trail with thoughts of my return and hoped-for success.

*

October 23, 2013

The 2013 federal government shutdown is finally over! These first few days back to work have unfolded in a flurry of excitement and questions (Will we get back pay for a shutdown that wasn't our fault? Will project deadlines be extended? How will we ever catch up after missing three weeks of work?), and I'm glad to escape to the woods. I return to Copper Creek with my coworker, Mary, and all the equipment we need to set up two remote cameras. Generously, I offer to carry the smelly items, including the chicken bait and skunk-oil lure. Mary has the locks for the cameras and wire cages for the bait. We each have a camera and our hiking poles. On my exploratory trip, I fell coming down the trail, my feet sliding out from under me at a particularly steep, slippery spot; poles should help to prevent such a repeat.

It's another beautiful day. Sunlight falls into the forest in an array of shapes and hues of gold and yellow. Copper Creek is still dry below the bridges. Up the trail, Mary and I stop to look across the channel. On the other side, square maws open into the mountain where early 20th-century miners excavated shafts to extract copper and manganese. It would take little effort, especially with the creek dry, to make our way over and investigate, but I know that getting up and down this trail is an all-day endeavor. Besides, I am generally not one for enclosed spaces. Also, there will be no martens living in the caves.

Just after we set off, Mary sees a rough-skinned newt on the trail. Although I was in the lead, I completely missed this salamander. "I only saw it because it moved," she explains. Such is the case with most wildlife, I think. The animals are there; *we* simply do not see them. I hope fervently that this holds true for the elusive marten. During the rest of the hike, we also observe several baby western toads when they move in front of us.

After eating lunch at the overlook, we search for a spot to install the first station. One challenging part of this process is finding two suitable trees, one for the camera and one for the bait. The tree for the bait can be of large diameter because the meat, wrapped in chicken wire, is simply nailed to the trunk. The camera unit, however, is strapped around the tree, so its girth can't be greater than the length of the strap that secures the camera. The two trees must also be a certain distance apart—not too close because that reduces the amount of area in the picture frame and not too far because it can then be difficult to see the photographed visitor. Additionally, the camera should face north, as sunlight can sometimes trigger it. Part scientific protocol and part artistic sensibility (looking for an animal that could be *anywhere* on the landscape is nothing if not art), the selection of just the right location can take some time.

We find two trees approximately 15 feet apart and begin. Soon, I realize that not only have I forgotten the nails to secure the bait, I've also put a memory card in one camera that is only 16 MB in size, not 16 GB. After the camera takes five test photos, the thing is full. My hopes plummet down the slope. Without bait to direct its interest, an animal will not move in front of the camera. Without a memory card, it won't matter if it does. I blame Congress and the government shutdown for my forgetfulness. Too many distractions, including a large amount of worry, have diminished my ability to concentrate, and now here we are, two hours up a difficult trail from all the spare supplies in the vehicle.

Fortunately, Mary is with me. She has flagging in her pack that we can use to hang the bait. She also has a memory card in her personal camera that will fit the remote one. Though terribly likely that the bait will be stolen by the first enterprising animal to come along, at least we will have photos of that individual. I keep my spirits up with thoughts that these are simply situations that help instill humility in a person. They also offer opportunities for accepting imperfection and compromise in our lives. With the camera and bait in place, our last task is to dribble the scent lure onto some cotton balls and hang them nearby. In two decades, the process of using the lure has not changed much. I still must hold my breath. I still must not think too much about the reasons behind why this product exists. More compromise.

The second station goes up relatively quickly. The bright, pink flagging holding the bait will help relocate the site if it manages to remain in place that long. Mary and I look forward to the check in two weeks. We might get nothing, or we might get a marten or fisher. We also might see something else unusual, like the trio of mountain lions that showed up during the citizen-science camera surveys this past spring. Or possibly the strangeness of the scene will inspire different species to approach together, like the varied thrush and chipmunk that were photographed together at a station just north of here.

It's now almost four o'clock in the afternoon, and the shadows in the canyon are long. Though autumn and winter are the best times to do carnivore surveys, they're also the most logistically challenging. We don't have snow to contend with yet, and in fact, the temperature at the lunch spot was a balmy 58 degrees Fahrenheit, but the amount of daylight is shrinking and shortening our workday. Mary and I give our knees a pep talk in anticipation of the return hike.

We see more small toads the color of coal along the trail and wonder how they have come to be on such a dry (*dry* being a relative term in the Olympic Mountains), steep hillside. Western toads lay their eggs in still water, such as ponds and lakes or quiet channels of creeks and rivers, so there must be such a spot somewhere nearby. But where, in this incredibly steep drainage? I am reminded that most of my trips to the forest lead to more questions than answers.

*

October 30, 2013

Despite my desire to accept the facts of imperfection and compromise in my life, I have brooded the past week over the camera stations. Mary is busy with other work, so I hike up Copper Creek by myself, this time with nails and more memory cards. Another unusually sunny morning has encouraged many feeding flocks of kinglets, chickadees, nuthatches, and juncos. They hurry through the treetops, calling and hanging upside down in their quest for insects and late-season seeds. Meanwhile, a group of red crossbills passes over, and a raven I cannot see gurgles a message for all to hear. On the ground, four Douglas's squirrels at different places along the trail run up to investigate me. One dances like a boxer on a log, daring me to step one foot off the trail into its territory.

In several places, the path is now hidden. Bigleaf maple leaves, curled and dry, many larger than a dinner plate, have fallen. They cover my boots as I walk, moving aside only reluctantly with a swishing sound. Today there are no newts or toads on the trail. Even though it is sunny, the temperature has dropped. I am barely at the lunch spot five minutes before the sweat on my body turns cold and I must don more clothes. The thermometer on my pack indicates 41 degrees, a substantial drop from last week's 58. Looking out across adjacent Elk Creek at the rock monoliths that make this landscape so inaccessible, I eat my peanut butter sandwich and consider this quest to find Olympic martens.

Locating martens hadn't been easy on the Siskiyou National Forest in southern Oregon either, but we did find them after one season of using the TrailMaster cameras. Here, however, the task has been an even bigger challenge. At this point, no one knows the exact reason for the apparent low density of Pacific martens in the Olympics. It may have to do with the isolation of the peninsula habitat from other mountain ranges. If the animals disappeared here due to overtrapping and timber harvest, as had happened with the fisher, then there are no connecting landscapes, as there are in the Cascade Range or the Siskiyou Mountains, to allow for immigration. It could also have to do with a lack of prey resources. Or, perhaps they were outcompeted by other small predators. Climate variation or long-term changes in weather patterns also may be responsible in some form, for martens are very adapted to living in snowy conditions. Less snowpack can facilitate more predators of martens moving into higher elevations, as is occurring with coyotes moving into Olympic marmot habitat.

The juvenile marten found dead at Mt. Rose in 2008 was the first confirmed detection on the Olympic Peninsula since 1990. That year, two individuals had been caught in live traps during a spotted owl prey study, and before that, in 1988, an animal was photographed dragging a snowshoe hare off the trail in The Brothers Wilderness. Off the national forest and national park, the first official marten record is from 1968 just north of Taholah, Washington, within one-quarter mile of the Pacific Ocean. The next earliest is from the late 1970s, when a trapper found a dead animal along State Highway 101 near Quilcene, Washington, in the northeast part of the forest. These two earliest records are from low elevations, but the remaining four, including the 2008 Mt. Rose record, have been from the higher country. One possibility is that if martens persist on the peninsula, then they likely do so in remote high-elevation portions of Olympic National Forest and Park. Thus, my reason for being at Copper Creek. Here the elevation is above 3,000 feet, the forest has never been harvested, and *there should be martens.*

Much to my surprise, the bait at both stations is still tied to the trees. It hasn't been taken because the sites haven't been visited. I install new bait with chicken wire and nails, refresh the lure, and make sure the camera is operational. I also move the second camera, which we'd installed a bit too close to the loop trail. At the new location, there is a good sign. An old bobcat scat sits on a log below where I hang the lure. Additionally, there are several giant, bleached snags in a nearby opening. *Some* animal must live in those dead trees, and hopefully, we will soon find out which one.

Back down at the footbridges, I wonder again at the vanishing water in Copper Creek. It doesn't resurface at any point between here and the road where my vehicle is parked. Likewise, the creek bed below the road is also dry. After my third trip up and down the mountain, I don't feel so exhausted. I put all my gear back into the truck, then continue down the creek looking for the water's reappearance.

The North Fork of the Skokomish, a wide river with its origins near Mt. Stone in Olympic National Park, is only one-quarter mile below the road. In a few minutes, I'm standing on its banks. Copper Creek is still dry, with no obvious outlet point that I can see. A bank of cottonwoods across the North Fork is a soft yellow against the gray-green landscape. Of birds, there are two: a bald eagle circling high above the other shore and an American dipper, very close to me, that is swimming and hopping about in the slower portions of the current. The dipper is an impressive species. The only songbird that swims, it navigates the slippery stones and bubbling froth with a dancer's ease. Perhaps owing to the watery environs it exploits, dippers rarely seem alarmed by my presence on shore. I watch it for many minutes, take a few photos that will show nothing but a small gray dot against a dark background, then begin walking back to the vehicle.

*

November 13, 2013

Fourth trip. Each time, I wonder, "Can I do this again?" My thighs burn going up, my knees coming down. Though these facts are always the same, nothing else on the trail is. Today, Copper Creek is flowing below the bridges. Rain that brought forth this outpouring has also made sodden the earlier carpet of dry leaves. Not until 1.3 miles up the trail, where a side path leads to an old miner's cabin site, do I begin to hear the feathery, high-pitched calls of the kinglets. The forest is again sunny and still, so where are all the birds? Once more, I realize, they are here; the exuberance of Copper Creek has simply drowned out most other sounds, at least to my hearing.

Rain and wind are often a pair in the Olympic Mountains, and the evidence for this partnership is apparent as I get closer to the top. Two fir trees have splintered partway up their trunks. The shiny, white cambium, now exposed and jagged, points up to the sky like an arrow. Insects and woodpeckers will soon find and use these opened trees, making the change from healthy, live organism to decadent one about transformation, not destruction. A chaotic design of broken branches, bark, and needles lie in a pile where the tops hit the ground.

In addition to this new forest material, there are also many pieces and parts of mushrooms on the trail. Some are more or less intact, having only been tipped over on their side. Others are shredded and lying in small piles. I suspect this is the work of the Douglas's squirrel, a great connoisseur of fungi and one to readily take advantage of seasonal abundance.

At the sites, I look quickly at each camera's memory card before replacing the bait and lure. A coyote has visited the first station, a squirrel the second. Back in the office later that afternoon, I download these photos to my computer and examine them more closely. The coyote stayed for 10 photographs. In the deep hours of the night, it had stood away from the bait tree and refused to approach any closer. The squirrel had come by briefly at about 8:30 in the morning; the camera took one photo when it was just a few feet away, then a second blurry image as it leapt out of view.

Susan, my supervisor, sees me looking at the photos and expresses interest. I explain what I've found, and she nods before returning to her work. Bless her heart for not saying, "You mean you just spent most of the day and a bunch of taxpayers' money to confirm that we have coyotes and squirrels on the forest?"

If I can't have martens on the cameras, then the next best thing is that the setups are all functioning between checks. The cameras had been working during the two weeks since my last visit, the bait had not been stolen, and the scent lure was still hanging from the tree. If a marten had come by, it would have gotten its picture taken. I can only conclude that a marten likely never came by.

*

December 3, 2013

New comments in the trail register read, "Whew!" and "Bring Advil." This morning is cold and clear, and very soon, Mary and I see a thin layer of snow covering the upper branches of several trees. Farther up, the trail also has a dusting. Today we will take down the cameras. More snow is coming, and below-freezing temperatures will make parts of the steep path too icy and treacherous for safe hiking.

Icicles hang from logs, stained with the orange and green colors of the fungi and moss growing on the wood. A hairy woodpecker flies above us and clings to the side of a small snag. Though winter is clearly upon us, there has been little rain since my last visit; Copper Creek below the bridges has returned to its underground course. Five times now I have been up this trail, and each time the sky has been filled with sunshine—a circumstance quite unusual in the Olympic Mountains!

Within the past month, a big change has occurred in the human world of wildlife conservation. In the Northwest, the Pacific marten is now divided into the Cascades and coastal populations. NatureServe, a nonprofit organization whose mission is to provide the scientific basis for effective conservation action, is responsible for this change. Based on input from the research community, this distinction enabled coastal martens (including those on the Olympic Peninsula) to be deemed "critically imperiled" while leaving the Cascade population animals as "apparently secure." In practical terms, this means that previously unavailable funding can now be used to study and conserve the coastal marten. This is very good news even as it's premised on an alarming situation.

The temperature at the lunch spot is 24 degrees Fahrenheit. We sit down to eat but don't stay long. The winterscape of Elk Creek is beautiful, the trees and stream and rock cliffs covered lightly with snow. A chickadee calls from somewhere below us. Tiny tracks of a deer mouse or vole mark the steps right before the very top. Many animals move to lower elevations once the ground freezes and the snow deepens; however, such is not the case yet here. Mary and I pack up our gear and head to the first station. We've both brought microspikes this time, anticipating icy conditions. The devices, attached to our boots and functioning much like tire chains on a car, give us more traction. I feel like these would have been useful even before the snow fell.

There are 22 photos on the first camera, but they are all from my last visit and today. Rodent tracks at the base of the bait tree, but no rodent photos, cause me to worry that something is wrong with the camera. Yet the camera worked when we walked into view just now. Mary takes down the wire cage holding the untouched bait while I unlock and pack up the camera. The scent lure, housed inside a yogurt container, is still smelly and goes into a sturdy plastic bag.

Along the knife ridge between stations, we find a bobcat scat on the trail. Though not fresh, it also wasn't here on my previous visit. Tracks in the snow show the animal coming from the direction of the second camera, and my hopes rise that we may at least have something for our efforts today. The cat's tracks are visible all along the trail, as are those of more rodents and possibly a varied thrush. At the turnoff to the station, however, the bobcat never deviated from the path. We check and sure enough, there are no photos on this camera either. Not only am I disappointed; I'm also puzzled. Bobcats, like martens in the Cascade Range, are frequent visitors at remote camera stations. They seem less wary than coyotes or mountain lions, and I have hundreds of photos from other camera stations of different cats trying to dislodge the bait. Perhaps this animal was focused only on following the tracks of live meals, or perhaps it had just eaten and simply wasn't curious about the smells coming from the station. Such a lack of interest undoubtedly happens all the time, yet on this occasion, because of the snow, we can verify that an animal *was* in the area but *was not* recorded on the camera.

The return hike is quiet. I reflect on the crucial importance of wildlife surveys as well as the inherent limitations of the information they provide. Soon, the one-inch layer of snow that holds the bobcat tracks will either melt or be buried by more snow. All evidence of the animal will then be gone. It may come back, or it may not. On another day, the cat, or another animal, might have been very interested in the bait. Or maybe not. Obtaining a photograph is obviously proof of an animal's presence at a site. The lack of a photograph, however, doesn't indicate its absence. The implications of this are, of course, enormous.

Part III

BEARING WITNESS

The aim of science is to discover and illuminate truth. And that, I take it, is the aim of literature, whether biography or history or fiction; it seems to me, then, that there can be no separate literature of science.

—Rachel Carson, marine biologist / conservationist / writer

20

Klondike Fire

Rogue River-Siskiyou National Forest, 2018

October 13, 2018, Agness, Oregon

As I arrive at the Klondike fire camp, the blue skies above the Rogue and Illinois rivers are slightly golden from the setting autumn sun. The sinking bronze hue has begun to settle on the slopes above the river valleys. The air is cool and clear. My return to a fire camp in Agness, Oregon, 31 years after the Silver Fire, feels surreal. Time seems to be collapsing on itself; how is it that I'm now closer to the end of my career than the beginning? Much has changed with wildfires during this time, including the fact that there were no resource advisors in 1987. I get out and stretch and feel very glad to be done with the 11-hour drive from the Olympic Peninsula. This is my second resource advisor assignment of the season.

The yurt tents for the various departments of wildfire management, including "Operations," "Facilities," and "Communication," are set up around the historic Agness Guard Station. I find the READ tent and meet Chad, the person I'll be replacing as lead READ. It's October 13, and Klondike has moved into repair mode rather than suppression, meaning the fire has been contained and fire activity is minimal. The READs have been monitoring repair work on the firelines created by bulldozers and hand crews, work that has included rehabilitation around wetlands and other sensitive areas. Chad shows me where he and the others have set up their tents. The sloping area sits beneath several apple trees not far from the guard station.

"This spot over here is about the flattest," he says, pointing to a relatively level area uphill from most of the trees and away from the porta-potties. It doesn't look like the best campsite, but I don't care. The cold and my tiredness will help with sleep tonight.

"You might want to get some dinner too," he adds, saying the mess tent, showers, and supply tents are all about one-quarter mile farther along the guard station loop road. Chad is tall and lanky, in his mid-30s, and from my old forest, the Mt. Hood. "Just come on over whenever you're done. We have our check-in meeting at 7:30 p.m."

After setting up my tent and eating a decent meal of stir-fry chicken and salad, I return to the guard station. I pass several buildings and wonder which one was the barn where we watched movies during the Silver Fire. The night sky is deep black with only a sliver of a moon and a few stars so far. When I get back, I see the READ tent has now filled. There are resource advisors as well as fire operations staff.

"Yes," Chad agrees, to my surprise at seeing the operations people. Most often, it's difficult getting much time with this department, as they're usually busy with an uncontrolled fire. "Ever since we moved into suppression," he continues, "they've been coming to our meetings. It's very helpful."

Chad then describes the usual ups and downs of being a resource advisor. "It was total anarchy when I got here," he says, shaking his head. "The previous lead READ wasn't very organized and people were just doing whatever they wanted. It was crazy."

None of this surprises me. Klondike has been burning for three months. There have been numerous resource advisors and numerous overhead management teams, and everyone has a little different way of doing things. Two bulging expando files attest to this long history, as do the many rolled-up maps piled in a corner.

"I've done my best to organize things," he finishes. "It's helped that we're doing repair work now and things are quieter. You should have a good, mellow assignment."

"I'm looking forward to that."

Three months earlier, I'd worked on the Sugar Pine Fire, approximately 80 miles northeast of Klondike and also along the Rogue River. As lead READ, I had managed six other resource advisors, and there'd been much to do. There were personnel issues, and I'd also spent time learning about new (to me) suppression equipment useful in minimizing resource damage. Unfortunately, we'd also lived for two solid weeks in smoke that never lifted. Though used to some level of smoke, I'd never experienced anything like the shroud that gave the landscape a distinctly apocalyptic feel. Many days I drove back and forth between the fire camp and the Prospect Ranger District office where the internet connection was better. These were dim, gray drives. Headlights indicated vehicles long before I could see the vehicles themselves, and barely visible livestock grazed in the highway's adjacent fields.

But now almost three months have passed. The southern Oregon fires are largely under control, and the skies have cleared. I have taken this Klondike assignment specifically because the work involves rehabilitation of the fire area rather than suppression. The assignment also appealed to me because of nostalgia. A lot had happened in the three decades since I'd worked on Silver. I'd resigned from and returned to the Forest Service. Wildfires had become bigger, were lasting longer, and were becoming even more unpredictable. Our understanding of ecosystem management had made important strides between the 1980s and the late 2010s, a time that included the adoption of the 1994 Northwest Forest Plan, while timber harvest, budgets, and staffing levels had all declined.

Personally, I'd also had my own evolution. The path I'd chosen, seemingly haphazard at times, in fact fit a pattern. In 1991, I'd begun surveying for martens and fishers in the Siskiyou Mountains, and I was still looking for them in the Olympics. I'd discovered my interest in amphibians and reptiles in the Siskiyous and still searched for them on the peninsula. I'd done my first three-week wildfire assignment here, and now was back in fire camp at the same spot. I'd also begun writing in this landscape and made the important decision to change course and follow that path, eventually devising a way to write and do biology at the same time. The Siskiyou Mountains, to use a biological term, were my natal ground, the place that had birthed me professionally. I'd learned much here, made many mistakes, and lost both of my parents while living here. There would never be another place like this for me, and I wanted to see it again. Even my old nemesis, poison oak, would be lovely (from a distance) as it turned an autumn red, brightening the slopes with its own kind of fire.

*

October 14, 2018, Klondike Fire Camp
A group of us walk to the mess tent for dinner. The air is now smoky, the night sky nowhere to be seen. I've been in the READ tent most of my first day, continuing to get up to speed on everything and preparing for the transition to the new fire management team coming in. At the morning briefing, I'd taken notes on the current size and scope of Klondike:

176,000 acres
72 percent contained

310 personnel
$90,000,000 budget

The main repair work includes fixing gravel forest roads damaged by three months of fire traffic. Additional needs include installing erosion control ditches onto constructed fire lines and seeding areas of bare ground. Possible bulldozer incursions into a roadless area and aerial retardant that may have gone into streams also need to be investigated. There are reports to complete, and I must check out a smartphone from the fire cache since my flip phone doesn't get reception here. That afternoon, I write an email to Barbara. All is busy but fine, I tell her.

"This doesn't look good," someone says, pointing to the glowing hillside behind camp. An hour later, when we come out of the mess tent, ash is falling from the sky and the mountain is clearly on fire. No one from operations comes to the resource advisor meeting at 7:30 p.m. We begin anyway, going over the day's repair work.

At 8:00 p.m., someone from operations stops in briefly. The situation is changing quickly, he explains. East winds have brought Klondike back to life. The fire is spotting six miles in front of the main body. The spots have been confirmed west of the Illinois River, putting our camp in between the older fire area and this new activity. The messenger advises us to be ready to evacuate in the morning.

I don't sleep well that night. The smell of smoke is thick inside my tent, and vehicles are moving around camp all night. In the morning, we hear that Klondike is an active fire again. Each department prepares to evacuate. I pack up my tent, then Chad and I organize the resource advisor files while two of the field READs continue getting ready to go home. They look simultaneously relieved at not having to return to suppression work and worried that all their efforts at repair may be for naught. The ones who are staying help pack up.

Late in the morning, plans change. Contracted personnel, including the caterers, people managing the shower trucks, and the camp staff, will evacuate back to the main camp in Gold Beach on the coast. The rest of us will remain in Agness. The new spot fires, including the largest, are all within a few miles of the guard station; it doesn't make sense to move everyone an hour's drive away. As for the danger inherent in now being in an evacuation zone, I don't feel too worried. The Agness Guard Station sits in a large, mostly grassy expanse of flat ground above the confluence of the Illinois and Rogue rivers. The area is grazed by livestock and qualifies as a fire "safety zone," where firefighters can survive without being injured from radiant and convective heat from the fire. Still, smoke will be an issue. Also, someone has scooped up my relatively flat site, and I must repitch my tent on a bumpy slope beneath one of the apple trees. Three deer munch on the fallen bounty nearby. They seem unperturbed by the fire, smoke, or people occupying their usually quiet feeding area.

*

In the coming days, more firefighting crews arrive. The smoke settles, and camp life assumes a familiar routine. Operations meetings begin at 5:30 a.m. followed by more meetings at 6:30. Each morning, I provide a two-minute briefing on resource protection to an audience of sleepy firefighters. Writing reports, responding to the unexpected, and ordering more staff to replace people rotating out fill the time. This last isn't as easy as it would be if it were earlier in the fire season. This year, like so many others recently, has been busy and long. People are tired and want to be home doing their regular jobs. I have only been on Klondike a few days and am already looking for my replacement, a challenging task as it turns out.

Chad has decided to stay a few extra days, so we share the duties of lead READ. I don't mind this as he has much more experience and knows more about heavy equipment than I do. He also knows Collector, a mobile data collection app connected with ArcGIS, our mapping program.

"Collector is great," Chad explains one morning after everyone has left for the fire. "Particularly with large fires where many people are working in different divisions, it enables us to get a lot of information organized quickly. For example, GPS points and photographs of areas that may need repair after the fire is contained and controlled. What's gathered by one person can be synced with that of other people, making a snapshot of the entire fire area available in real time. It also helps to minimize people duplicating work."

On Sugar Pine, I'd gotten an online Collector account, but I hadn't used it yet in the field. I ask Chad if he could give me a lesson. We spend two afternoons mapping firelines still in need of repair, as well as the Pine Grove historic trail that had been expanded as a fire break with a bulldozer and will need mitigation.

The east winds continue spreading Klondike. Spot fires and new firelines are mapped, as well as those that have been reopened after they'd been repaired.

This is disheartening but can hardly be helped. The anxiety level around the community of Agness is high. The residents have lived with smoke and the threat of their homes burning up since July. Even though evacuation level three means "Go," and that fire "danger to your area is current and imminent," and that people should leave immediately, this is not enforceable by law, and most choose to stay. Many homes are substantial distances from this new round of spot fires. Others are closer, and it seems risky not to leave. Yet I understand people's reluctance. This has indeed been another long season.

The first night after the evacuation order, everyone remaining in camp eats dinner at the Singing Springs Resort in Agness. Though we all have a fine meal and encounter helpful, patient people at the resort, this arrangement isn't tenable for the several days the evacuation might be in place. For one thing, there is little parking available. For another, the dark, narrow, winding road along the Rogue River from the guard station to Agness is too dangerous for tired people who have just worked extremely long shifts to drive. Consequently, the caterer, now in Gold Beach, begins sending tins of hot food upriver to the camp.

*

October 19, 2018

As I stand in line to get dinner from the tins, most people around me are looking at their phones. The line inches forward, and I think about the 1987 Silver Fire. Only five miles upstream along the Illinois River is Briggs Ranch, where my crew and I stayed in spike camp for a week. We'd spent those days improving an old trail that connected the natural fire break of Briggs with Silver Prairie, two miles to the south. Two weeks later, we flew into the Kalmiopsis Wilderness and did much the same. Both assignments involved tins of scrambled eggs or spaghetti if we were lucky and the helicopter could fly or MREs if it couldn't. The recollections of the freeze-dried food make me grateful now for these tins, lukewarm or not.

One evening as I walk to dinner, I notice a man coming out of a rather large tent. Not only is it a tent he can stand up in; it's also on flat ground! I stop and consider whether I should go to the effort of relocating.

"You're camped in a very good spot," I say as he joins me on the road.

"In some ways," he says. "It is flat, but it's also noisy here. Everyone around me is snoring."

I nod sympathetically. Snoring is a given in fire camp and a reason I always have my earplugs handy. Maybe my sloping apple orchard is just fine. This man and I walk together, and I ask him where he's from.

"Portland," he replies. "But originally, I'm from Kabul, Afghanistan."

His name is Sam, and he's working as night security at the camp. We fall into easy conversation as I ask him how he came to be in Portland.

"I was an interpreter for the U.S. military," he explains. "My work qualified me for a priority visa to come to the States. I was very glad to come, but initially, I couldn't bring my family, so I had to go back."

"Were they eventually able to come as well?"

"Yes, but it took a long time for the paperwork to go through. For six months while we waited, I stayed up at night with a loaded gun in my hands." He pauses. "If it's not the terrorists creating chaos, then it's the small thieves trying to rob you."

"That must have been very hard," I say.

"It was. I still have the PTSD."

"I'm sure."

We arrive at the junction of the dining area and supply tent, which has recently returned to camp. Sam looks over at the people beginning to line up for dinner.

"I am surprised," he says, "when I hear the complaints about having cans of food instead of the caterers. At least people here aren't shooting at you or exploding bombs."

This beats my simple gratefulness for not having to eat freeze-dried food because it's not very tasty. It's one thing to hear stories in the news about Kabul and the war that has now been going on for 17 years. It's another thing entirely to hear about them from a real person. Someone I just happened to meet in the middle of a fire camp, almost as far as one could be from Afghanistan.

*

One of the biggest challenges of resource advising on the Klondike Fire involves a small water mold with the scientific name, *Phytophthora lateralis*. I had an intimate history with this plant pathogen, a nonnative species believed to have originated in Asia and first noted in Seattle, Washington, in the 1920s. Because *Phytophthora* most commonly causes root rot in trees in the cypress genus, *Chamaecyparis*, and because Lawson Cypress, also known as Port-Orford-cedar, is common in the Powers Ranger District, I knew it well from my years working on the Siskiyou.

Port-Orford-cedar is an impressive conifer. It's the only species in its genus that is native to North America, and its range is small, including just southwest Oregon and northwest California. POC, as we commonly referred to it, is an ecologically important tree as it is one of the few conifers that thrive in serpentine soils, which are notable for their challenging growing conditions. Several rare plant species are associated with POC communities, and the trees provide important shade and stability in the areas they inhabit along streams. POC is also an important tree in the wood industry as it's light but strong, fine-grained, and insect-resistant. As *Phytophthora* travels around the landscape via the natural movement of water in streams and rivers, as well as by attaching to vehicles and people's boots during wet weather, the mold kills POC trees by infecting their roots. It's difficult, if not impossible, to eradicate from an area once it's established.

Consequently, prevention is the best method of protection. Washing vehicles and equipment before they enter "clean" areas, as well as closing off areas to traffic during wet times of year, can both be effective measures for limiting *Phytophthora*'s spread. During emergencies, however, these strategies are not so easily implemented. Chad had maps showing infected and noninfected watersheds and where washing stations had been set up. But Klondike had been burning for three months and was a huge fire. Keeping on top of this issue had been tough.

Additionally, fire management teams bristle at the idea of anything preventing them from attacking fires with every tool available. When people, homes, and other resources of value—including, for example, healthy stands of POC—are at risk, this makes sense. However, whether the trees are killed by fire or the root disease, either way, they are gone. I spend time studying the maps and refreshing my mind on an issue I hadn't thought about for many years. *Phytophthora* is a challenge to manage when it's simply moving on its own. During a fire, *we* are also moving it by transporting water, via the ground or air, to dump on the fire. Water taken from infected watersheds had to be sanitized before it could be used in uninfected watersheds. This can be done by bleaching the water before it is put on the ground, but it requires that each division supervisor monitor the activity closely. As a resource advisor, I could explain the reasoning behind the process and emphasize its importance, but I couldn't be out there every day to make sure the mitigations got done. In my time away from the Siskiyou National Forest,

I had forgotten about *Phytophthora*, yet the overwhelming reality of trying to contain such an insidious force feels very familiar.

*

Five days after Klondike blows up, a public meeting is held at the Agness library. The fire management team provides information on operations, weather, safety, and fire behavior. I attend to be available for questions and also to see what people are saying and how they're coping. Fires have been burning for months in northern California and southwest Oregon. People are tired and angry, and they want answers. Why is Klondike roaring again? Where are all the people that should be working on this? *Why isn't the Forest Service doing more?*

The crowd is sizable since almost no one has heeded the evacuation order. Everyone is civil, but the words from the team do little to assuage people's concerns. Not until the sheriff, a local Agness man, offers up praise for the firefighters, as well as compassion for the people, do the residents grow calmer. He does an impressive job, and I tell him so afterward.

"This is my home," he says, simply. "These are my friends and family."

A group of women come over and begin talking with him. They ignore me in a way that reminds me of my outsider status. I drift away, speaking to a few others before heading back down the road to the fire camp.

*

October 23, 2018

My old home is on my mind as I meet several people who are either from Powers or currently working there. Like many small Northwest towns that have been dependent on timber harvesting, Powers hasn't adapted well to the decrease in cutting on federal lands. I haven't visited since 2002, so I know only what people have told me. Unemployment is among the many problems plaguing the little town. One person advising the Klondike management team on road repair tells me that drugs are also currently a big issue. I meet two young men working on Klondike whose parents I worked with in the 1990s. I find that the two men have embodied how their parents did, or didn't, adapt to the changes in forest management that began in the 1980s. From one, I hear a positive report, his mother is well and enjoying retirement. From the other, the news is more negative. His father had a stroke, and the recovery is slow.

"Dad never got over all the trouble the owl caused," this man tells me, his mouth tight, his eyes not quite meeting mine.

I remember his father well. He was the person who often referred disparagingly to my work as "going out to look for dickey birds." I'm sorry for my old coworker, but I really dislike this spurious blame placed upon the spotted owl. The changes to the timber industry are far more complex in origin than that of a single species' needs upending the entire system. From my perspective, based on my understanding of ecosystem function and integrity, I believe the changes have moved in the right direction. Yet I don't want to get into an argument, which would undoubtedly make little difference in this man's opinion. I listen and try not to pass judgment. We have all lived through a tumultuous time in the management of Pacific Northwest forests, and the story isn't over yet.

*

October 24, 2018

Michael, my replacement, has arrived. As a recently retired botanist with the Bureau of Land Management, he is happy to come to Klondike for two weeks. Michael also has substantial experience as a resource advisor, and I feel confident leaving the situation in his hands. I spend several hours before his arrival writing the READ transition plan. This document includes notes on the Port-Orford-cedar situation, descriptions of the two national historic trails impacted by the fire, fire suppression activities that have affected the wilderness and inventoried roadless areas in the national forest, aerial retardant misapplications in both terrestrial and aquatic environments, the availability of straw and seed for erosion control purposes, general repair work left to do, and a list of local contacts. The plan grows to eight pages. I go through everything with Michael in the READ tent before we head over for the evening briefing where I'll introduce him to the incident management team.

This meeting doesn't go particularly well. There is one individual on the team whom I feel has never cared for me and certainly has felt no obligation to follow our recommendations for preventing the spread of the water mold. I've come to expect aggression from him. Yet it's another person who speaks up now as I go over some concerns around washing vehicles and equipment.

"It's all just a waste of time," he says, flatly. "There are too many ways for something to slip through the cracks. A truck that doesn't get washed, or a person who forgets to sanitize his boots. There are new vehicles arriving every day! Even worse, it's begun to rain. It will be impossible to keep track of everything!"

The group is looking at me. There are just three other women in this room of 25 or more men. Chad has left, and I see in an instant that I haven't made enough allies here. No one else counters these declarations or offers a different assessment of the situation on the ground. For my part, I can't disagree that it's a challenging task, but his surrendering, as well as aggrieved, tone doesn't suit me either.

"It's not a perfect system," I say after a moment to acknowledge his concerns. "But we are here to serve the national forest. Port-Orford-cedar is a valuable tree, and the forest leadership team has decided these measures will help to conserve the species, and we must implement those measures as best we can. It won't be very useful to prevent the trees from burning up only to have them die from a disease they got because of suppression activities."

There is only tepid acknowledgment to my words, and soon we are on to another topic. After the briefing, two of the operations supervisors introduce themselves to Michael and welcome him personally to the team. At the same time, the planning section chief, the only woman in an upper-level fire position, comes over to me.

"You're so calm!" she says admiringly. I'm surprised by this given that I feel anything but calm. She then thanks me for my work on Klondike. "It's been good to have you here, Betsy."

"Thank you."

I appreciate her words but also feel depressed. The world of wildland firefighting is still very much a man's world. Though my discomforts and experiences are small compared to women who have suffered abuse and even violence in these environments, it's still wrong to experience sexism in 2018. While women's roles in the Forest Service have grown and been elevated in scope and degree these last 30 years, the fire world has lagged. At the same time, I've had positive, affirming experiences on fires working with both men and women. These must be acknowledged along with the harder ones.

The following morning's briefing is held under a large "circus" tent raised the day before to accommodate the increase in people on Klondike. A PA system has also been set up to make sure everyone can hear. The caterers have returned, as have the shower trucks. I attend the briefing, expecting to introduce Michael, but the team does that for me. Consequently, as he begins his two-minute briefing on natural and cultural resources affected by Klondike, I leave. I'm not sorry I've come to Klondike, though the assignment wasn't at all what I expected. It was great to see the Siskiyou Mountains again and to think about all that the land and the people here have given me. As always, the fire challenged me in different ways, and I'm not sorry about that either. Still, as I drive back down the Rogue River toward the coast and then north, I look forward to returning to the Olympic Peninsula.

The Mountain Goat

Olympic National Forest, 2019

The circle of people before me are all here at 5:30 a.m. on this rainy July morning in 2019 to participate in the Olympic Mountain Goat Translocation project. At the moment, we're standing in an old rock quarry in the Olympic National Forest located just north of the Hamma Hamma River. Into this quarry will soon arrive helicopters carrying mountain goats (*Oreamnos americanus*) in slings that have been captured from the surrounding high country. They will be examined and prepared for their move by truck from the Olympics, where they aren't native, to the Cascade Range 130 miles away, where they are. Needless to say, this is a massive effort. Anytime you're capturing and moving wild animals, the process involves many agencies and people and years of planning, analysis, and public involvement. Dozens of wildlife biologists, veterinarians, contractors, and volunteers are ready now to get to work.

But that may not be today. The clouds are low and the drizzle fine. Overhead, marbled murrelets are "keering" as they fly, west or east, south or north—it's difficult to tell with the cloud layer so low. The dawn avian choir begins to sing with its familiar members: the stalwart robin, a plaintive towhee, an enthusiastic Pacific wren, and several pragmatic juncos. One person in our group comments on the murrelets.

"The clouds have pushed them down," explains Scott Gremel, a longtime spotted owl researcher with Olympic National Park and an expert birder. "But they're just flying through, since there's no structure here." By "structure" he means old-growth forest, stands with centuries-old trees that have large, mossy limbs and cover.

Bryan, the site manager for the goat project at Hamma Hamma and a district wildlife biologist with the WDFW, addresses the group at 6:00 a.m.

"We'll wait an hour or so and see if things improve and the clouds lift," he says. "But it doesn't look good. We might have to call it off for today."

"How is it at Hurricane?" someone asks, referring to Hurricane Ridge in Olympic National Park where the other staging area is located.

"Good," Bryan says, smiling. "It's sunny and clear. They're flying there."

Hurricane Ridge, 35 miles northwest of Hamma Hamma, sits at 5,200 feet elevation, well above the clouds and rain. The situation is disappointing, but most of us here have lived and worked on the peninsula a long time. Rain is a near-constant companion. A friend when one is, for example, doing salamander surveys, a hindrance if one needs to fly a helicopter.

An hour later, we pack up to leave. The supplies for processing the goats are put away, and the exam tables are covered. People begin driving off with plans to meet up again the following morning.

*

In biologist and author Douglas Chadwick's seminal 1983 book about the mountain goat, *A Beast the Color of Winter*, he writes about our Olympic animals.

> Numerically, the Olympic group represents the most successful intro-duction to date anywhere—so successful that the Olympic Peninsula has become the one place in the solar system where you will hear complaints about being overrun with *Oreamnos*. The Olympic goats are descended from a handful of Canada- and Alaska-born animals. I've met them several times and discovered them to be good-looking, friendly, and well-enough-mannered by goat standards. And no one really minds too much that they exemplify the questionable aspects of transplanting . . . mixing up geographic gradations, or clines, of physical traits (the transplanters could at least have taken nearby goats from the Cascades) and skewing the natu-ral evolutionary process. (175)

Chadwick spent years studying goats and also had close calls with animals that weren't so accepting of his presence. As for our "well-mannered" Olympic beasts, time passes and events occur. In recent years, the introduced goats have increased in number and become more problematic. Brought here in the 1920s to provide hunting opportunities, over the decades they'd also become popular as "watchable wildlife." Yet mountain goats aren't like blacktail deer or Roosevelt elk. They don't mind people for the most part and will allow national park and forest visitors to get quite close. At certain times of the year, this is strategic. Unlike deer or elk, goats have a great need for salt. Where they are native in the Cascade Range of Washington, there are more natural sources of salt, but such is not the case in the Olympics. Consequently, the goats must seek this important mineral elsewhere, including where people have peed and/or left their sweaty clothes and packs.

Yet mountain goats *are* wild animals. They are large, muscular creatures and are adept in the mountains in ways that humans are not. Both males and females grow horns that are very sharp (often described as "rapier-like"), which aren't shed and can be lethal weapons used against other goats, predators, or humans. In October 2010, Robert Boardman, a peninsula resident and experienced backcountry enthusiast, was gored to death by a billy goat on Klahanie Ridge near Hurricane Ridge. Though Olympic National Park has always recommended safe practices when hiking around goats, this tragedy increased the concerns of people and these animals overlapping. Analysis began shortly after this to remove the mountain goats from the peninsula once and for all.

The story of the goats' arrival in the Olympics, their subsequent success and population growth, and the uneasy intersection between large, wild animal and human, as well as herbivore and plant, is complicated. Still, the complexity shouldn't completely overshadow the remarkable animals themselves. Living in a vertical world without wings is impressive. Mountain goats have toes that spread wide and hooves with the flexibility to hook into small cracks and rough-textured surfaces that provide friction on smooth rock and ice. They are also well adapted for moving up and down rock faces and other steep pitches. With adeptness and fearlessness, mountain goats cling to, dance along, and leap between ledges and rocky points in ways that defy the notion of limitation. One of the most impressive photographs I've ever seen was on the cover of *National Geographic* some years ago. It showed a goat stretched out between two points in front of a concave cliff face. Joel Sartore, a photographer and the founder of the Photo Ark project, an effort to create a photo archive of global biodiversity, captured this animal in Glacier National Park. The nanny is reaching across open space to lick salt; she seems to float on air, and one can't help but wonder what happened *after* the photograph was taken. Sartore describes her exit as simply retracing her steps, "placing all four feet on the same little ledge [where her back legs had remained], turning around slowly until she could exit, uphill and to the left" (Sartore 2024).

Douglas Chadwick also describes in *A Beast the Color of Winter* watching a billy goat effectively do a cartwheel to get turned around and out of a dead-end situation.

At that point its footing had dwindled so seriously that the animal was no longer able to simply turn around. It did not even seem to be able to lean out far enough to see over its shoulder in order to back up. (1983, 54)

After some tentative foot shuffling the mountaineer braced its front hooves on the ledge and slowly raised the rear of its body off the ground. I watched the beast lift its hindquarters higher and higher and begin to roll them straight over its head. The rear hooves touched the wall here and there for an instant, yet what the creature had effectively carried off by the time it was finished was a complete slow-motion cartwheel, or, technically, what gymnasts call a rollover. I put down my binoculars and remembered to breathe, and this mountain goat, an average-sized billy, strolled off in the direction from which it had come. (1983, 55)

Not only are mountain goats acrobats of the high-country cliffs, but they're also able to live in harsh conditions where snow and cold dominate much of the year. I don't know anyone who hasn't enjoyed seeing the animals in the Olympics. However, most people agree it would be best if they were gone, returned to where they are native and where there are more resources for them. The benefits of removal are many. Alpine vegetation in the Olympics will recover, as will the Cascade Range's population of goats, which has shown declines in recent years due to overhunting. Like most transitions, however, the project will have its negative aspects. Some goats will die during the process. Stress is terrific on the animals as they're captured, sedated, and handled. Finally, after being transported to another land, they must learn quickly of new dangers and opportunities as well as identify new allies and enemies. For people doing the work, the emphasis is on doing everything possible to minimize goat casualties. It's also about accepting that some animals will unfortunately not survive.

*

That evening, rain pours from the heavens. Several of us are staying at one of Olympic National Forest's rental cabins a mile from the staging area. The Hamma Hamma Guard Station was constructed in the mid-1930s by the Civilian Conservation Corps. In the early years, it was used as an administrative site for fire and trail crews before it became a rental cabin for forest visitors. For these two weeks of goat operations, the cabin is reserved for those of us working on the project. Several tents, including mine, are pitched around the building, while a few people sleep inside. The cabin's kitchen and living area are dark, lit dimly by a few gaslights on the walls. Scott and one of his Olympic National Park coworkers, Bill, are staying here, as am I; my supervisor, Susan; and another Forest Service biologist from eastern Washington, Mark. From the WDFW, there's Shelly, a longtime biologist on the North Olympic Peninsula, and Cliff, a retired biologist who entertains us later that night playing his guitar and singing his ballad, "Mountain Goat Promenade."

As Cliff sings, the rain continues. Over the years, I have spent many days out in such weather. As long as it's somewhat warm, I enjoy the wet. Still, it's also great to be warm *and* dry during a rainstorm. We've had a nice meal and have no obligations now beyond relaxing and listening to the music.

Suddenly, something moving fast outside catches my attention. Large windows fill three walls in the living area of the cabin. As I look, another dark flash emerges from the eaves and into the rain. Then another. Bats! I look over at Shelly, who has done bat surveys around the peninsula for many years. She's noticed too and smiles at me. I knew there were bats living at the cabin, and some years ago my coworker Kurt installed a bat box above the building in the hopes of encouraging the animals to occupy it instead of the cabin's roof. In my opinion, it wasn't bad to have bats living in the Hamma Hamma cabin, but there were potential issues, for the bats and for the people staying here. I look out the other window and see them coming from that part of the roof too. They are undeterred by the weather and we watch a few dozen fly out. This is many more than I realized were living here.

*

My fingers sink into the long, thick fur of the tranquilized mountain goat. After a second day of work being canceled due to rain, we are finally on! The nanny before me is quiet but still aware and moving some. Logan, a veterinarian student from Washington State University, has called me over to help hold the animal. Logan is in his early 20s, with short red hair and a perpetual smile. He and a WDFW veterinarian are the "vet team" for this animal. They assess the goat's body condition, draw a blood sample, inject prophylactic medications and fluids, and attach an ear tag. After they finish, another group, the "wildlife team," will take measurements of the goat's horns (and estimate her age), the neck girth, chest girth, and total length. This team also fits her with a radio collar. After all is completed on the table, the goat is carried to a crate where she'll wait until the truck arrives to transport her to the Cascades.

With other goats, I work as the data recorder—a hard job, I'm told. It's vital to get all the information recorded accurately, and several people can be providing numbers and descriptions all at once. One biologist says to me, "I'd rather deal with the goat's kicking legs any day!" However, I'm not worried. I'm a detail person and love recording information. When a helicopter arrives with a goat, I grab three things: the processing form, a green card that goes on the crate the goat will go into, and a bag with all the medications to be given to the vet team. After the goat is weighed on a scale, it's carried to a table for the bulk of the work. At some point, the helicopter crew will pass me the form showing where the animal was captured, the time captured, and the drugs it received. This form will go with the green card on the crate so that the receiving team in the Cascades knows the details of each animal.

Once an animal is on the table, the entire area becomes a "quiet zone." Only the teams assigned to that goat are allowed to be close, and everyone speaks in low voices. If nothing unexpected is found, the process takes approximately 15–20 minutes. The priority of everyone here is the well-being of the animals. Though the goats are sedated, they're also still aware of the strange situation they find themselves in. Once in the crate, they're in a quiet area away from people. If a nanny and kid should come in together, they're put in adjacent crates with "howdy doors," screened windows on the ends, where they can see each other.

All the people I'm working with have much experience handling wild animals. They work calmly and efficiently, and the process is seamless, though not completely without drama. Getting the goats into the crates is one of the trickier parts. After the animal is carried to an open crate, Bryan attaches three pieces of parachute cord, each with a carabiner, to the blindfold and the two ropes that are tying the legs. The wildlife team eases the goat into the crate as far as possible then loosens the ropes and the blindfold. The horn guards are removed last. At the same time that the goat realizes it's no longer restrained, Bryan yanks the three parachute cords, pulling off the blindfold and the hobbles. The goat jumps forward into the crate, and the door is closed. This part goes smoothly most of the time, but one time it doesn't. A 300-pound billy, being coaxed into his crate, suddenly escapes the handlers and the hobbles that have bound his legs. Fortunately, such a possibility had been anticipated. The empty crates have all been arranged to form a corral of sorts. The billy is stopped by this half-circle, restrained a second time, and successfully encouraged into the crate.

After everything is done, the tables are cleaned and readied for the next animal. We all return to our camp chairs and books, waiting for the sound of the helicopter. Susan has organized a "snack shack" several hundred feet from the goat area, complete with more chairs and food, all set up beneath a tent should the rain return. People chat or read; I make notes in my journal.

I'm impressed with everyone here, their years of hands-on experience working with wildlife, their dedication and compassion. I'm not the only one who feels privileged to be able to see a mountain goat up close. I also may not be the only one to feel some ambivalence about the work. When I mention to one person that it makes me uncomfortable to see animals in these circumstances, he nods in agreement.

"Yes," he says. "But I guess it's the difference between concern for the population and concern for the individual."

Though I don't believe these two considerations have to be mutually exclusive, I know what he means. The decision has been made to move these mountain goats. The environmental impact statement outlined a program to capture and translocate as many goats as possible, then lethally remove individuals that can't be captured safely. From an individual or population perspective, the work happening now has the most benefits. Also, the released animals seem to be taking well to their new home, though there have been mortalities. I was part of the fisher reintroduction, and we all knew that those first animals coming from Canada would have challenges getting established here. In wildlife management, as in life, there are compromises to accept in the service of a larger goal.

*

This wasn't my first time being close to a mountain goat. In 2015, at Lake of the Angels in Olympic National Park, less than 10 miles from the staging area, I had an unexpected night encounter with a curious goat. During a marmot survey with my friend and backpacking partner, Carrie, we found ourselves in an area frequented by goats. Though park employees had hazed the animals before our arrival, this had had little effect. I didn't like the idea of throwing rocks at the animals, but this is one of the recommended ways to discourage goats from coming closer. Shouting and waving one's arms are other ways. We did all three, and the visiting goats, eager to access our kitchen area, moved off only reluctantly.

During our trip, I'd been kept awake by Carrie's snoring. One night at about 2:00 a.m., I grabbed my sleeping pad and bag and moved away from the tents. A nearly full moon brightened the sky, but a few stars still popped in the darkness. They flickered and reminded me of the vastness of time and space and my very small place in both continuums. The deep night further emphasized the aptness of this area being named the Valley of Heaven.

I had just closed my eyes and begun to fall asleep when I heard footsteps. I listened for a minute as the heavy footfalls came closer. I didn't need my head-lamp to see the huge frame of a mountain goat standing 15 feet from me; its massive, white presence filled my vision. The goat didn't seem aggressive, and I wasn't particularly worried, though I didn't care for the idea of being licked or having my sleeping bag chewed on (Dave Shea had once told me of a fire lookout in Glacier National Park who woke one morning to find a mountain goat in the structure licking his toes).

Reluctantly, I stood up, gathered my stuff, and headed back to the tent. The goat, meanwhile, moved into our kitchen area and started nosing around the pots. I yelled once, but it continued its investigations. We had washed everything thoroughly, and our food was in bear canisters, so it wouldn't get any tasty rewards from these humans. In any case, it was now 2:30 a.m. and I couldn't be chasing a goat around in the middle of the night. Between Carrie snoring on one side of me and the goat rattling around the kitchen on the other, I would have to find sleep somehow.

*

Capturing goats and processing them ends by early afternoon. Any later and it becomes too warm, and the well-furred animals can easily overheat from the stress. The refrigerator truck has arrived, and the process of loading the crates begins. The goats, quiet and not appearing particularly anxious, look out through the howdy doors. A father and daughter from Monroe, Washington, have arrived as volunteer drivers. They live close to where the goats will be released and are pleased to be helping on the project. After all the crates are loaded and tied securely, the truck's back door is closed. We wish the people and goats a safe journey.

Everyone disperses for the rest of the day. I drive up the Hamma Hamma valley. The area isn't closed to the public, and we have employees meeting visitors and explaining the goat project and fielding questions. Just the summer before, most of the Hamma Hamma watershed *had* been closed to visitors. The Maple Fire, started in early August by bigleaf maple tree thieves, had shut down the watershed for the firefighting efforts that ensued. As I worked on Maple as a resource advisor, I drove one afternoon along the river to look for some different views of the fire as it burned along the north face of Jefferson Ridge (an unusual occurrence compared to the Bear Gulch and Big Hump Fires, which had burned primarily along south-facing slopes).

As I drove around a bend that day, I saw farther up the road a big, white, fluffy dog sniffing around in the fire ring of a dispersed campsite. I slowed down to pick up the dog and try to return it to its owner; however, when I got closer I saw the animal was a mountain goat! I couldn't believe I was seeing a goat so far down from the cliffs and the high country that protect them from predators such as cougars and bears. I stopped, got several photos, then encouraged it to move on (without throwing rocks). Upon investigation of the fire ring, I found many discarded oyster shells, the draw for an animal requiring salt.

*

The next morning, we're all up before light, getting ready and watching the bats return to the cabin after their night of foraging. The skies are clear, and all indications point to good weather for capturing goats. People are in high spirits; the news from the Cascades is that the releases have gone well. At the staging area, several new volunteers have arrived. The snack shack is hopping with everyone getting coffee and treats. I continue recording data, but I also assist in carrying one animal from where it's placed by the helicopter on the ground in the sling to the scale where it will be weighed. This animal is a billy, and he's heavy. Another animal this morning has "prolonged time on the table" due to having mouth sores, which the vet team treats and stitches up.

The last animal I work on is another billy, a beautiful male with all of his winter coat shed away and new, clean white fur taking its place. I write down all the vet team tells me about the treatments he's getting, the samples taken, and his general body condition. The wildlife team moves in to estimate age, take measurements, and attach the radio collar. Cliff, the composer of Mt. Goat Promenade, examines the horns for the age estimate. After a minute or so, he tells me, "Five to six years."

I next copy information from the helicopter team's intake form to the processing form. This animal was captured on Mt. Stone, one of the peaks above Lake of the Angels. A five-or-six-year-old animal means that it was alive and an adult when Carrie and I did our marmot survey there in 2015. As I staple the form and green card to the crate, I look briefly in the howdy door at the billy, wondering if he's the one I met that night in the dark four years before.

*

During my last evening on the project, Susan and Mark drive to the Hamma Hamma Store on the Hood Canal and buy a few dozen oysters. That night we build a big fire, grill oysters, and watch the bats come and go. Not only have they been emerging from the roof and the bat box, but they're also flying out from behind the window shutters, which have been fastened open. Mark takes a small flashlight and looks behind one shutter.

"Hey, there are pups back here," he whispers, excitedly.

Sure enough, several young bats along with the adults are squeezed behind the protective space. Apart from having more bats than we realized, the Hamma Hamma cabin is also a maternal colony. During the evening oyster feast, Andrew, a biologist with the Quinault Indian Nation, counts more than 100 bats leaving the bat box above the building. I stand for 10 minutes on the south side and count 35 leaving the eaves and shutters.

Later that night in my tent, my thoughts are spinning with goats and bats and even barred owls, since Mark and Susan found a pair and two juveniles near the cabin. Additionally, someone is snoring loudly from another tent. Though I put in my earplugs, I can still hear him. After some deliberation, I take my sleeping bag and go inside the building.

The couch in the living room is free, and I settle in. I ponder the many people who have slept here over the decades. From the crews who first built the cabin, to the many forest workers who managed the land before us, to the guests who come to get away from their busy lives and enjoy the natural world. I'm nearly asleep when I hear scratching from inside the walls. The bats are leaving or returning; I'm not sure which, but it's a comforting sound.

The Barred Owl

Olympic National Forest, 2020–22

One evening, during the winter of 2020, I encountered a barred owl sitting on the bird feeder in our garden. I'd been taking the garbage out, lost in thought, when I suddenly looked up to see the owl perched just five feet away. The bird didn't move as I stopped abruptly. We stared at each other in the dim glow from the porchlight. Rustling noises in our viburnum bushes took the owl's focus from me, and I knew then that it was here for the rats that enjoyed free meals of birdseed. Though I'd been able to live trap a few of the rats and transport them to a nearby wild area, some remained.

I backed away quietly. Leaving the garbage temporarily on the porch, I went to tell my wife, Barbara. We then watched the owl from inside the house. A paragon of patience, the bird remained on the curved metal hanger where the feeder dangled, turning around occasionally, ever alert. Unfortunately, our garden was just too lush; finding a clear path to the rat probably wasn't going to happen.

*

Over the years, I have met so many barred owls that I feel I know them better than spotted owls, the species that helped set my career in motion. They have responded during spotted owl surveys and called unbidden during backpacking trips. I've seen individuals dust bathing on national forest roads, flying in front of my car, and being mobbed by robins (the robins' vocalizing being the only way I knew of the owl's presence). During one warm day, while I drove to a project site with the window rolled down, I heard the distinctive whistle begging call of a juvenile owl. Stopping, I easily found two barred owlets that had fledged and left the nest but were still dependent on their parents for food.

Barred owls are also no longer only found in the landscapes of national forests and parks. Near our home, pairs of owls sing duets at night, and I observed one, shortly after the encounter at the bird feeder, sitting on the electrical line above our garden. Another time, I saw a bird in the state park near our home that had just grabbed a very large rat. On yet another occasion, a woman staying with us said that a barred owl "dive-bombed" her while she walked around the track at the nearby middle school. This last is not an uncommon interaction between barred owls and people in urban settings.

The lives of northern spotted owls and barred owls are now intertwined in a complex, rapidly evolving way. In the 1980s, the spotted owl in the Pacific Northwest came to symbolize a tremendous shift in the management of the region's temperate old-growth forests. Studies during the prior decade began showing that populations of these owls were declining due to overharvesting of the ancient forest. This world beneath 300-foot-tall trees provided what the owls required: centuries-old, broken-topped Douglas fir and western hemlock trees for nesting, multiple canopy layers that fostered stable microclimates, and plentiful prey such as woodrats, flying squirrels, and red tree voles. Until European Americans began harvesting these forests, the northern spotted owl lived in a relatively stable environment alongside other species with which it had long coevolved.

Yet while northern spotted owls have undeniably been negatively impacted by the loss of habitat then and now, particularly as we enter an age of unprecedented forest loss to mega wildfires, there is also another grave concern to the species. The barred owl, or *Strix varia*, named for the varied directions their "bars" assume on their undersides, has become a primary threat. A member of the same genus as spotted owls, barred owls are native to eastern North America but are also now present in many habitats across the Pacific Northwest. In just a few short decades, the conservation of northern spotted owls has grown from focusing mostly on the maintenance and even creation of older forests to also removing an invasive species.

*

When I began working for the Forest Service in western Oregon conducting spotted owl inventories, we occasionally heard barred owls. They looked nearly identical to spotted owls, with their solid, dark eyes and similar size (though barred owls are slightly larger); however, they didn't behave the same. Spotted owls came readily to our calls. They took the mice we offered, the method employed to locate nest trees, and often stayed with us, unperturbed by our presence, long after their interest in the mice had waned. By contrast, though barred owls also responded to our calls, they exhibited none of the "friendliness" of spotted owls. They remained high in the canopy, guarded but vocal. Hearing a barred owl (we rarely saw them) was noted on our survey forms along with other owl species of the Pacific Northwest.

In the 1983 editions of both *National Geographic* and *Golden Field Guides to Birds of North America* (reference books I used when I began surveying), the range maps for barred owls didn't include the West Coast of North America. The *Golden* guide described the owl as "common in southern swamps and river bottoms; less common, but widespread, in northern woods" (176). The *National Geographic* guide acknowledged that the "northwestern portion of range is expanding rapidly; may soon overlap range of similar Spotted Owl" (240). Both guides did show the barred owl's presence at that time throughout the boreal forest in Canada.

These descriptions align with what my mentor Dave Shea knew from personal experience. Dave's work in Glacier National Park in Montana in the 1960s and 1970s had brought him into contact with the westward-moving owl, a previously unknown resident of the area. In the summer 1974 issue of the *Condor*, he described observing or hearing barred owls at least 13 different times and concluded that "there is good evidence for a southwestern extension of range [from eastern Montana] and that this species is a permanent resident within Glacier National Park" (222). Two years later, Avery Taylor Jr. and Eric Forsman, the latter of whom became a preeminent spotted owl biologist and was the first to document the owls' dependence on older forests, described continuing movements of the barred owl, including the first records for Washington and Oregon. Taylor and Forsman wrote in the winter issue of the *Condor*, "It seems doubtful that two species so similar in general food habits and habitat requirements could coexist in the same areas for long, but this relationship remains to be investigated" (1976, 560–61).

There are other examples of wildlife species expanding their ranges, but few have done so with the speed of the barred owl. The species' adaptability and strength are eerily human-like in this regard. In fact, the best theory as to the birds' motivations for moving west is that they were simply following the European settlers across the northern Great Plains. The massive expanse of open country—maintained in part by fire, natural and human-caused, and unsuitable for a forest bird—suddenly grew dotted with new towns and communities where people had planted trees. These miniforests provided cover and nesting structures, while human presence necessarily fostered growth in rat and mouse populations. As these early European Americans began to exclude and suppress natural fires, more forests grew. The larger great-horned owl has perhaps, by the smaller owl avoiding the larger, helped keep the barred owl from permanently taking up residence in parts of the Midwest; additionally, the increase in forests has helped the barred owl to avoid the great-horned owl.

Fifty years after Dave Shea's first encounters with the birds in Glacier National Park, *Strix varia* now occupy many forested habitats in western North America and Canada. They are found in towns as well as wilderness landscapes, along river bottoms and at higher elevations. They are aggressive and, like any wildlife species, determined to secure resources for themselves. They will kill spotted owls and other smaller owls in their quest for territories, nest trees, and food. Barred owls have smaller home ranges than spotted owls, can use a wider range of habitats and live at greater densities than spotted owls, and are generalist predators, able to eat a wide variety of other species in addition to the arboreal rodents that spotted owls depend on. Recent range maps illustrate these geographic changes: British Columbia, a thicker swath of land across the middle of Canada, the Coastal Mountains and Cascade Range of Washington and Oregon to northwestern California, eastern Washington, northern Idaho, and more of western Montana all now have barred owls. Very importantly, the barred owl's range now completely overlaps that of the northern spotted owl.

*

Our understanding of the conservation needs of the northern spotted owl, and translating what we know into management actions to maintain viable populations of the owl, have evolved during the last four decades. In the 1990 decision to list the northern spotted owl under the Endangered Species Act, loss of nesting habitat from timber harvest was the primary concern. Four years later, the 1994 Northwest Forest Plan outlined long-term management strategies to maintain and restore habitat for old-growth dependent species. A wealth of knowledge went into developing different alternatives to manage millions of acres of forested landscape within the range of the species. There was much to consider: different ownerships and different management goals within those ownerships; the biology of the owl and its need for complex forests, stable microclimates, adequate prey populations, and protection from predators; and the economic needs of rural communities. Though the Northwest Forest Plan addressed the requirements of hundreds of species, the northern spotted owl was a primary focus. As such, monitoring of owl populations would be crucial in evaluating the success of this plan.

In 1999, the Northern Spotted Owl Effectiveness Monitoring Plan described two objectives: assessing changes in spotted owl populations and trends and assessing changes in the amount and distribution of habitat. There was no mention of barred owls. However, in 2005, the Northwest Forest Plan's 10-year status report noted two emerging issues potentially contributing to the loss of northern spotted owls: West Nile virus and the "apparent negative interaction between barred owls and spotted owls" (Lint 2005, v).

It's hard not to be impressed by the barred owl and what it has achieved as a species. And if its arrival in the Pacific Northwest hadn't precipitated intense interference and competition with northern spotted owls, as well as other owl species, it might remain cautiously admired. Yet the barred owl's presence here is consequential, and the potential loss of a top native predator is no small thing for an ecosystem. Additionally, very recent research in 2023 has shown that barred owls may be having even broader ecological impacts on Northwest forest ecosystems. With their generalist diet and ability to use more habitat types, as many as three to four barred owl pairs have been observed living in the area of one spotted owl territory in the Oregon Coast Range. Consequently, barred owls are exerting novel predation pressure on some species of arthropods and amphibians that spotted owls don't typically eat, including the rough-skinned newt, a salamander toxic to most would-be predators.

*

Removing a species from the landscape once it's established is a great challenge for land managers. Unless the work is taking place in a largely closed environment, for example, an island, it's virtually impossible to achieve complete eradication. Yet it's work that is often undertaken because the impacts to native fauna can be so serious. Invasive animals and their associated effects, including the extinctions of native species and the alterations of ecosystems, are important causes of global losses of biodiversity.

During the spring of 2022, I observed barred owls on four occasions in the space of two weeks. One incident involved robins mobbing an owl. As I watched, one particularly bold (or suicidal) robin body-slammed into the owl. Another involved an owl flying directly in front of my car with a robin nestling in its talons (and a group of robins in hot pursuit). After these observations, I decided to write more about this amazing, and, in the Pacific Northwest, problematic species. I contacted Dave Wiens, a research wildlife biologist with the U.S. Geological Survey in Corvallis, Oregon, who has studied the interactions between barred owls and northern spotted owls since 2006. In 2015, Dave and his colleagues began an experiment across the range of the northern spotted owl to see if the lethal removal of barred owls (using shotguns) could benefit spotted owl populations. The goals of the work were to see if (1) competitive interactions with barred owls caused population declines of spotted owls, and (2) if they did, to see if the removal of barred owls could be an effective tool in the long-term management of both species. The work took place in five areas of Oregon, Washington, and California that had nearly 30 years of demography data on spotted owls, information crucial to putting the results of the removals into context, and where, prior to the experiment, strong declines in resident spotted owls had been observed. These study areas were divided into treatment, or removal, areas, and control, or no removal, areas. From 2015–19, nearly 2,500 barred owls were removed from the treatment areas.

The results of these removals showed consistent or increasing numbers of resident spotted owls in treatment areas and sharp decreases in areas without removals. Specifically, removing barred owls resulted in a strong positive effect on northern spotted owl survival and a weaker, but still positive, effect on spotted owl dispersal and recruitment.

"We've clearly shown that removals can slow or arrest population declines of northern spotted owls at localized scales," Dave told me. "So removals implemented under a carefully designed, adaptive management strategy in select areas would at the very least provide options for recovery of spotted owls. This would also provide time to develop novel alternatives to removal."

By the time the Northwest Forest Plan's 25-year status report on spotted owl populations was published in 2021 in the journal *Biological Conservation*, what had long been suspected was stated definitively: barred owls were, and are, having a significant impact on northern spotted owls. Occupancy modeling corroborated other analyses showing that if barred owls are present in a landscape, spotted owls are likely to abandon territories and less likely to recolonize sites. The report concluded that "without removal or reduction of [barred owl] populations, the more realistic scenario is probably that [northern spotted owls] will become extirpated from portions of their range and possibly linger on as small populations in other areas until those populations are eliminated because of catastrophic events, resulting in the extinction of this subspecies" (Franklin et al. 2021, 18–19). One example of such catastrophic events includes the 2020 Labor Day wildfires in the Pacific Northwest that burned 8,900 square kilometers of forest, including 1,510 square kilometers of spotted owl nesting and roosting habitat.

*

Owls evoke mystery and awe and often strong emotions in people. In July 2022, the U.S. Fish & Wildlife Service published a notice of intent in the *Federal Register* to prepare an environmental impact statement for a barred owl management strategy, which would include removal. Several online responses describe anger and disgust that the killing of one animal is the primary solution to saving another. Some feel the real issue is the loss of habitat and that that's where conservation efforts should focus. Commenters associated with land or wildlife management agencies were more supportive of removal programs, yet the fact remains that the situation, and the story of how we got to this critical juncture, are very complicated.

Most biologists I know feel ambivalent about removing barred owls. The science is clear—this nonnative species is having irrevocable impacts on northern spotted owls. The science also seems clear that barred owls are not the ecological equivalent of northern spotted owls, a counter to the argument that one owl species is simply replacing another. Ryan Baumbusch's doctoral research, published in 2023, at Oregon State University analyzing the diet of individual barred owls obtained during the removal experiments documented a staggering variety and amount of prey taken. All these prey species now have a new predator to deal with, and the consequences to the forest ecosystem may be quite serious and not fully known until they happen. Yet for all that *is* known about spotted owls, barred owls, and their prey, wildlife management is rarely about science alone. It's about people with different opinions, ecosystems that are rapidly evolving, and tremendous uncertainty. Additionally, just removing barred owls, a management strategy that would necessarily have to be ongoing, will not be enough to recover northern spotted owl populations. The availability of suitable nesting, foraging, and dispersal habitat well-distributed across the owl's range is still crucial.

Wildlife management is also about what we as humans uniquely understand among the world's organisms: that there are issues of ethics and responsibility and the need at times for action based on well-designed and analyzed scientific endeavors. Changes in habitat, including the loss of old-growth forests in the Pacific Northwest, the development of treed landscapes across the northern Great Plains, and barred owls moving through the boreal forest in Canada, have connected the fates of these closely related owls. People may not have physically carried barred owls to western North America, but we have facilitated their migration and altered the landscapes they found upon arriving. What is our role now? No matter what we do or don't do in the coming years, one or both species are going to be affected.

Barred owls, like spotted owls, are beautiful, amazing raptors. They are also strong and resourceful. As he's studied both species over the years, Dave Wiens says he's been amazed by the barred owls. In addition to the rough-skinned newts observed in barred owl stomachs, the skull of a red-tailed hawk was also found. Another surprising aspect has been the scope of their population expansion. "While many owls and raptors are in trouble these days," reflects Dave, "barred owls are flourishing."

23

Bearing Witness

Olympic National Forest, 2019–20

Like Debaran Kelso, Scott Gremel is one of the few people who has worked with northern spotted owls for most of his career. When I told him recently that I'd also begun my career with the Forest Service surveying for owls, he laughed and said, "Yes, and like a normal person, you went on to other things!"

Perhaps, but I admire the focus and dedication of those who devote their lives to one animal. I've known Scott since I started working on the peninsula, but I haven't known him well. Fortunately, during the mountain goat project, I got an opportunity to talk with him more.

Most days, after the capture work had finished, Scott spent the afternoons placing passive autonomous recording units, or ARUs, in the Hamma Hamma watershed. These devices, each about half the size of a cereal box, are part of a new remote owl survey method, which Scott has been coordinating for both Olympic National Forest and Park. A successful pilot study in 2017 of the ARUs efficacy in detecting spotted owls and other species began a gradual move away from the mark-recapture methods Debaran Kelso did for many years or the callback surveys I was hired to do in 1986. Since we no longer harvest old-growth trees (i.e., nesting habitat for spotted owls) on the Olympic, we simply assume that all older forest near our project areas is occupied. We plan mitigations that will minimize disturbance from noise and human activities to any birds potentially living nearby. This is the safest approach from a management perspective. While the demography study yielded much information at specific owl sites, there have always been large parts of the forest and park where we don't know the current status of the owls. The hope is that information from ARUs, which can cover more of the landscape, will help fill in these gaps in our knowledge.

One afternoon after finishing with the goats, I accompanied Scott in the field while he set up the recorders. There were three stations above the Hamma Hamma cabin, and we drove up the road that switchbacks along Cabin Creek, a tributary to the river. After parking, we hiked a short distance upslope to the first station. Scott has worked in Olympic National Park since 1994. He told me that he grew up in Indiana, was interested in birds from an early age, and had been inspired by a well-known birder named, appropriately, Bud Starling.

"He was a scamp but also a great guy," Scott said. "Bud did these birding walks in local parks and most everyone who went was older, so I think he appreciated having this young teenager along too. He kind of took me under his wing, so to speak."

With Bud Starling, Scott went on bird-a-thons around the Midwest and learned to bird by ear. After getting an undergraduate degree with a focus on studying bird communities in forested areas following clearcut harvest, Scott found himself in the Pacific Northwest. He worked for a few different agencies doing spotted owl surveys and forestry work before landing a job in 1994 as a crew member on the Olympic National Park owl survey team.

"When I got this job, working with owls in the Olympics," he said with a smile, "I thought that was the coolest thing ever."

In the 1980s and early 1990s, Olympic National Park conducted trail-based spotted owl surveys, and the resulting estimate of their numbers was low. This was partly because many of the park's trails are along rivers near large, open floodplains, but that's not where the owls were living. After the listing of the owl under the Endangered Species Act in 1990, a more thorough inventory began. Approximately 30 random plots of 2,000 acres each were placed across the landscape, with six to seven three-mile-long flag lines per plot. Stations one-quarter-mile apart were then established along each flag line. Scott explained that the crew hiked these transects four times, once for the initial setup and three times to survey. It was labor-intensive work, but it resulted in a better estimate of the number of spotted owls in the park, which was approximately 230 pairs. The crew also detected a few barred owls, but these weren't heard often.

"We thought of barred owls as an edge species," Scott said, "and that they wouldn't come into pristine old growth. Of course, we were wrong."

By 2019, "the coolest job ever" had evolved into a 25-year relationship between Scott, the mountains, and the owls. When I asked him about particularly memorable experiences he's had with the birds, he found it hard to pinpoint just one. But after a moment, he described sitting on a slope observing a female owl below him. Suddenly, she flew down to a branch just above the ground and started making the barking alarm call. In the next moment, a bobcat walked by below her. The bobcat never noticed Scott and didn't seem disturbed by the owl.

"For all I know," Scott mused, "this interaction happened every day."

The first ARU station was not far from the road, but I still lagged behind Scott and his long legs. When I caught up with him, he was pulling the unit out of his pack.

"There's really not much to setting these up," he explained. "It's nothing like doing remote cameras."

Scott was referring to the remote camera setup that requires finding the right size trees the right distance apart and getting the bait and camera attached and the camera aimed properly. "With these," he said, "you just need to make sure they're programmed for the correct recording times. For this protocol, we record during two four-hour blocks each night and also 10 minutes every hour to get some periodic daytime information."

I took photos while Scott attached the microphones to each side of the device and then tied it to the tree. The ARU looked a bit like a square-headed gremlin with two large ears. The work took only a few minutes, and then Scott was ready for the next site. Several months after this trip in the Hamma Hamma, he and I met for coffee. I wanted to know what he thought about using ARUs compared to traditional survey methods for finding spotted owls.

"The biggest concern I have," Scott told me, "is that we're losing the personal experience with the species, and with that a certain kind of understanding of the animals. We'll get occupancy data for them, but we won't have any survival or reproductive information like we get with the mark-recapture work. Basically, there's no information generated at all about individuals. For example, we might get high numbers for occupancy, but we won't know which birds are being recorded with the ARUs. Something we've seen over the years is the movement of adults between territories, which is pretty unusual. This shows them being driven out by barred owls. Those kinds of details won't come to light with the recorders.

"Still, there are positive aspects to surveying this way," Scott continued. "We can get a landscape scale estimate of occupancy, and we can also detect other species. We also get much better data on the presence of barred owls. Having these recordings creates a permanent record so the data can be analyzed differently in the future if new analysis tools are developed. A really important piece also is that this work is noninvasive. In some areas, the birds get hooted a lot, and that's hard on them."

I thought about this last part, which is something all of us in the profession have talked about for years. Hooting to call in a spotted owl works because you,

Scott Gremel of Olympic National Park setting up an autonomous recording unit in Olympic National Forest, 2019. USDA Forest Service by Betsy L. Howell.

Autonomous recording unit currently being used in Olympic National Forest and Park. USDA Forest Service by Betsy L. Howell.

the surveyor, are imitating an intruder in the bird's territory. An owl flies in and, in this case, finds a mouse and a free meal, but the impetus to come is still about defending its territory, which is stressful. Additionally, there have always been ethical issues for biologists about feeding mice to the birds.

"I think using recorders is a good complement to traditional surveys," Scott added. "It seems to work best for determining when spotted owls *aren't* there—that is, nonoccupancy. And when spotted owls *are* found, it would be best to have people visiting the stands to confirm the identity of the individuals and their breeding status."

*

In early 2020, I also talked with Damon Lesmeister, the research team leader for the Bioacoustics Laboratory at the Forest Service's Pacific Northwest Research Station in Corvallis, Oregon. He was coordinating the range-wide effort to use bioacoustics to monitor northern spotted owl populations. Damon told me that while acoustic technology for wildlife surveys has been around for several decades, it's just in the last 10 years or so that the field equipment has become rugged, portable, and reliable enough to deploy in the forests of the Pacific Northwest. Advances in processing the data generated from ARUs have also been key.

"Only in the past year," Damon said, "do we have high-throughput methods to rapidly process and automatically identify spotted owl calls from large volumes of sound recordings. We are also quite meticulous about not having any false-positives in the data that are analyzed. We validate all detections of spotted owls with trained human observers, filtering out any non–spotted owl calls. This is especially important at sites where we have only a few spotted owl calls. We want to be 100 percent sure those are indeed spotted owls. We're also filtering out any human callback surveys that are recorded."

Damon was less skeptical of the technology than Scott and explained the advantages of using ARUs, many of which Scott had acknowledged too. These include the noninvasive aspect, the ability to gather much more sound data over a longer period of time, being able to record the vocalizations of multiple species and to document the complex inter- and intraspecific interactions among them in a natural setting. In addition, the fieldwork is safer for technicians because it can be done during the day.

Some of the cons associated with bioacoustic monitoring are the mirror images of the pros. The knowledge and experience provided by long-term owl researchers, who know individual birds, histories, and territories intimately, would be lost by using only bioacoustic methods. Bioacoustics provides a powerful means to assess occupancy and trends (from site-level colonization and extinction rates) at the population level. However, the recorders don't capture detailed data on survival, nesting status, or the movement of individual owls that can provide more insight into the mechanisms driving those trends. The upfront costs of purchasing bioacoustic equipment can be steep for large-scale monitoring, yet over multiple years, using recorders is a cost-effective survey method. ARUs also need to be replaced as they wear out or are lost due to theft, wildlife damage, or wildfire events.

"For the same or less time in the field," Damon explained, "we're now obtaining 1,400 hours of recordings spread over six weeks at each site. But all of these sound files need to be processed, validated, managed, and stored, all of which are time-consuming and add to the costs associated with bioacoustics. Yet I do see bioacoustics becoming the primary method for studying owls. I think about how valuable it would be if we had recordings from several decades ago, before forests went through massive changes due to disturbance and invasive species."

Beyond the pros and cons of the ARUs compared to traditional survey methods, and questions about which one works best as budgets shrink, is the reality of spotted owls continuing to decline on the Olympic Peninsula. For this situation, Scott also had a bigger question.

"I wonder about the utility of doing surveys to watch a species go extinct," he said bluntly. "What do you do with a study when your animal goes extinct? What other species has this happened to? I don't know any."

I remembered my conversations with Debaran and her experiences with the owls becoming more silent over the years, which might translate into them being recorded less readily by the ARUs. "Maybe the situation is better than we think," I offered. "Maybe there are more owls out there than we know?"

Scott considered this. "I think Debaran is more optimistic than me. But the other thing I wonder is why monitor a species if you're not going to do anything different management-wise? Options for improving conditions for spotted owls are either habitat protection or barred owl removal, and Olympic National Park currently isn't doing either of these. Are we just bearing witness to their demise? And is that useful? I think at this point it would be more help-

ful to take the monitoring funds and put them into something more worthwhile, like barred owl control."

I thought about this. To be fair, the national park is already a protected
landscape, but I understood Scott's statement that the park wasn't involved in
new efforts to conserve habitats.

"How do you feel about that?" I asked him. "That is, about the demise of
the spotted owl?"

Scott didn't hesitate. "Oh, I'm over it," he said. I must have looked shocked,
for he added quickly, "I've been living with this for a long time."

*

One month after having coffee with Scott and talking with Damon in February
2020, I invited Debaran over as well. It had been almost six years since I'd accompanied her on her surveys and wrote the article for *American Forests*. We talked
fairly regularly, but it had also been a long time since I'd been properly updated on
her work and the owls she knew so well. Debaran had begun doing limited ARU
work at 6 sites where she'd also received funding to monitor in the traditional way
(the other 18 sites she'd usually monitored were now being surveyed solely with
ARUs). Initially reluctant to work with the ARUs after decades of knowing the
owls in her study area so well, Debaran still felt grateful; without approval to use
the standard methods in conjunction with the ARUs, she wouldn't be doing any
surveys with owls. Also, she saw the potential advantage of using the two methods
together, which can reveal more information than either one alone. She would
install one ARU as close as possible to the nest trees at her sites.

"It's still very important to know who the birds are," she said, voicing the
same concerns as Scott. "I worry about there not being people on the ground.
Researchers and managers need to have an intimate connection with the landscape and the species."

To demonstrate this, Debaran shared an update about the female owl I had
met when I went out in the field with her in 2014. She found this same individual in 2019, and while the owl didn't seem to have nested, it was also late in
the season when she was found. Debaran reminded me that she first banded
this female in 2005 and at that time had estimated her to have been a subadult.
So at their last meeting, the owl was 16 years old.

"She looked a bit old," Debaran said, "and white in the face, but of course,
lovely as ever!"

At another site I visited with Debaran in 2015, where the owls had been nesting in a grandmother Alaskan yellow cedar tree, the pair also nested in 2019. Debaran documented the male taking mice to the tree but could learn no more. Later in the season, hikers reported seeing an owl in the area. When Debaran returned, however, she couldn't find any birds.

In a third area, the spotted owl pair nested, and later Debaran found one youngster that had been killed. When the female at that site flew in, she offered a mouse, which the bird then took to a second juvenile. This youngster had been quiet until its parent offered the meal.

"The recorder likely wouldn't have picked up the juvenile," Debaran said. "Therefore, I don't think we would have known if the pair had successfully nested without me, or someone, being there to observe the young. And we definitely wouldn't have known about the mortality."

While ARUs are out for several weeks on the landscape, they aren't usually out for an entire breeding season. They also don't record continuously. With Debaran's juvenile in this example, it might have called at another time, and the sound would have been recorded. Or, perhaps not. There are simply many events and interactions going on in the forest that humans never see or hear. But that doesn't mean they're not happening.

*

My conversations with Scott, Damon, and Debaran made me reflect on my own work on the peninsula, which has been varied but also focused mostly on Pacific martens. By the summer of 2019, after using remote cameras to look intensively for this small mustelid for 11 years, we had only four remote camera stations that had photographed a marten out of hundreds placed in Olympic National Forest and Park as well as across other ownerships for other species' inventories. All four detections were in the same location in Olympic National Park, in the upper Hoh watershed near the base of Mt. Olympus. Similar to Scott's question with spotted owls, I've also wondered whether we've been surveying only to document the demise of the marten from the peninsula. And if so, is this useful? Is bearing witness the best we can do? I have remained hopeful of finding martens, or at least, I haven't been fully convinced that they were gone as a population. However, a few animals in the Hoh, and one photographed opportunistically in 2015 by a rock climber on Mt. Cruiser, 27 miles from the Hoh, do not constitute a functioning population.

Still, having hope in what we don't know or don't completely understand doesn't have to be considered naive. In late 2018, the scientific journal *Conservation Genetics* published a paper by Cody Aylward and colleagues about martens that were rediscovered in southern Vermont after having gone undetected for several years despite systematic monitoring after animals were reintroduced to the area. While the authors couldn't definitively say the rediscovered martens, whose DNA was analyzed via tissue samples, represented the translocated animals or a relictual population, they did state that "both of these scenarios indicate that marten persisted in southern Vermont largely undetected from 1989 to 2010, even when systematically monitored" (Aylward, Muroch, and Kilpatrick 2018, 284).

In another study by Jennifer Grauer et al. published the year before in *Biological Conservation*, the genetic composition of martens reintroduced to Wisconsin from source populations in Colorado, Minnesota, and Ontario, Canada, was found to reflect the Minnesota and Ontario transplants, but the signatures from the Colorado animals had disappeared. The researchers also detected genetic clusters that could not be attributed to any of the populations from which the transplants originated. The authors wrote that these clusters potentially arose "from an early reintroduction attempt or the persistence of a cryptic native population of martens" (Grauer et al. 2017, 246).

There are other examples as well of species that were believed to be extirpated from a particular area but were subsequently found. After fishers were thought to be gone from western Montana during the middle of the last century, animals were translocated to the region in the early 1960s and late 1980s from British Columbia, Minnesota, and Wisconsin. From 1993 to 2005, the genetic composition of 85 trapped fishers was examined. Similar to the reintroduced martens in Wisconsin, almost half of these fishers had groups of genes not found in any of the British Columbia, Minnesota, or Wisconsin populations, demonstrating that they were, in fact, descendants of a relic population. In other situations, animals once gone from certain areas may return on their own if the forces that precipitated their disappearance have been removed. In Washington, this has happened with wolves, bald eagles, and wolverines. Almost immediately following the deconstruction of the Elwha River dams in Olympic National Park, salmon and bull trout were observed swimming in upstream waters where they'd not been seen for a century.

With tremendous advances in technology, including remote cameras, acoustic sensing, and genetic analyses, scientists and managers now know more about many wildlife species than we ever have before. Nonetheless, cryptic

populations, which generally occur at low densities, can be exceedingly difficult to find no matter what survey technique is used. And while we understand
fairly well the threats depressing the northern spotted owl, including previous
harvests of old-growth forests, the invasive and now ubiquitous barred owl,
and habitat removal from regular massive wildfires, it is not yet clear what
is happening with Pacific martens on the Olympic Peninsula. For this small
mustelid, we needed to find more animals to even begin to formulate hypoth-
eses regarding its low numbers.

24

Dodger Point

Olympic National Park, 2019

August 7, 2019. I am with seven old and new friends and coworkers at Dodger Point lookout, high above the Elwha River in Olympic National Park. We are blessed with sunny blue skies, little wind, and no wildfire smoke (an issue the last two summers on the peninsula). Mt. Olympus is a regal presence to the west; Windfall and McCartney Peaks reside to the east. Three in our party, Kurt, Chris, and Pam, completed a marmot survey today on the slopes below the lookout. They observed occupied burrows, distinguished by fresh digging at the entrances, but no marmots. Steven and Liz, both Olympic National Park employees and the youngest and fittest in our group, collected six remote camera stations that were installed around Dodger Point a year ago in August 2018. My backpacking partner, Carrie; Patti Happe, wildlife branch chief for Olympic National Park; and I accompanied Liz and Steven to two of the stations. We are hopeful that this new effort will document martens. The stations are all above 5,000 feet elevation, and they've been recording the local wildlife for the last year.

It's now evening, and several of us are taking turns scrolling through 4,000 photos on the memory card from one of the cameras. Flying squirrels, mice, a bobcat, and one deer are all we see. True, the card reader screen is small, and looking at the images outside with some glare from sunlight is challenging. There *could* be a little marten face hiding in the shadows.

"We'll look at these again, and the rest of the cards, back in the office on the computer," says Patti, disappointed.

I'm disappointed too but not surprised. I'm also more bothered by the fact that some of the camera stations failed to function during the entire year they were out; this will bear more investigation later. In the meantime, there are two more stations to collect tomorrow. Additionally, in August and September another 21 cameras will be retrieved from three other high-elevation areas in the park: the upper Hoh River (just below Mt. Olympus), Anderson Pass (which divides the Dosewallips and Quinault watersheds), and High Divide (above the Sol Duc and Hoh Rivers). Uncertainty abounds and questions will remain no matter what we find. I am hopeful but not overly optimistic. The view from Dodger Point shows all too clearly what we are up against.

*

The investigation into the status of martens on the Olympic Peninsula has made enormous strides in recent years. After the volunteer efforts from 2009 to 2014, two martens were photographed in 2015. The first was captured on a fisher monitoring camera in the upper Hoh River near, appropriately enough, Martin Creek, two miles below the base of Mt. Olympus. Only a few ghostly images showed a marten that didn't stay long at the site. Later that month, a rock climber sent us a photo he'd snapped with his phone 40 feet below the summit of Mt. Cruiser (elevation 6,100 feet). This popular climbing peak sits above the headwaters of the Hamma Hamma River on the boundary between Olympic National Park and Forest. Shem Harding of the Mazamas, a nonprofit mountaineering education organization out of Portland, Oregon, told us they'd stopped for lunch before the final push to the top when a marten popped out from the rocks above them. The animal watched the people curiously for a minute or two as Shem took photos, then it zipped back into its hiding space.

In 2015, it had been nearly seven years since the juvenile marten had been found on Mt. Rose. Now in one month, two martens had been detected in two different areas! Everyone felt renewed hope. We also felt that our earlier theories were correct—we needed to get up high to find the martens.

*

It's 13.5 miles from the Whiskey Bend Trailhead to the Dodger Point lookout. Now, however, it's an even longer trip due to the Elwha River having washed out the road eight miles below the trailhead. In November 2015, after the two dams along the Elwha were removed in 2012 and 2014, the river took the road out. In response, the park installed a temporary bridge and repaved portions of the road. In November 2017, this fix was also destroyed. From an ecological standpoint, it's fantastic to see the river getting to once again be its river self. From a survey and general access perspective, it makes things more complicated. Fortunately, the park had vehicles above the washout to transport us to the trailhead.

The first evening, we hike 2.5 miles to Humes Ranch, a large, grassy area and an early European American homestead site along the Elwha. Normally, Humes would be full of backpackers, but due to the washout, we have the place to ourselves. That evening, we watch the inspiring acrobatics of common nighthawks and listen to their buzzy calls. The Elwha provides background sounds as it flows on the far side of the floodplain. The river is free! If anything during the last several years has given me hope for a potentially bright future for natural ecosystems, it's been the removal of the dams and the restoration of the Elwha River.

After we're all in our tents, the nighthawks continue calling. Suddenly, a barred owl joins in. The owl's distinctive call, which sounds like someone asking the question "Who cooks for you?" comes from the treetops. Not much later we hear a whistle, the begging call of a juvenile owl. The young one keeps whistling and sounds very close. The next morning, Patti tells us there haven't been spotted owls heard here in at least 10 years. There was a time when the intact forests of watersheds like the Elwha had no barred owls, but this is no longer true. Barred owls are everywhere, in managed forests and untouched forests, in wildernesses and in towns. The landscape and its ecological communities are ever-changing, a circumstance that has always been true but that is now happening at an unprecedented pace due to past and present human activities. Wildlife researchers are trying to document these changes, but the task is daunting. The barred owl is here, and the Elwha River flows naturally once more. As I fall asleep that night, I know that these are the only conclusions I can make with any certainty.

*

The trail up Long Ridge from Humes Ranch to Dodger Point is, well, long. We all spread out along the way finding our own individual pace. It's late summer, and the forest is mostly quiet. A few chickadees, nuthatches, and juncos call in soft tones. I move banana slugs off the trail to ensure they don't get stepped on. Two slugs, already off the trail, are curled together in a yin-yang shape of mating activity. Mushrooms of many sizes, shapes, and colors are bursting from below ground. Several clumps of ghost pipe are interspersed in areas of sword fern. Because ghost pipe feed on the roots of live trees via mycorrhizal fungi, they have no need to photosynthesize. Consequently, they're not green but rather a brilliant, sometimes almost translucent, white. The flowers of some of the pipes are still pointed downward, as they are when they first emerge. Others are beginning to straighten as they mature and prepare to release their seeds. Some Indigenous tribes believed that ghost pipe grew wherever a wolf had urinated. Though wolves haven't been on the peninsula for almost a century, perhaps the echoes of their presence remain.

At six miles, there is a trickle of a stream, and we stop to fill water bottles. After another two miles, we break out of the forest. Warm, summer fragrances welcome us: lupines, asters, subalpine fir. Since my first summer with the Forest Service hiking in the alpine meadows around Timberline Lodge on Oregon's Mt. Hood, I've loved the high, open country of the Northwest forests. To emerge into the bright, blue skies on a clear, warm day, even with a hungry bug population accompanying me, is one of the best moments ever.

*

Four of the eight stations around Dodger Point are southeast of the lookout along a ridge that descends toward the river. Liz and Steven have left camp early to pull down the two farthest stations before meeting Carrie, Patti, and me at two closer sites. Even off trail, the walking isn't difficult until we get to a slope of rock scree. After the rocks, we arrive at a saddle, and the way is clear but for a few dense patches of young subalpine fir. As we get closer to the GPS coordinates for the first station, we start looking up into the trees for the cameras and bait.

"There it is!" I shout.

The camera, about 20 feet up the bole of a mature fir, is attached below a small roof made of plastic sheeting to keep the snow off. On a second tree 12 feet from the camera hangs a lure dispenser box and a small piece of cow bone at the same height. Most of our camera stations over the years have been hung only as high as we could reach from the ground. Because these Dodger Point stations, as well as the others at High Divide, the upper Hoh, and Anderson Pass, were to remain out all winter, they had to be up above the snowline. This required climbing the trees the previous year. It had also involved some important new technology.

After the coastal marten's conservation status changed to "critically imperiled" in 2013, more funding became available to study the animals. In 2015, the Olympic Peninsula marten team formed, which included Patti Happe of Olympic National Park; Kurt Jenkins, a research scientist with U.S. Geological Survey working in the park; Keith Aubry, a research scientist and long-time mustelid biologist with the Forest Service's Pacific Northwest Research Station in Olympia; Katie Moriarty, a recent PhD graduate who had completed her dissertation on martens in California; and me, a resource manager with little experience in formal research but able to boast a long association with martens and camera surveys. (As of 2023, Patti, Kurt, and Keith are all now retired, though they still remain involved as consultants with marten work on the peninsula.)

Together, we wrote a proposal and received funding to do intensive surveys at higher elevations in the park and forest as well as along the park's coastal strip adjacent to the Pacific Ocean. Though only one of the historic marten detections at that time on the peninsula was from lower elevations (the 1968 Taholah record along the Pacific coast didn't come to our attention until 2018 when it was discovered by chance), Katie had been finding martens in Oregon less than a mile from the saltwater. In late 2015 and 2016, we installed 193 camera stations along the coast and at high elevations in the upper Hoh and on the east side of the park and forest. The coastal stations operated during the winter when the bears and skunks would be less active, the high-elevation sites during the late summer when access was easier and safer. All stations stayed up for only six weeks. Among nearly 400,000 photographs, less than five were of one marten from one station, again in the upper Hoh, near the fisher camera that had documented an animal in 2015. This effort proved cameras had to be installed at higher elevations. We also felt they should be left out longer to increase the possibility of a marten coming by. But how, when they needed to be checked every two weeks to replace bait and lure?

In February 2017, I met Robert Long, a senior conservation scientist at Woodland Park Zoo in Seattle. Robert and his wife, Paula MacKay, a carnivore conservation specialist with the zoo and a fellow writer, had been studying wolverines in the Cascade Range since 2013. They too had encountered the twin problems of needing to keep cameras out over the winter and being hampered by environmental conditions that prevented them from accessing the stations safely. In 2015, Robert began working with a biologist from Idaho Fish & Game and an engineer from Microsoft Research to develop a device that would automatically dispense a predetermined amount of scent lure. Within a 12"-by-18" weatherproof metal box, a bag of lure is attached to a hose that is managed by a small control board powered by lithium batteries. At a set time each day, a small amount of scent lure is delivered to a bone hung on the tree below the dispenser box (the bone provides a substrate for the lure and a visual attractant for the animal). In this manner, the station is refreshed with lure and, along with a large memory card and more lithium batteries for the camera, remains functional for many months. This automated scent dispenser, Robert told me, had been a "game-changer" for documenting wolverine presence in the Cascades and elsewhere.

I asked Robert if they'd be interested in trying their dispenser technology in the Olympics. We had the same issues with winter access and safety, as well as a mesocarnivore that now seemed to exist at very low densities. If we could get the dispensers and cameras in the right areas, they could remain in the backcountry for several months, providing a longer period of time for an animal to find them. Fortunately for the Olympic martens, Paula and Robert were eager to join the effort.

In summer 2017, we installed six dispensers and camera stations in the upper Hoh River drainage in the national park and at Mt. Rose and Mildred Lakes (just north of Mt. Rose) in the national forest. In summer 2018, we checked the stations. A marten had come to both stations in the upper Hoh. This animal, or possibly two animals, had been photographed in September and December, one and four months, respectively, after we'd set up the stations. The two Mildred Lakes stations captured two different fishers in May, 10 months after installation (one fisher also had a radio collar, meaning it was one of the founder animals and had to be at least nine years old, which is at the upper age range for these animals). If these cameras had only been on the landscape for a few weeks, we wouldn't have gotten any martens or fishers. The opportunity to understand more fully what was happening with Olympic martens had suddenly increased greatly. In 2018, we received additional funding to install more camera stations with dispensers, including those we were now checking at Dodger Point.

*

Liz and Steven have collected the two farthest stations and met up with us again in record time. This is Steven's third day on the job, while Liz is a long-time park employee with many years of experience in the Olympics. As they screw the tree steps into the camera and bait trees to climb up to the equipment, I thank them for their hard work.

"You don't need to thank me," says Steven, smiling. "This isn't what I expected to be doing, but it's fantastic!"

Patti had hired Steven to help with nuisance-animal situations, for example, bears in campgrounds or mountain goats along trails, but since he also has climbing experience, he was immediately recruited for the marten project.

I thank him again, just for being so enthusiastic, adding, "At least the surprise work wasn't, 'Here, read this government document!'"

We all laugh. Though writing and reviewing reports are important, they aren't why we got into this field. Most biologists I know entered the profession to spend time in the natural world, not in an office. In terms of having greater understanding, and thus being able to make informed management recommendations, one must spend time in these environments. So many ecological processes are happening all at once, species are interacting and affecting each other in obvious (e.g., predation) and subtle (displacement) ways, and the broader environment is transforming rapidly, sometimes predictably and at other times surprisingly. Even after years of study, fantastic new technology, and a great team working on Pacific martens in the Olympics, questions remain. This latest iteration in our survey effort has achieved the goal of being able to leave the cameras out all winter, and it also has documented our elusive friends at other sites.

As we watch the sunset that evening behind Mt. Olympus, we know it's only eight miles straight-line distance to the Hoh martens. But what an eight miles! Up and down the slopes of Ludden Peak and Mt. Scott, across the Bailey Range, around and over the glaciers and chasms of Mt. Olympus. If there is a subpopulation of martens around Dodger Point, would it be connected to the martens in the Hoh? How big are the home ranges of these animals? What are they eating? How are they surviving as the winters grow more variable and the snowpack less? It's hard to stop the flood of questions. Yet we have only one task at the moment: find the animals. The memory card with 4,000 photos and no martens is not a good start.

*

On the hike out, we all carry something from the camera stations. I have a lure dispenser strapped to the outside of my backpack. Occasionally, the breeze pushes an odor of skunk in front of me, but it's not strong. Several of the mushrooms along the trail have now been excavated and left upside down. Some appear slightly chewed on, others not at all. I think this is the handiwork of

Pacific marten, Olympic National Park, February 2019. Olympic Marten Project.

the Douglas's squirrel but don't know that for sure. As for the ghost pipe, the tops are now pointed upward, ready to release the seeds for next year's plants.

Everyone is hiking out today but Carrie and me; she and I will spend another evening with the nighthawks at Humes Ranch. After setting up camp, we cross the floodplain to where the Elwha River is flowing. There is a sandy path to the water, through willows and rocks and logs that long ago were carried down during high water. This coming winter, everything will change. More rocks and logs will be deposited, others shifted around, many piled together in massive clumps.

We filter water and then wade up to our knees. The Elwha water doesn't look glacial, with that slate-gray color of early spring runoff, but it's still very cold. I want to jump in because it will feel good on my bug bites and other scratches and scrapes. I also like the idea of a cleansing, a renewal, of having a direct connection to the river that has brought life to these mountains for millennia. After a bit of hesitation, I go for it. The water *is* freezing. It's also refreshing and brilliant, but I still crawl back out quickly.

"Your eyebrows got very tall," Carrie says, laughing.

That evening, we eat our supper watching the nighthawk show. As always, it takes a minute to pinpoint the birds in the sky. With moves so rapid and limitless space behind them, the nighthawks don't make an easy object for the human eye to focus on. A few swifts appear as well. All are taking advantage of the abundant insect life of the meadow. It isn't a massacre though. Plenty of mosquitoes are surviving the birds' predations and finding their own meals in Carrie and me.

In the middle of the night, I wake up to the barred owl calling. Over and over, it asks its question, "Who cooks for you?" The owl repeats this so many times that even after it stops, I still hear the call. Suddenly, I try to remember what the spotted owl's four-note location call sounds like. It's been more than two decades since I've heard a spotted owl (when I was out with Debaran Kelso five years ago, the female never hooted after coming in). Now I can't remember how their call goes. This upsets me, but I know it's partially because I'm half asleep. As the juvenile begins whistling and a nighthawk joins in with growling sounds as it dives, I eventually fall back asleep.

*

The next day, after hiking out, Carrie and I stop by park headquarters. Patti is in her office looking rather well-rested and clean. She asks me if I will see the other crew that will be going to retrieve the cameras and dispensers from High Divide and Anderson Pass.

"Yes," I say, and she gives me their backpacking permit.

"Oh, yeah, there are these too," she adds, casually handing me more papers before returning to her computer screen. I glance down.

I expect to see more government forms, but instead, there are several photos of a marten in the snow! One of the cameras below the Dodger Point lookout captured the animal beside the tree and also peeking out from behind it! I shout and begin jumping up and down in Patti's office doing my "marten dance." She laughs and says, "Congratulations!"

As we would soon learn, three of the eight stations at Dodger Point photographed martens. Later that summer, after all the cameras had been collected and the memory cards examined, a grand total of 11 of 31 sites, and all 4 of the areas where we installed cameras, had been visited by martens. Not only that, but after our Dodger Point trip, two incidental marten photos were taken by visitors in August and October of 2019, one in the park and one in the forest. In only one year, our marten records for the Olympic Peninsula had more than doubled.

25

Flight

Olympic National Forest and Park, 2017

Bat Survey

Our summer intern, Halle, hadn't been in the office 10 minutes before my coworker, Karen, and I whisked her out again to do a bat survey. It was May 2017, and this was Halle's first day. She'd come to us through the Student Conservation Association, a nonprofit organization that works to build the next generation of conservation leaders by arranging work for young people in practical field assignments. Halle was 20 years old and had just finished her sophomore year at the University of Wisconsin. She'd spent the last several days driving across the country to accept this position. She'd mostly be working with Karen doing inventories for pollinators, including the Taylor's checkerspot butterfly (*Euphydryas editha taylori*), a federally endangered species.

Karen and I have worked together on the Olympic since 2005. Interestingly, our careers have overlapped throughout the years: we attended Washington State University at the same time, and we also served in the Peace Corps in Argentina at the same time. She has worked, as I have, with spotted owls and marbled murrelets since the 1980s and in recent years has done much inventory work with invertebrates as well as bats. Karen now handed Halle a pair of gloves and several plastic containers. "We need to collect some bat guano from the attic of one of the buildings here. Do you want to come?"

"Sure!" she said, looking only slightly confused. Halle wore her blue SCA T-shirt and was tall with long, dark hair and a big smile. She surely expected this morning to be doing the usual paperwork before beginning a new job.

In the back compound of the Quilcene Ranger Station, the auto shop building has housed dozens of bats for many years. Recently, we've done "exit surveys" each summer to count them as they leave their roosting sites. This work involves the pleasant circumstances of sitting in a camp chair in the evening and counting bats as they fly out from the roof and eaves to forage. Though we couldn't identify all the species for certain with this method, we knew that there were little brown (*Myotis lucifugus*) and big brown bats (*Epte-*

sicus fuscus). Now, however, we also needed to know more than just which species were living there.

In addition to the two chytrid fungi affecting frogs and salamanders (*Bd* and *Bsal*), there is also another fungus with an ominous scientific name, *Pseudogymnoascus destructans*, or *Pd*. This fungus affects bats and has devastated some populations in eastern North America. It's a cold-loving organism and will grow readily on the muzzles (giving rise to its common name, "white-nosed syndrome," or WNS) and wings of bats that are hibernating in caves. The fungus causes such damage to the skin that the bats wake up and use energy that they need to make it through the winter. First identified in 2006 in New York, the fungus has since spread rapidly to numerous states and Canadian provinces, mostly in the east. However, in 2016, it was also documented on a little brown bat in Washington State.

After this discovery, Karen began working with WDFW personnel to organize tests of guano from our auto shop bats. Though we weren't completely sure bats were hibernating in the shop, we wanted to test anyway. Some weeks before Halle's arrival, Karen had placed plastic sheeting on the floor of the attic to find the guano more easily. Though this area was still being used for storage, it had also been largely left to the bats.

"Have you been to the Northwest before?" I asked Halle as we walked to the back compound.

"No. I was in California last summer with the organization American Conservation Experience, but I've never been here." Halle explained she was getting a double major in conservation biology and Spanish. "Next year, I hope to do a semester in Spain," she added.

In the attic, we didn't find much guano. Karen collected what there was into small containers. Halle recorded information provided by Karen, and I took photos. In another few weeks, the lab results would fortunately come back negative for WNS. (Unfortunately, in 2022, *Pd* was detected from five bats [no clinical signs of WNS] at the Hamma Hamma cabin, and in 2023, a euthanized bat showing clinical signs of WNS in Quilcene also tested positive for the fungus.)

*

One month later, Karen, Halle, and I, along with another summer intern, a Forest Service biologist from our regional office in Portland, Oregon, and two biologists from the WDFW, carried our camp chairs to the back compound. The air was pleasantly warm, the evening still. Common nighthawks called from above; mosquitoes, good food for bats if nothing else, hummed around our ears and faces. While Karen began the overview for the evening, I donned a light coat I didn't really need just to minimize the surface area available to the ravenous insects.

"Sunset is at 9:14 p.m.," she explained. "We'll begin the survey 30 minutes before then. The survey will last until 45 minutes after sunset, or until 10 minutes after we see the last bat, whichever is longer. We'll each take a section of the building and sit in front of it. You count each bat that comes out, and if you see a bat go back *in*, then you record that too. If you want to generally note whether the bats look larger or smaller, that's great too, though we won't be identifying them to species." Karen looked around. "Does anyone need a clicker for counting the bats?"

I raised my hand. Not having a smartphone, I didn't have the counting app that the others would be using. There were a few good-natured comments about this, but I didn't mind. It was a point of pride for me that I still managed with only a flip phone. The next task involved assigning people to different parts of the building. I had the good fortune of getting the south side, which generally always had the most bats. Two of us split this long area, which included three dormers. With camp chairs in place, headlamps available for later, clickers in hand or phones opened to the app, notebooks and pencils ready to record bats going back in or other nighttime visitors in the surrounding forest, for example, barred owls, we were ready!

A universal experience in the study of wild animals involves waiting—waiting for the breeding birds to sing, waiting for the frogs to chorus, waiting for the day to warm and the butterflies to fly, waiting for the night to grow deep and dark enough for the owls to hoot. Often these hours are spent in less-than-ideal comfort for the observer. Either it's cold or raining or snowing, or maybe one must remain still and in a cramped sitting or standing position. It's the price a person pays for choosing to enter an animal's world on its terms, and most biologists accept the discomfort knowing the potential reward is worth it. Still, sitting in a camp chair and being warm and dry while waiting is *nice*. True, the mosquitoes were pesky, but soon the bats would emerge to help reduce their numbers. I settled into my chair, clicker in hand, eyes trained upon the eaves and dormers of the auto shop roof.

Twenty minutes after beginning the survey, the first bat emerged from the building. This animal flew only inches above my head as it moved out into the nighttime world. I hit the clicker. For the next 35 minutes, we counted a total of 50 bats leaving the auto shop; I tallied the second-highest total at 19. We could hear the bats scratching around in the roof as they prepared to exit. We also heard some high-pitched squeaks. One bat was observed returning to the building though it may have exited later.

*

Bumble Bee Survey

The Dennie Ahl Seed Orchard sits in an area of historic prairie in the South Fork Skokomish River watershed of Olympic National Forest. During the middle of the 20th century, when regeneration, also called clearcut, harvest was in full swing on the Olympic Peninsula, seed orchards were constructed as part of the Forest Service's tree improvement program. The basic idea was to provide an area dedicated to growing healthy, vigorous trees. These would then be used to replant harvested landscapes. Named after an early log scaler for the forest, the Dennie Ahl Seed Orchard produced abundant and easily harvested crops of trees grown from known superior parent trees found in the natural stands.

In recent years, owing to the changes in harvest and timber management, the seed orchard has been used less, though it is still maintained by the forest. Because of its open habitats and flowering plants and shrubs, Dennie Ahl has become an important area for pollinators. In July, Karen arranged a class at the seed orchard on how to inventory and identify bumble bees. Rich Hatfield, senior endangered species conservation biologist and the bumble bee conservation lead with the Xerces Society, agreed to come and teach a two-day course. The Xerces Society for Invertebrate Conservation is an international nonprofit organization dedicated to protecting the natural world through the conservation of invertebrates and their habitats. The name of the society comes from the Xerces blue butterfly, *Glaucopsyche xerces*, the first butterfly known to go extinct in North America as a result of human activities.

The class of 10 women were all biologists, and most of us came from Olympic National Forest; one person worked for the WDFW. Halle and another summer intern were the youngest and newest to the Forest Service. A few of us, like Karen and another seasonal employee who had studied entomology, had some experience surveying for bumble bees. Cheryl, the forest botanist, and I had taken one class before on bees but hadn't yet put what we'd learned

Bumble bee identification training on Olympic National Forest, 2017. USDA Forest Service by Betsy L. Howell.

into practice. Apart from the general concern over the health of bumble bee populations, the specific impetus for this training was to learn how to identify the western bumble bee (*Bombus occidentalis*), a regionally sensitive species. Learning to identify other local species was also necessary as they would more likely be the ones we found. Currently, habitat loss, climate change, disease, and pesticide use have put all bumble bees in peril.

Karen gave a safety talk and asked if anyone was allergic to bees. Then Rich began with an overview of the various species we'd be likely to see, including the yellow-faced bumble bee (*Bombus vosnesenskii*), the yellow-fronted or yellow-head bumble bee (*B. flavifrons*), and the obscure bumble bee (*B. caliginosus*). The yellow-faced bee is a very neat, tidy-looking bee with a clean yellow stripe on its posterior end and a black belly. The obscure bumble bee is similar to the yellow-faced but has a cloudy belly with some yellow hairs mixed in with the black. The many species of bumble bees in the Pacific Northwest can be organized into groups based on general appearance: red-tailed (has red hairs on the abdomen), black-tailed (the posterior of the abdomen is mostly black), striped (the abdomen is mostly black with one or more yellow stripes), and white (has white hairs somewhere on the body). Two "difficult species groups" include the yellow-faced bumble bees and the cuckoo bees. This last is a category that encompasses lineages of bees that lay their eggs in other bees' nests. To add to the mix are the species not native to North America, including the honeybee.

A season in the lives of bumble bees begins with the emergence of the queen from hibernation in late winter. She looks for a nest, often a rodent burrow or some sort of hole in the ground, where she lays her eggs. When these bees, mostly females, hatch and emerge from the nest, they begin collecting pollen. Females are the only ones to collect pollen for the colony, and they make a small amount of honey to keep the colony going (since bumble bees hibernate, they don't need large food resources over the winter as honeybees do). Later in the season, the colony produces new queens, as well as males that then consume the stores of honey and leave to find mating opportunities with the new queens. By late autumn, all the bees die except for the new queens, which then go into hibernation. Rich explained that at this time of year, we would mostly likely be finding females.

There began to be questions about what exactly the males contributed.

"Very little," Rich said. "However, they are crucial to the mating process." He paused. "Also, they do support themselves once they're out of the nest. That is, they gather their own pollen and nectar to eat."

Bumble bees are much larger, stouter, and hairier than honeybees. They also behave differently, with an annual life cycle and the fact that they nest in the ground. Very importantly, bumble bees are native to North America, while honeybees are not. Rich spoke about the myth that raising nonnative honeybees helps conserve bee populations.

"This is akin," he said, "to raising chickens to help wild bird populations. There's no doubt that honeybees are important for many reasons, but helping to conserve native bees is not one of them."

After the brief lecture, we followed Rich to an area of spiraea and rose bushes to watch a demonstration on bee-capture technique.

"It's very easy to catch a bumble bee," he explained. "First, you wait for the bee to land on a flower." He waited, and when a bee alighted on the pink blooms of the spiraea in front of him, he stepped nearer. "Second, you quickly sweep her up in your net." With one swift motion, Rich had the bee in the net. He began waving the net back and forth to push the bee down toward the bottom. "You want to get her into the smallest space possible, then close the area off with your hand."

After the bee was corralled in the bottom of the net, Rich took a small vial from his pocket with his free hand. He popped the top off, then placed the container where the fingers of his other hand were keeping the bee in the bottom of the net. In no time at all, the bee and the flower she had been on were inside the vial.

"That's all there is to it. Very easy." Rich said. "This vial then goes into the cooler of ice packs we brought. After 20 minutes or so, she'll slow down enough to be removed and examined." Everyone moved in closer to look at the bee dancing in the vial.

"How do you know it's a 'she'?" someone asked.

"For one thing, you can easily see the pollen sacs on her legs," he explained. "Males have very skinny legs, and since they don't collect pollen for the colony, they don't need sacs. Also, why not default to using the feminine?" He gave a slight grin. "Particularly since I am with all women."

"What about getting stung?" another person asked.

"I've rarely gotten stung," Rich said. "Keep your eye on the bee and stay aware and focused. With practice and patience, soon the bee will be in the vial."

Each of us grabbed a net and several vials and fanned out into the meadow. Though I wasn't worried about getting stung, I also wasn't sure that catching a bee was that easy. It *looked* easy, but Rich had obviously been doing this a long time.

*

Surveys for bumble bees and butterflies, important pollinators, are measures of how far ecosystem management has come in just a few decades. Wildlife inventories in the national forests from the 1960s mostly focused on economically important game species such as elk, deer, grouse, and quail. I remember even in the '80s when we weren't thinking at all about pollinators or other lesser-known species that now play a larger role in our environmental analysis process. With the adoption of the Northwest Forest Plan in 1994 and greater emphasis on ecosystem sustainability, biologists in Washington, Oregon, and northern California were suddenly learning how to inventory for a broader suite of sensitive species, including mollusks and salamanders, red tree voles and bats. Nonvascular members of the plant kingdom such as lichen, fungi, and bryophytes, also began to get more attention as they were rare and little known. In 1998, I did my first mollusk and red tree vole surveys in the Siskiyou National Forest. Both involved looking for the smallest of the small on the forest floor including, for tree voles, clumps of resin ducts of fir needles that the animals discard after eating the needles. For mollusks, we examined the undersides of squares of cardboard that had been set out the previous evening. Some mollusk species are as small as .04 inches (one millimeter) in diameter. Lee Webb, the forest biologist in the Siskiyou, had happily said one afternoon as we dug around in the forest floor, "I can't believe I'm doing a survey for slugs and snails!"

With its focus on old-growth forest-associated species, the 1994 Northwest Forest Plan didn't address pollinators as a group, which typically use more early seral habitats. However, with the observed collapse in recent years of native bee populations across North America and the clear need of these species for the pollination of human food supplies, concern regarding their conservation status has increased. Additionally, in Pacific Northwest moist coniferous forests, the understanding of the need for a balance of early- and late-seral habitat stages has been growing.

*

I found my own area of spiraea and went to work. Much to my surprise, on the first swipe of my net, I had a bee! I swung the net through the air a couple of times, coaxing the bee into the bottom. Getting it into the vial took a little longer, but as Rich had predicted, the process wasn't hard. On my next few attempts, I encountered faster bees and they got away. However, soon enough I had a second bee. The protocol for a bumble bee survey directed that the survey be 90 minutes long per one surveyor over one hectare of habitat. If there are three surveyors, then the search time is 30 minutes. Since we had 11 people, the survey time would be only 10 minutes. Before we knew it, Karen announced the end, and we returned to the cooler to deposit our bees. We ate lunch while waiting for the bees to cool so we could begin the identification process.

Rich set one bee at a time on top of the cooler lid, which was white and provided a good background. The 11 we'd caught were all females, with large, triangular legs, and full pollen sacs. The sacs were bright yellow or orange depending on which plant they'd been collecting pollen from. We'd captured only one yellow-faced bumble bee but five of the obscure bumble bees. The others included the yellow-fronted bumble bee, and the fuzzy-horned bumble bee, *B. mixtus*.

Given that so many species had "yellow" in the common name, we used the scientific species names to discuss these animals. *B. flavifrons* had a bright yellow abdomen and a long, horse-like face, whereas *B. mixtus* had a cloudy thorax. Each species was obviously different, but identification still required patience and practice examining the various characteristics up close with the hand lens.

After identification, we set each bee on a notebook to continue warming up. Some took longer than others, so several might be in the recovery ward at any one time. As they warmed, some lifted their front legs straight up in a defensive posture. Then they'd begin walking around. Eventually, they flew away, undoubtedly wondering what all *that* had been about.

*

At our second survey site in the orchard, we caught more bees, a little fewer than half of them males. Most were *B. mixtus*. One new species was *B. rufocinctus*, the red-belted bumble bee, named for the red hairs on its otherwise yellow abdomen. We also observed honeybees and wondered where their hive was located. Rich said that, in general, these bees aren't found too far from their hives, usually less than three miles, though sometimes they might roam farther.

The third and last survey area for the day yielded the most: 39 bees captured, 37 females and 2 males. This time, most were *B. rufocinctus* (18) with *B. caliginosus*, the obscure bumble bee, coming in second at 13.

"I can't believe I'm holding a bee," said Halle, delighted as the small creature rested on the tip of her finger. The worry over being stung had vanished. It helped, of course, that the bees were incapacitated, but our comfortableness also came from beginning to know and understand the animals. "They are really cute," she added. "Look at that face!"

As we continued discussing the bees and taking notes, one of the male bees in the recovery ward began to waken. At first, not much notice was given to this individual. Soon, however, he had made his way over to one of the females.

"Hey, what's going on?" I asked, suddenly aware that the male was now right next to the female. He then reached out a leg to touch her. Then he touched her pollen sac. Rich leaned in and looked closer.

"Hmm," he said. "I think he might be trying to steal her pollen."

"What?" someone asked in a loud voice. Then Halle and I both shouted at the same time, "Get off her!"

Of course, the male bee paid no attention to us. He kept taking pollen while the female tried to move away. "Stop it!" Halle cried again.

"She's worked hard for that pollen!" I said.

"Yeah," Cheryl laughed. "Get your own pollen, asshole!"

Though we all were fascinated by this interaction, it was also viscerally upsetting to watch the thievery. We could have easily separated the two bees, and maybe we should have since this was not a "natural" encounter. Fortunately, however, the female soon woke fully and took a few steps away. Then she flew off.

"Fascinating," said Rich, shaking his head. "I've never seen that before."

*

We'd hired Halle to work primarily on pollinator inventories, but she also enthusiastically helped me swab rough-skinned newts to test for the chytrid fungus, *Bsal*. This process was similar to that used for testing amphibians for *Bd*. Halle and I donned rubber boots and visited different wetlands to find the newts. We captured them with aquarium nets, then gently rubbed parts of their bodies with a Q-tip before letting them go (all of the 33 newts we swabbed tested negative for the *Bsal* fungus, however 9 tested positive for *Bd*). Though Halle was quite a bit younger than me, I found her an easy person to talk to, with a keen eye for observation, a good sense of humor, and a compassionate outlook.

As we got to know each other more over the summer, I decided it would be nice if my wife, Barbara, could meet Halle. We met at a local restaurant one evening and ate outside, taking advantage of a rare, warm night in western Washington.

As we chatted, small birds hopped around our table looking for tidbits. Most of these were European house sparrows, but at one point I noticed an Oregon junco, a common species and a friendly presence, in the mix. After a minute, I looked again at the junco, and this time a larger bird stood right next to it. Something was amiss, and it took me a second to realize what.

"Hey, is that a cowbird chick?" I asked, directing Halle's and Barbara's attention to the goings-on.

"Ack!" said Halle in a loud voice. "It is!"

"Oh, no!"

Sure enough, the little adult junco had gotten roped into the responsibility of feeding this cowbird young, which was much bigger than itself and whose true mother had laid her egg in the junco's nest, likely removing the junco eggs in the process.

"We should get it," said Halle.

"What? What's going on?" asked Barbara.

I explained how brown-headed cowbirds get others to do all the work of raising their young by laying their eggs in different birds' nests, a strategy known as brood parasitism. Even worse, they often destroy the eggs and young of the parents. Though brown-headed cowbirds are native to North America, they've also, like barred owls, expanded their range as humans have altered the landscape and removed forests. Sadly, the irresponsible parental behavior of cowbirds has had devastating impacts on some songbird species. Halle reiterated a desire to kill the cowbird chick. Barbara looked horrified.

"I feel I must speak out for the little one," she said.

"I worked on a project surveying for Kirtland's warbler last summer," Halle said, undeterred. "I've seen the damage cowbirds cause."

Kirtland's warbler was listed as federally endangered for many years due in part to the effects of cowbird parasitism (in 2019, it was delisted due to a remarkable recovery from decades of active management to restore the species).

Eventually, the junco flew away, and the chick followed after it. The observation was upsetting to me and Halle, but as both birds had flown, there was little we could do about it. Yet if they hadn't, *would* we have done something? Throughout my career, I've often heard people say that it's wrong to interfere with natural events taking place, yet I've often disagreed with this position. Humans have already interfered tremendously in the lives of other animals, and many of our actions have precipitated the interactions we're now observing between different species. Careful consideration, of course, must be given to any further action on our part, but I think it's often worth investigating the possibilities.

*

Marmot Survey

In July, I invited Halle to join my friend Carrie and me on a four-day backpacking trip. For our second volunteer marmot survey with Olympic National Park, we'd chosen Appleton Pass 10 miles north of Mt. Olympus. We decided to go the last week of July when the snow should have mostly been melted.

"She sounds great," said Carrie when I mentioned inviting Halle.

"She is great." I thought a moment. "Young people are smarter now, aren't they? They're so aware politically, and many are so mature. Halle is way more together than I ever was at that age. She knows what she wants and is organizing the experience she needs to get there. I think I just got lucky that way, was in the right place at the right time and met the right people, but she's making it all happen." I paused again. "You know, if I could have been guaranteed of having a daughter like her, I might have considered having children."

Carrie laughed. "There are no guarantees, though."

"No, there aren't."

As predicted by me, Carrie and Halle hit it off immediately. We did the final organizing of gear at the trailhead then joined the stream of wilderness enthusiasts heading up the Sol Duc River. Some had come out just for the day, wearing only sandals and carrying no water. Others had planned for several days out, looking as if they'd just emerged from the pages of an REI catalog.

*

The winter of 2016–17 brought more snow than we'd had in recent years, and it had also stayed around longer. We left the Sol Duc River (and most of the crowds that were headed to the very popular Seven Lakes Basin) and began the ascent toward Appleton Pass and Oyster Lake. As we reached 4,000 feet elevation, patches of snow appeared in the shady areas. Alpine ponds had filled where melting had begun, and avalanche lilies poked up at the edges waving at us as we passed by. Juncos flitted through the salal and heather. Mountain chickadees, pine siskins, and red crossbills called and flew above us. Ravens, too, let us know of their presence. Though ravens may be seen in many habitats and at different elevations, they are less numerous than they used to be. I am always glad to hear their heavy wingbeats and quorks, bringing news of the high country.

We arrived at a tributary to the Sol Duc River. The water flowed too fast and too high for crossing by simple rock-hopping. An old-growth tree up the slope from the trail had come down, however, and formed a bridge of sorts. Halle easily hopped up on the log and walked down it to the other side. Carrie and I were more careful. We slid down the log on our butts, a less stylish but equally successful method of crossing.

That evening we pitched our tents on the edges of the snowfield that hid Oyster Lake. Only a trail of footprints and the slightly bluish cast at the lowest point confirmed the waterbody and our source of water for the next few days. Word of our arrival spread quickly in the bug community. Horseflies, gnats, and mosquitoes all arrived to help with the camp setup. Fortunately, they proved less abundant out on the snow. After getting settled, I started boiling water and asked Halle if she needed some too. We'd all brought our own food, and I had volunteered to bring the stove.

"No," she replied. "I'll just eat mine cold."

"Are you sure?"

"Yeah, it's fine."

Carrie and I ate our substantial meals of noodles and curry lentil soup, while Halle seemed to have only a Tasty Bite meal. We discussed the days ahead, and Halle expressed her hope of seeing a bear. I said that seemed very likely since we were in the national park where bears weren't hunted and hadn't learned to be afraid of humans.

After dinner, we hung our food on the bear wire the park had installed. There we met three other women backpackers, who'd been here a few days. They'd named a blacktail deer and frequent visitor to their camp Seamus and a mountain goat that also liked to make an appearance Jeffery (this was before the goat translocation project had begun in 2018). So far, we hadn't seen any goats other than two on the far slopes of Mt. Appleton. A large herd of elk also rested on a snowfield below the mountain, no doubt finding respite there from the bugs.

*

We had eight survey polygons to do over the next three days, and it looked as if some parts of them would be covered in snow. We began with the ones closest to camp below the trail that led north to Boulder Creek, a tributary to the Elwha River. After scanning the ground where the snow had melted, we stopped for a break and filled out the data form. Halle was our scribe while Carrie and I continued scanning. We discussed how much of the area was covered in snow, how confident we were in our observations, and what other comments might be useful to note on the form. I took GPS points at abandoned burrows, and we all took photos. As we finished, there was some discussion about the names of nearby peaks.

"Let's look at my peak finder app," said Halle.

This was new to me, since I didn't have a smartphone and am not up on the latest apps. I'm also inherently suspicious of too much technology. Yet I had to admit, the peak finder app was pretty cool and helped answer our questions.

In one area blanketed by avalanche lilies, we found what appeared to be the tunnels and possible burrows of Olympic pocket gophers (*Thomomys mazama pugetensis*), another endemic species to the peninsula. We also examined a nearby pond for amphibians. No marmots. The next two days we traveled to the farther polygons finding similar situations: much snow, brilliant wildflowers (lilies, lupines, chartreuse paintbrush, and penstemon), few burrows (all appearing abandoned), and a few possible pocket gopher sites. For Halle's sake, as well as mine and Carrie's, I had really hoped to find marmots. Still, I've spent much more of my career *not* finding animals than finding them. And because negative results are important information too, I've never been too bothered by them. I was glad to see they didn't bother Halle either.

As the days unfolded, so did the natural world's stories, not all of which we fully understood. The intentions of the insects seemed very clear, and they drove us into our tents to escape. We also watched poor Seamus trying to outrun the beasts. Similarly, the elk had remained on the far snowfield, no doubt more at ease there than if they'd been in the trees. One morning, we observed a cow elk lying down, and when we returned that evening, she was still in the same place. As the temperature dropped, the herd began to move off the snowfield. The cow remained behind. After several minutes, a few animals came back toward her. Then they moved off again. Was she ill and dying? Would we be witnesses to her demise? Though I try to be dispassionate while working in my profession, I also find it difficult to watch animals suffer. Fortunately, the cow eventually stood and followed the herd down the slope. Whatever had ailed her, if anything at all, would remain a mystery to us.

Our last survey area included a steep hillside bursting with wildflowers as well as many abandoned burrows, one of which appeared to have fresh dirt kicked out of its entrance. We still rated the site as abandoned but also took many photos to show Patti Happe. After finishing the survey, we hiked up to the pass between the Sol Duc and Hoh watersheds. There, Mt. Olympus appeared in all its splendor. Cat Peak and Mt. Carrie also stood prominently to the east.

"Hey, there's your bear, Halle!" I shouted.

Not far below us, a big, healthy-looking black bear, completely uninterested in us, ambled along feeding. After watching the bear for many minutes, a snowberry checkerspot butterfly (*Euphydryas colon*) came by, perhaps to remind Halle where her true responsibilities were this summer. Or perhaps the butterfly wanted to remind us that bears weren't the only important ones around here. Or maybe, in fact probably, it had simply found a good plant on which to drink nectar.

*

That evening after dinner, we hiked up a side trail that went to an overlook above Oyster Lake. A mountain goat had been enjoying the spot but dashed off immediately at our appearance. There wasn't much room at the top, and the drops below were a little too perpendicular for my liking, but the view was worth it. With the wind blowing, the bugs were nonexistent. Carrie and I found some comfortable rocks to sit on and enjoy the sunset. Meanwhile, Halle explored around the overlook's edges, trying to get another view of the goat.

"Uh, maybe that's not . . ." I began my warning as she moved farther away from us, "such a good idea."

My words faded among the breezes, and she didn't hear me. Even though I was more than 30 years older than Halle and she easily *could* have been my daughter, I saw her more as my younger pal. Besides, Halle was smart and sensible. She didn't need me instilling *my* fears on *her* experience. After poking around for a bit, she found a spot to sit as well.

The next day, we hiked out, not having seen any marmots but still having completed good survey work and having had a great time. Warm breezes enveloped us with the scents of subalpine fir and mountain hemlock. The forest's breath is deeply familiar to me. I first experienced it as a child when my parents and I went camping and in the woods around our home and then later as a college student working for the Mt. Hood National Forest. Whether the land is soaked in rain and the clouds hang up in the trees, or the sun shines deeply into the dark interior, I love being in these forests. It's partly the timelessness of the landscape that appeals, the connection I can feel to an earlier world where humans were not the dominant and destructive force that we are today. In the forest, my individual experience seems less important, since it's hard to put too much emphasis on one's short existence while standing next to an 800-year-old tree. I can think a lot when I'm hiking. But every time I return to the present moment, there are the trees and the plants, the birds and maybe a Douglas's squirrel to remind me that I, like them, am just passing through this world. Where it's all leading is rarely clear to me, but for now, the goal is returning to the trailhead. Beyond that, I can't predict much.

Despite the warmth, the weather was changing. The clear skies we'd enjoyed had begun to fill with clouds. A storm hadn't been predicted, but then one never knew with the weather in the Olympic Mountains. And in fact, the clouds and winds picking up as we left Appleton Pass didn't just bring in cooler weather. The following week, in early August, smoke from wildfires burning in British Columbia and eastern Washington arrived in the Olympic Mountains and covered the region for several weeks. We'd done our survey just in time.

Epilogue

Olympic National Forest, 2020

For as long as I've worked in the Olympic National Forest, I've wanted to get to Goat Lake. Described to me as a "jewel" in the mountains and accessible only by an unmaintained trail used by fisher people and hearty adventurers, Goat Lake, and three other smaller, nearby lakes, sits high above the Dungeness River. The water bodies are only a mile and a half from the main river trail, but the path gains 2,000 feet in elevation. It's not an easy destination, and one needs a reason to go there. In August of 2020, I finally had that reason.

My coworker, Marc, a fisheries biologist; our seasonal biological technician, Conor; and I made the steep, three-and-a-half-hour trek to Goat Lake to do an environmental DNA survey. This technology, also referred to as "eDNA," is another noninvasive survey method to determine the presence of wildlife species that can be difficult to detect visually. The premise is simple. All living organisms are constantly shedding bits of genetic material, including skin, hair, and bodily fluids. If this material can be captured and saved so that it doesn't degrade, then it can be analyzed in a lab to determine genetic sequences unique to wildlife species. eDNA has most often been used through collecting water samples in lakes and streams to confirm the presence of amphibians and fish. More recently, it has also been used to find snakes and small mammals (collecting DNA from soil), bats (from the air), and bumble bees (from flowers).

Our goal this summer was to visit high-elevation lakes that Marc first surveyed in the 1990s. We wanted to look at the presence of native versus nonnative fish and amphibian species. Native amphibians are particularly vulnerable to predation by introduced fish that have been stocked in western high mountain lakes since the first part of the 20th century. Research in recent years has shown salamanders and frogs seeking shallower, warmer waters that will not support fish yet are also ephemeral and more vulnerable to drying and disappearing seasonally in the face of declining snowpacks and increasing temperatures. The combined impacts on amphibians from predatory fish and changing environmental conditions have been called the "climate vise" by scientists.

After the 1994 Northwest Forest Plan came into being, regeneration harvest, a.k.a. clearcutting, on the Olympic National Forest had stopped, and a more holistic approach to land management had begun. But these changes affected lower-elevation ecosystems more than higher ones. We wanted to know what was happening to species in areas not vied over for timber and other commodities. We wanted to determine a baseline for species presence now in areas very affected by climate change. Ultimately, we want to maintain biological diversity in these sensitive ecosystems, where a seemingly small change or impact can have lasting effects.

*

Goat Lake is all that we expect it to be, a perfect blue gem in the Olympic Mountains. At almost 6,000 feet elevation (high for the Olympics!), the slopes surrounding the lake are open and rocky. Fingers of forest and lush mountain meadows provide green colors against the grayscape. Larger than many high-elevation lakes at a little more than seven acres, Goat Lake was first stocked with rainbow trout in 1971. A 1972 survey showed impressive growth of the fish. The surveyors surmised this was due to the presence of freshwater shrimp, which "the trout feed on all winter under the ice cap" (Johnston 1972, 131). They also observed "large numbers of two species of newts" (128; this statement may refer to the rough-skinned newt and the long-toed salamander) around the shore. After Atlantic salmon were also stocked in Goat Lake in 1985, additional plantings of rainbow trout occurred in the 1990s and 2000s. While the salmon have been fished out of Goat Lake, the trout remain, and I don't expect to find much amphibian presence.

We make our way to the western shore of the lake where there is a wide, open area. Each one-liter water sample we collect must be filtered, and then the filter is analyzed later in the lab. To facilitate this process, we've carried up a flask, a cordless drill, and a small pump. It takes about an hour to filter the needed four samples at each lake, so we don't dawdle eating lunch. The trips up and back to Goat Lake alone will consume seven hours. Conor gets the equipment set up, and Marc sets off to collect the samples. I follow more slowly, looking for amphibians on the shoreline.

Marc, Conor, and I have been on our own "COVID raft" now for two months, and I can't think of two better people to be with during this time. I've worked with Marc, a smart, capable biologist with a great sense of humor, for 15 years. He has done extensive habitat enhancement work for fish in several rivers in the forest, as well as the earlier lake surveys, so he knows much history of the landscape. Conor is returning for his second season with the forest. He's an enthusiastic young biologist and also very happy to be out in the woods. Per Forest Service policy during the pandemic, we must drive to our field sites in separate vehicles. We also must wear masks and social distance. The eDNA sampling protocol requires a level of cleanliness to prevent contamination of the samples that dovetails well with COVID precautions. While each of us has partners at home, the office has been closed since March, and being isolated from coworkers hasn't been easy. It's also been challenging to implement field-work in this new world. Yet we feel fortunate. The high lakes surveys have saved our mental health during this experience of living through a pandemic.

I don't see any amphibians on my walk about the lake. While Marc is collecting one of the samples, he hears a *plop* into the water. After filtering the samples, we move to "Goat North Pond," a small, shallow waterbody a few hundred feet from the main lake. Here we observe frogs and a juvenile long-toed salamander. Several months later, when we get the eDNA lab results, Goat North Pond, unsurprisingly, shows evidence of Cascades frogs, *Ambystoma* salamanders (so either the long-toed or the northwestern species), and newts. Unexpectedly, it also seems to have fish. Similarly, we learn that rough-skinned newts are present in Goat Lake despite the fact that we didn't see them.

*

There have been times in my career when the survey work and data collection seem like simply carving the landscape up into bits of information. I feel this most often when I'm especially perplexed by the questions. When there are too few answers and any conclusions have many caveats and assumptions. When dots and lines on a map become too much the focus, or when the time spent processing paperwork exceeds the time spent outside. I won't ever stop taking notes, or photos, or participating in research, or watching and waiting and working toward the moment when the mysteries of the forest reveal themselves. Yet information by itself will always provide only part of what is needed.

Science is critical to help us understand cause and effect and the vast complexity of the world around us. Yet human beings, including scientists, are emotional creatures. It won't only be facts and figures that move people to act on behalf of the environment and the other species that live on the planet. Change will come from how humans *feel* about the natural world. I believe we'll widen our circle of compassion when we feel more community-minded and less individualistic. We'll write letters and demand action energized by how we connect with our hearts. We'll even change our lifestyles and behavior when we believe that the lives of the ensatinas, rattlesnakes, spotted owls, Pacific martens, and Olympic marmots are just as important as our own. Science can foster this transformation by illuminating connections. Knowledge can be the pathway for a relationship with nature, a connection the author and scientist Robin Wall Kimmerer describes as one of reciprocity, of giving as much as we are given.

When I think about the many challenges the world and its inhabitants are facing, I can be confronted with both overwhelm and heartbreak. When these feelings come in the night, I know I may not get back to sleep, or if I do, it will be a restless sleep. Population declines, invasive species, disease, loss of habitat and biodiversity, a changing climate, and more extreme weather events are all issues that I, along with my biologist and forester colleagues, have worked with firsthand. To be sure, I've observed many successes. Changes in policy, recovery for some species, habitat improvement and restoration, and increased awareness through education and experiences in nature have been key to advancements in conservation. Still, many problems are only growing more complex. When my thoughts grow burdened with these complexities and the uncertain outcomes we're facing, I always return to the many people I know working toward a better future. During my career, I have been consistently impressed by the energy and enthusiasm of those I've worked with during species inventories and habitat projects. It takes all of us, including the senior scientists, the young people, the managers, and the volunteers, to get this work done and bring about the changes we want to see. That I know so many of these people personally and have worked alongside them for so many years is one aspect of living in today's world that always calms me.

In the Pacific Northwest, vast changes in federal land management in the last 30 years have been facilitated by science increasing our capacity to understand how humans have impacted, and continue to impact, the landscape. They've also come about because people have demanded a new approach to broaden natural resource and ecosystem sustainability. There is still much to learn, and the situation isn't static. Our understanding today is only a stepping stone to tomorrow's insights. Rapidly advancing technology is making this understanding possible. I am amazed at the equipment I use now compared to what I had during my first years with the Forest Service. We know much more than we did 30 years ago, and our ability to see into the intricate lives of animals has never been greater, yet many questions remain. Still, I think, for me, the fact that sometimes animals are present even though we can't see or hear them may be what gives me the greatest hope of all.

Selected Bibliography

Aylward, Cody M., James D. Murdoch, and C. William Kilpatrick. "Genetic Legacies of Trans-
    location and Relictual Populations of American Marten at the Southeastern Margin of
    Their Distribution." *Conservation Genetics* 20, no. 2 (December 10, 2018): 275–86. https://
    link.springer.com/article/10.1007/s10592-018-1130-3.

Chadwick, Douglas H. *A Beast the Color of Winter*. San Francisco: Sierra Club Books, 1983.

Dillard, Annie. *The Writing Life*. New York: Harper Perennial, 1989.

Di Vincenzo, Mark. "Ore. Salamander Hitchhikes to Nn." *Daily Press*, December 1, 1999.
    https://www.dailypress.com/1999/12/01/ore-salamander-hitchhikes-to-nn/.

Federal Register. *12-Month Finding for the Northern Spotted Owl* 85, no. 241 (December 15,
    2020): 81144–52. https://www.federalregister.gov/documents/2020/12/15/2020-27198/
    endangered-and-threatened-wildlife-and-plants-12-month-finding-for-the-northern
    -spotted-owl.

Forsman, Eric. "Eric Forsman Oral History Interview." Northwest Forest Plan Oral History
    Collection (OH 48), December 5, 2016. https://scarc.library.oregonstate.edu/omeka/
    exhibits/show/forestryvoices/item/34846.

Franklin, Alan B., Katie M. Dugger, Damon B. Lesmeister, Raymond J. Davis, J. David Wiens,
    Gary C. White, James D. Nichols, et al. "Range-Wide Declines of Northern Spot-
    ted Owl Populations in the Pacific Northwest: A Meta-Analysis." *Biological Conserva-
    tion* 259, no. 109168 (2021): 1–20. https://www.sciencedirect.com/science/article/pii/
    S0006320721002202?via%3Dihub.

Gibbs, George. *Dictionary of the Chinook Jargon, or, Trade Language of Oregon*. eBook #15672,
    2005 (updated 2020).

Golden Books. *Birds of North America: A Guide to Field Identification*. New York: Golden Press,
    1983.

Grauer, Jennifer A., Jonathan H. Gilbert, James E. Woodford, Daniel Eklund, Scott Anderson,
    and Jonathan N. Pauli. "Unexpected Genetic Composition of a Reintroduced Carnivore
    Population." *Biological Conservation* 215 (2017): 246–53.

Johnston, James M. *High Lake and Stream Survey Report, Olympic National Forest*. Olympia,
    WA: Washington State Game Department, 1972.

Kimmerer, Robin Wall. *Braiding Sweetgrass: Indigenous Wisdom, Scientific Knowledge, and the
    Teachings of Plants*. Minneapolis: Milkweed, 2013.

Leopold, Aldo. *A Sand County Almanac, and Sketches Here and There*. Special commemorative
    ed. New York: Oxford University Press, 1989.

Lint, Joseph. "Northwest Forest Plan—the First 10 Years (1994–2003): Status and Trends of
    Northern Spotted Owl Populations and Habitat." Gen. Tech. Rep. PNW-GTR-648. Port-

land, OR: U.S. Department of Agriculture, Forest Service, Pacific Northwest Research Station. 2005.

National Geographic Society. *Field Guide to the Birds of North America*. Washington, DC: National Geographic Society, 1983.

National Wildfire Coordinating Group. *Resource Advisor's Guide for Wildland Fire*. Boise, ID: National Interagency Fire Center, 1996.

Oregon Zoo. *Medical Note: Northwestern Salamander Intake*. Portland, OR. January 19, 2000.

Peterson, Roger Tory. *A Field Guide to Western Birds*. Boston, MA: Houghton Mifflin, 1961.

Sartore, Joel. "MIG003–00001." Joel Sartore, National Geographic Photographer and Speaker, 2024. https://www.joelsartore.com/mig003-00001/.

Scheffer, Victor. "Mammals of the Olympic National Park and Vicinity (1949)." *Northwest Fauna* 2 (1995): 5–133.

Shea, Dave S. "Barred Owl Records in Western Montana." *Condor* 76, no. 2 (1974): 222.

Shea, Dave. *Chief Mountain, Home of the Thunderbird: Physical, Historical, and Spiritual Perspectives*. Myrtle Point, OR: Myrtle Point Printing, 2007.

Stebbins, Robert C. *The Peterson Field Guide Series: A Field Guide to Western Reptiles and Amphibians*. 3rd ed. New York: Houghton Mifflin, 2003.

Taylor, Avery L., Jr., and Eric D. Forsman. "Recent Range Extensions of the Barred Owl in Western North America, Including the First Records for Oregon." *Condor* 78, no. 4 (1976): 560–61.

Thomas, Jack Ward. *The Journals of a Forest Service Chief*, edited by Harold K. Steen. Seattle: University of Washington Press, 2004.

Further Reading

Dietrich, William. *The Final Forest: The Battle for the Last Great Trees of the Pacific Northwest.* New York: Simon and Schuster, 1992.

Johnson, K. Norman, Jerry F. Franklin, and Gordon H. Reeves. *The Making of the Northwest Forest Plan: The Wild Science of Saving Old Growth Ecosystems.* Corvallis: Oregon State University Press, 2023.

Luoma, Jon R. *The Hidden Forest: The Biography of an Ecosystem.* Corvallis: Oregon State University Press, 2006.

Maser, Chris. *The Redesigned Forest.* San Pedro, CA: R. & E. Miles, 1988.

Mathews, Daniel. *Cascade-Olympic Natural History: A Trailside Reference.* Portland, OR: Raven Editions, 1999.

McNulty, Tim. *Olympic National Park: A Natural History.* 4th ed. Seattle: University of Washington Press, 2018.

Mudd Ruth, Maria. *Rare Bird: Pursuing the Mystery of the Marbled Murrelet.* Seattle, WA: Mountaineers Books, 2013.

Olson, Deanna H., and Beatrice Van Horne, eds. *People, Forests, and Change.* Washington, DC: Island Press, 2017.

Powell, Roger A. *The Fisher: Life History, Ecology, and Behavior.* Minneapolis: University of Minnesota Press, 1993.

Wildung Reinhart, Karen. *Yellowstone's Rebirth by Fire: Rising from the Ashes of the 1988 Wildfires.* Helena, MT: Farcountry, 2008.

About the Author

Betsy L. Howell is a wildlife biologist and author living on Washington State's Olympic Peninsula. Her writing has appeared in *American Forests, Earth Island Journal, The Wildlife Professional, Women in Natural Resources*, and more. She is the author of a memoir, *Acoustic Shadows*, and a novel, *The Marvelous Orange Tree*. https://betsylhowell.com/.